As per New CHSE Syllabus

FUNDAMENTALS OF
MICRO & MACRO ECONOMICS

CLASS–XII

(FOR ARTS, SCIENCE AND COMMERCE)

(Written as Per the Syllabus Prescribed by CHSE, Odisha)

S.M. LOKMAN
Lect.-in-Economics
Regional College, Rambag
Jajpur, ODISHA

KALYANI PUBLISHERS
LUDHIANA – NEW DELHI – NOIDA (U.P.) – HYDERABAD – CHENNAI
KOLKATA – CUTTACK – GUWAHATI – KOCHI – BENGALURU

KALYANI PUBLISHERS

Head Office :

3251-B, Gurdev Nagar, **Ludhiana**-141 001 • Ph : 0161-2760031, 2745756, 5025883
E-mail : kalyanibooks @ yahoo.co.in **Website :** www.kalyanipublishers.co.in

Administration Office :

4779/23, Ansari Road, Daryaganj, **New Delhi**-110 002 • Ph : 011-23271469, 23274393
E-mail : kalyani_delhi @ yahoo.co.in, kalyani_delhi @ kalyanipublishers.in

Works :

B-16, Sector 8, **Noida (U.P.)**

Branch Offices :

1, Mahalakshmi Street, T. Nagar, **Chennai**-600 017 • Ph : 044-24344684

110/111, Bharatia Towers, Badambadi, **Cuttack**-753 009 (Odisha) • Ph : 0671-2311391

H.No. 4-3-65/2/A, Behind H.V.S. Public School, Raghunath Bagh, Sultan Bazar, **Hyderabad**-500 095
E-mail : kalyanipublishershyd@gmail.com

10/2B, Ramanath Mazumdar Street, **Kolkata**-700 009 • Ph : 033-22416024

Arunalaya, 1st Floor, Saraswati Road, Pan Bazar, **Guwahati**-781 001 • Ph : 0361-2731274

Koratti Parambil House, Convent Road, **Kochi**-682 035 • Ph : 0484-2367189

No. 24 & 25, 1st Floor, Hameed Shah Complex, Cubbonpet Main Road, **Bengaluru**-560 002

T 38738 05

14+334=348, 20X30, 43.5 FHARMA

U-40683 05

Reprinted, 2024

Reprinted, 2025

Reprinted, 2026

TYPESETTING AT
(MISC-2023-MME-OD2)
Gautam Graphic Printers

PRINTED IN INDIA
At B.H. Brothers, Plot No. D3, Sector-B3, Tronica City

DEDICATED TO

My Loving parents Mv. S.A. Mannan,
Freedom Fighter and Parishtani Khatun
For their Blessing from the Heaven.

– S.M. Lokman

PREFACE

It gives me immense pleasure in presenting this book entitled **'Fundamental of Micro and Macro Economics'** for the students of class–XII, Arts, Science and Commerce studying under the Council of Higher Secondary Education (CHSE), Odisha. The book is written strictly in accordance with the syllabus prescribed by the CHSE, Odisha. I have taken utmost care to present the texts in a very simple and convincing language for the clear understanding of the students. At the end of each chapter the summary given in the form of 'What we learnt' and the 'Questions for review', I think, are the special features of this book and will be very helpful for the students. The questions given at the end of each chapter are as per the council pattern to acquaint the students with the question pattern they are going to face in the annual council examination. CHSE question papers of 2023, for Arts/Science and commerce Students are added at the end of the book for the benefit of the students. I shall be very happy if the book serves the purpose of the students for whom it is meant and be recommended by our esteemed teachers.

On the occasion of the Publication of this book I would like to express my gratitude to my principal Sri Anil Kumar Mohanty and my colleagues for their constant support and encouragement rendered to me. I would also like to express my gratitude to my brothers, Sisters, Friends and relatives and my students for their well-wishes. My Special thanks to K.M. Zuberi, my better half, my dearest daughters Nafisha, Nahida and Khusnuma for their help in preparing the script.

Last but not the least, my special thanks to Mr. Ramesh Chandra Swain, Regional Manager ***Kalyani Publishers,*** Cuttack, for his sincere effort to bring out this book well in time.

Suggestions for further improvement of the book will be highly solicited.

2023 **S.M. LOKMAN**

SYLLABUS

CLASS–XII (ARTS, SCIENCE and COMMERCE)
ELEMENTARY MICRO AND MACRO ECONOMICS

A. INTRODUCTORY MICROECONOMICS

UNITS	CONTENTS	PERIODS	MARKS
I	**Introduction :** • Definition, Scope and Subject Matter of Economics • Meaning of Economy and Central Problems of an Economy–Scarcity and Choice, What, How and For Whom to Produce ? • Basic Concepts –Wants, Utility, Goods, Value, Price and Wealth	10	10
II.	**Consumption and Demand :** • Laws of consumption–Marginal and Total Utility, Law of Diminishing Marginal Utility, Law of Equi-marginal Utility and Conditions of Consumer's Equilibrium • Demand–Meaning and Determinants, Individual and Market Demand, Demand Schedule and Demand Curve, Movement along and Shifts in the Demand Curve. • Price Elasticity of Demand–Concept, Determinants, Measurement of Price Elasticity of Demand, Percentage and Geometric Method (Linear Demand curve) Relation of Price Elasticity of Demand with Total Expenditure.	14	15
III.	**Production :** • Meaning of Production and Production Function. Short-run and Long-run. • Total, Average and Marginal Product • Law of Variable Proportion and Returns to a factor	10	10
IV.	**Cost, Revenue and Supply :** • Cost –Money and Real Cost, Implicit and Explicit Cost, Fixed and Variable Cost, Total, Average and Marginal Costs in Short run and their Relationship (Simple Analysis) • Revenue–Total, Average and Marginal Revenue and their relationship. • Supply–Meaning and Law of Supply.	12	10

V.	**Market :** • Meaning and forms of Market, Pure and Perfect Competition, Price determination under perfect competition and Effects of Shifts in Demand and Supply. • Meaning and Features of Monopoly, Monopolistic Competition and Oligopoly.	**8**	**10**
B. INTRODUCTORY MACROECONOMICS			
VI.	• Meaning of Macroeconomics. Distinction between Macro and Microeconomics, Subject matter of Macroeconomics.	**4**	**5**
VII.	**National Income** • Meaning and Aggregates related to National Income–GDP, GNP, NDP, NNP at Market Price and Factor Cost. • National Disposable Income (Gross and Net), Private Income, Personal Income, Personal Disposable Income. Nominal and Real National Income. • Income Determination–Aggregate Demand and Aggregate Supply and their components, Simple Keynesian Theory of Income determination.	**10**	**15**
VIII.	**Money, Banking and Public Finance** • Meaning and Functions of Money • Meaning and Functions of Commercial Banks • Meaning and Functions of Central Bank • Meaning of Public Finance, Difference between Public Finance and Private Finance. • Budget–Meaning and Objectives, Balanced and Unbalanced Budget, Surplus and Deficit Budget.	**12**	**20**
	Question Pattern 15 Multiple Choice Questions 1 × 15 = 15 15 Correct the statements 1 × 15 = 15 11 Questions out of 13 to answer in 2-3 sentences each 2×11 = 22 6 Distinguish between out of 8 in 6 sentences each 3 × 6 = 18 4 Long answer type Questions out of 6 7 ½ × 4 = 30 **Total 100**		

CONTENTS

UNIT – I

1. DEFINITION, SCOPE AND SUBJECT MATTER OF ECONOMICS

2. BASIC CONCEPTS (WANTS, UTILITY, GOODS, VALUE, PRICE AND WEALTH)

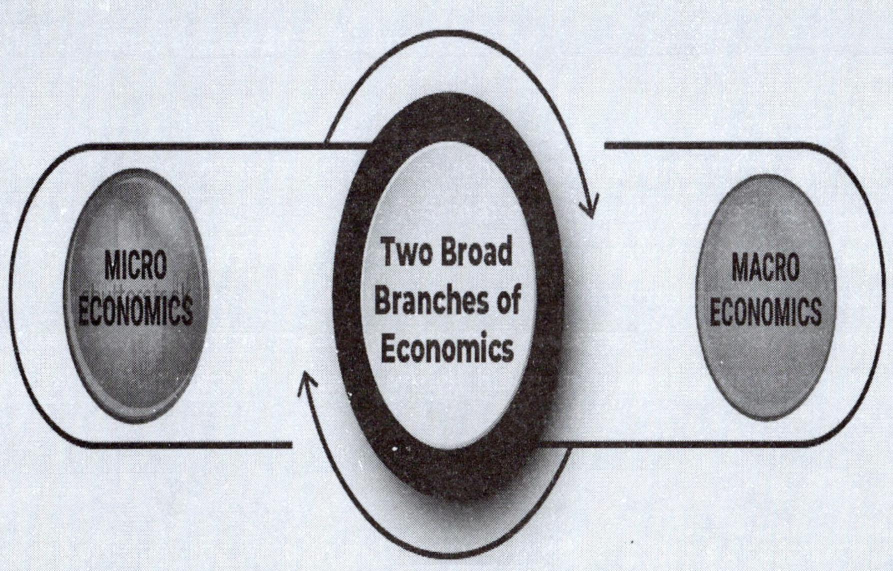

DEFINITION, SCOPE AND SUBJECT MATTER OF ECONOMICS

Economics as a Social Science is the oldest among all Social Sciences. Practically it has been in existence since the very first day of human existence on the earth. Because, what the first human on the earth would have done must have been related to the fulfillment of his want for food and this 'want' is the core of economics. Had there been no 'want', our subject would not have developed. Definitely man must have involved himself first in economic activity, then must have performed other activities, such as social, political, cultural, spiritual and other innumerable activities. In this sense we can say that 'Economics is the father of all social sciences'. But, unfortunately our subject was neglected till 1776 as it had not got a separate identity of its own till that date. Of course, there were economic activities and economic thinkings but no thinking on economics. Those who were indulged in economic activities and economic thinkings were known in different names, such as the mercantilists, the Phisiocrats and like. But thinking on economics started with **Adam Smith**, a Scotish economists, who for the first time wrote a systematic book on economics, named **"An Enquiry into the Nature and Causes of the Wealth of Nations"**, Shortly, known as **'Wealth of Nations'**, which was published in the year 1776. This is the reason why Adam Smith is called as the father of economics and his monumental work. 'The Wealth of Nations' is as sacred as the Bible for the students of economics.

The term 'Economics' is originated from the Greek word **'Oikonomia'**, which is the congregation of two words—**'Oikos'**, meaning 'household' and **'Nemein'**, meaning 'management'. Thus, the evolution of our subject started from the 'household management'. But being a dynamic subject the concept of Oikonomia has become too narrow to mean our subjects as its scope has been expanding day by day. Now it has become a subject of management of firms, industries, trade and commerce, different economies and different economic institutions and international organisations. But the objective has been the same, i.e. managing with the limited resources available.

Definitions

To explain in precise what a subject is about, it is customary to give a definition of the subject. In this sense the definition of economics will provide the beginners of the subject a tentative idea on what economics is about ?

Of course, our subject is so vast and its scope is so wide spread that it is too difficult to present what economics is about, in sentence or two in the form of a definition. Broadly speaking, 'economics is a decision-making science in the arena of consumption, production, distribution and efficient allocation of scarce resources', Yet this is too narrow. However, from time to time different economists have put forward different definitions of economics. Here for the sake of simplicity for the beginners, let us start with the definition of economics given by the Father of economics.

Adam Smith's Definition (Wealth Definition)

***Adam Smith**, the Father of economics, for the first time presented the concept and definition of economics in his book, **"An Enquiry into the Nature and causes of Wealth of Nations'**, published in the year 1776. In the title of the book he has made it clear that what 'economics' is about. The title suggests that economics is a study of **'nature and causes of wealth'** According to him, "Economics is a science of wealth, it enriches both people and the king."*

An analytical study of Adam Smith's definition on economics implies that economics as a science teaches how to make wealth. By Wealth he meant only the material goods which are scarce in relation to demand. The second aspect of his definition, 'it enriches both people and the king' implies that economic people are rational and guided by self-interest. Guided by self-interest when people earn wealth and become rich the king or the state obviously becomes rich. Thus 'making' and 'spending' wealth is the prime objective of the study of economics. Since Adam Smith put much emphasis on 'Wealth' in his definition, his definition on economics is famous as **'wealth definition'.**

Some early classical economists like **J.B. Say, J.S. Mill, N.W. Senior** and others also accepted and propagated the wealth definition of Adam Smith and they defined economics in Adam Smith's line putting emphasis on wealth but in a different manner.

UNIT – I

1. DEFINITION, SCOPE AND SUBJECT MATTER OF ECONOMICS

2. BASIC CONCEPTS

(WANTS, UTILITY, GOODS, VALUE, PRICE AND WEALTH)

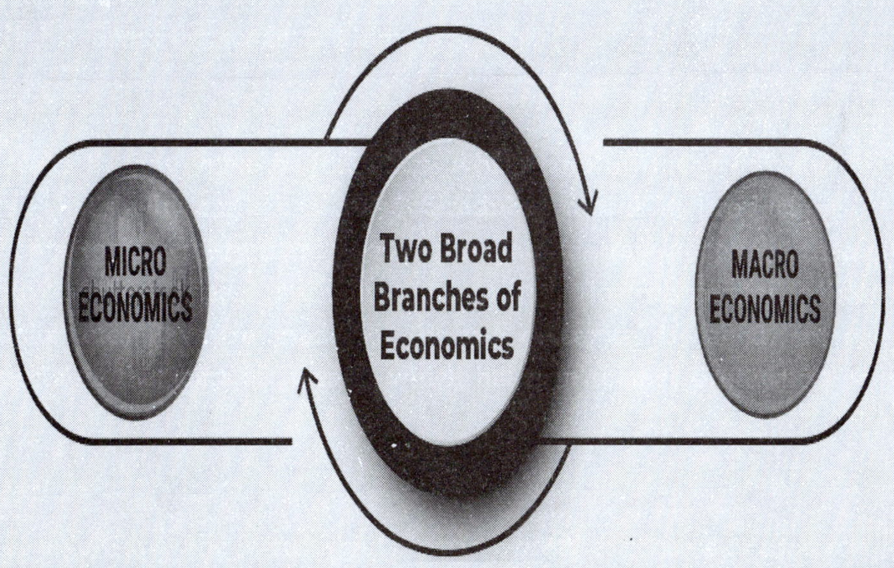

***J.B. Say** defined our subject as, "Economics is science which treats of wealth".*

*According to **J.S. Mill,** "Economics investigates the nature of wealth and the laws of Production and its distribution."*

***Francis A. Walker** defined our subject as, "Economics is the name of that part of knowledge which relates to wealth".*

Thus, the classical economists considered 'wealth' as the center stage of the subject matter of economics. The importance of 'Wealth', in the form of precious metals and other material goods which are scaree is evident from Adam Smith's definition that, "....; it enriches both people and the king'. So to make the state health the classicals put emphasis on the accumulation of wealth. The accumulation of wealth depends on production and the use of factors of production.

The main feathers of wealth definition which are inherent in it are-

1. Economics is a study of wealth.
2. Wealth refers to such material goods which are scarce in relation to demand.
3. Economics studies the nature and causes of wealth, changes in wealth through accumulation, which obviously implies economic development.
4. Production and accumulation of wealth depends upon the extent of the domestic and foreign market.
5. Individual interest is conducive to social interest.

Criticisms

Though the wealth definition of Adam Smith, supported by other classical economists, deeply influenced the writings of other economists for a good long time, yet it was severely criticised by a number of social reformers and writers like Carlyle, Ruskin, Maurice and others. Keeping in view the too much emphasis on accumulation of Wealth given by Adam Smith and his followers Carlyle branded our subject as ' a dismal science', as it encouraged wealth making and also called our subject as the 'Gospel of Mammon',. Ruskin even went upto branding our subject as 'Economics a Bastard Science', as importance was given on making wealth without considering the way. Later, Alfred Marshall, an eminent English economist, systematically criticized Adam Smith's wealth definition on the following important grounds :

1. **Too Much Importance to Wealth :** The wealth definition of Adam Smith and other classical economists gave undue importance to wealth than man. The question is why man earns wealth ? Does he earn wealth merely to pile it or to fill his coffer ?

Certainly not. He earns wealth to satisfy his wants. So, making wealth is not the end but merely a means to an end and 'Man' or his welfare is the end. But the wealth definition has given 'Wealth' the primary position and 'Man' the secondary position. According to Marshall economics must emphasize 'man' more, than 'Wealth'. In his words, "Economics on the one side is a study of wealth, and on the other and more important side, a part of the study of man". But neglecting 'man' , the definition has given too much importance to wealth.

2. **Narrow Meaning of Wealth :** Adam Smith and other classical economists, supporting the Wealth definition, interpreted 'wealth' in the sense of material goods and precious metals which are scarce in supply. They have excluded different services, like the service of teachers, doctors, Singers, dancers etc., which are called as non-material goods from the purview of the study of economics. By his they have narrowed down the meaning of wealth and the scope of economics. Services, i.e. the non-material goods do satisfy our wants. How can we exclude them from the scope of economics ?

3. **Individual Interest Not Always Conducive to Social Interest :** Wealth definition is based on the assumption that each individual earns wealth for his self-interest and when each individual earn more and more wealth the state is enriched. That is, individual interest promotes social interests. But Practically, individual interest is not always conducive to social interest, rather, often individual interest is detrimental to social interest. Earning wealth for self-interest makes economics a study of selfish economic man. But Marshall considers economics as a study of common man.

   Though the wealth definition narrowed down the scope of economics, narrowed down the meaning of wealth, neglected 'man' and the concept of 'welfare', made economics a selfish science and was not accepted by many writers, social reformers and economists, yet credit goes to Adam Smith, the Father of our subject who first set the ball in the field which attracted others to dribble with it.

Alfred Marshall's Definition (Welfare Definition)

Pointing out the frailties of the wealth definition, Alfred Marshall, a Famous English economist and the pioneer of the Neo-classical school of economists, put forward a new definition of economics in his book **'Principles of Economics',** published in the year 1890. In his definition on economics Marshall tried to divert the attention of those who criticized economics as a dismal Science, a selfish science, a science of bread and butter and so on, by shifting the importance on 'wealth' to 'welfare'. In his definition, putting emphasis on man as 'Primary' he pointed out that, economics is on the one side a study of wealth, and on the other and more important side, a part of the study of man. To him, wealth is just a means to an end and the end is 'Welfare'.

Marshall *defined economics as, "Political economy or Economics is a study of mankind in ordinary business of life; it examines that part of individual and social action which is most closely connected with the attainment and with the use of material requisites of well-being".*

Some other neo-classical economists and followers of ***Alfred Marshall****, also defined economics putting emphasis on 'Welfare' aspect of wealth. According to* ***A.C. Pigou****, "Economics is a study of that part of social welfare which can be brought directly or indirectly into relation and with the measuring rod of money".*

In the words of ***Prof. Cannan,*** *"The aim of political economy is the explanation of general causes on which the material welfare of human beings depends".*

More precisely ***Prof. Penson*** *defined our subject as, "Economics is a science of material welfare".*

An analytical study of Marshall's definition of economics, which is popularly known as 'Welfare definition', gives rise to the following features of his definition.

1. Economics is a study of an ordinary or common man's individual and social activities under taken by him in his day to day life.
2. Economics does not study all the activities of mankind.
3. Economics studies only that part of his activities, individual or social, which fulfills his material needs or wants.
4. Only those material goods' acquisition and use come with in the purview of economics which promote welfare.

Thus, according to Marshall, it is not acquisition of wealth, rather promotion of welfare' which is more important and material wealth is just a means to promote welfare. Man in his day to day life earns material wealth to lead a better life, which is nothing but welfare. Thus, by putting emphasis on the welfare aspect of wealth he made economics more logical and acceptable.

Criticisms

The acceptability of Marshall's 'Welfare definition continued more or less till 1932. In this year an another English economist Lionel Robbins, in his book 'An Essay on the Nature and Significance of Economic Science' severely criticized the welfare definition of the neo-classicals on the following heads.

1. **Narrowed down the scope of Economics :** According to Robbins by defining economics as a study of ".... Material requisites of well-being", Marshall has narrowed down the scope of economics in two ways. Firstly, as per his definition, the material goods which do not promote welfare, like the production and distribution of intoxicants, weapons etc. fall outside the purview of economics. Secondly, the non-material goods, like different services, which, though promote welfare do not come with in the purview of economics. In this sense Marshall has confined the scope of economics more than what Adam Smith had done by referring 'Wealth' to scarce material goods.

2. **Concept of Welfare is not clear :** The concept of material welfare in Marshall's definition is not clear in the sense that a material good, like deadly weapon or say war heads, which do not promote individual welfare from Marshall's view point, is conducive to individual welfare from society's view point or from defence view point. Moreover, a particular material good may not bring welfare for all individual in the society. Similarly, 'welfare' is not a static concept, rather a dynamic one which changes with the changes in time, place and circumstances. But Marshal has not made it clear in his definition.

3. **Welfare is a Subjective Concept :** In the welfare definition of the neo-classicals, particularly of Pigou, attempt is made to measure 'Welfare' with the measuring rod of money. But 'welfare' being a subjective concept cannot be measured in terms of money. Because Psychology differs from person to person and the value of money also differs from person to person and from time to time, on the basis of the economic condition and urgency of the situation. So, money cannot be an appropriate measuring rod of 'welfare'.

4. **Economics is rather a Human Science :** According to Marshall economics studies the day-to-day activities of mankind related to society and thus makes economics a social science only. But this is not acceptable on the ground that those who are living outside the society, such as saints or one who is living in exile are not falling will in the purview of economics as they are not indulged in the activities related to society. But the fact is they are also subject to the Fundamental Principles and laws of economics. They have wants, they are also guided by welfare concept and so on. So, economics should rather be treated as a human science, not merely a social science.

In spite of the criticisms, credit goes to Marshall for integrating economics with human welfare, for shifting importance from 'wealth' to 'welfare' and making the study of economics more acceptable. In comparison to Adam Smith's definition many economists considered Marshall's definition more suitable.

Lionel Robins's Definition (Scarcity Definition)

Prof. Lionel Robins of London School of Economics, in his book, 'An Essay on the Nature and Significance of Economic Science', published in the year 1932, gave a completely different definition of economic, which he called an analytical definition. His definition of economics is analytical in the sense that he has provided the reasons for the study of economics.

*According to **Robins,** "Economics is the science which studies human behaviour as a relationship between ends and scarce means which have alternative uses."*

An analytical study of Robins definition of economics makes it clear that the definition is based on the facts of man's life which is equally applicable to the society as a whole. It makes each man an economists and makes economics a study of human behaviour or his response to the problems arising out of his unlimited wants and limited resources which are capable of alternative uses. By this he has tried to make our subject more realistic and analytical.

Features

A close observation of Robins's definition of 'Economics' as a Science gives the following features of the definition and the matters of study in economics :

1. **Unlimited Wants :** In Robins's definition 'ends' refer to 'wants', which are unlimited, both from the individual and society's view point. Wants are unlimited in the sense that as one want is satisfied, an another crops up and the chain of wants continues in a never ending manner. It is not possible to satisfy all our wants. Had it been possible, then there was no need of studying economics. Yet, as an economic man, each of us try to satisfy some of our wants as far as possible.
2. **Scarce Resources :** 'Resources' or 'means' are meant to satisfy wants. These resources, be it money or time or energy or in any other form, are scarce or limited in relation to their requirement or demand. This is the reason, why we become able

to satisfy some of our wants, not all. If resources were unlimited, wants would not have been unlimited. It is the scarcity of resources which gives rise to all economic problems. What is true for an individual is also true for society or the economy as a whole.

3. **Resources are capable of alternative Uses :** The resources at man's disposal are not only scarce but also capable of alternative uses, making the economic problems more complex. A piece of land, for example, can be put into several uses putting its owner in a dilemma as to how he will use it. Thus, the alternative uses capability of resources gives rise to the problem of allocation of resources. Because, be it an individual or a society, motto is the optimum use of scarce resources, so that maximum utility or satisfaction or welfare is achieved.

4. **Choice is the Solution :** An economic man is a rational man. According to Robins, on the backdrop of the above stated problems how an economic man behaves (also a society or economy) is studied in economics. As stated above, as man wants optimum utilisation of his scarce resources in the attempt to satisfy his unlimited wants, he makes the choice of his wants on the basis of their urgency. Keeping in view the resources at his disposal, he gives priority to the most urgent wants pushing behind the less urgent and least urgent wants, and goes on satisfying the wants so long his resources permit him.

Thus, according to Robins, 'choice' is the solution to all economic problems. The economic problems, whether related to consumption or production or distribution or any other aspect of economics are innumerable and all cannot be satisfied due to the 'Scarcity' of resources. But we can make the best uses of our scarce resources, what the economic science teaches us, is through choice. That's why, "economics can be best treated as a science of choice". Since the question of 'choice' arises due to 'scarcity' of resources, his definition of economics is popular as 'scarcity and choice' definition.

In appreciation of Robins's definition of economics we can say that his definition gave economics a new touch. His definition raised a problem, studied in economics, that is universal-allocation of scarce resources optimally. His definition provided a more analytical scope to economics as it has given rise to the problems which are central to the science of economics. Even the modern economists like Harvey, scitovsky, stigler and others have also appreciated Robin's definition of economics saying, it touches a broad field of economics than the earlier definitions.

In spite of all appreciation Robbins definition is subject to certain criticism which are discussed below.

Criticisms

Though many economists appreciated Robins's definition of economics, yet economists like Prof. A.C. Pigou, Fraser, Eric Roll, Samuelson and others criticised the Scarcity definition of the following grounds.

1. **Makes Economics only a positive science :** While defining economics as a 'Science of choice' Robins, it seems, has not taken into account the pros and cons of the art of choice'. It seems, while making choice an economic agent (a man or household or firm....) is only guided by the principle of 'What is', or 'What should be' and thus makes economics only a positive science. But critics are of the opinion that as a social science it should also take in to account the normative aspects, like 'What ought to be' (from maximisation of satisfaction or welfare) while making choice.

2. **Affluence may also create Economic Problems :** In his definition Robins pointed out that all economic Problems arise due to scarcity of resources but could not visualize that economic problems may also arise due to affluency or abundance of resources. Even he could not visualize the Great Depression of his times, that occurred in Europe and America in 1930s. The economic crisis of 1930s was not due to the scarcity of resources, rather due to abundance of resources. By this he narrowed down the purview of economic problems to scarcity of resources only.

3. **Made economics a static subject :** In his definition Robins has made our subject a static one by discussing it as a study of how scarce resources having alternative uses are allocated among unlimited wants. He has not taken into account an another important aspect of the study that how the resources will grow, i.e., how there will be economic development. This aspect of economics makes our subject dynamic. But his definition has made economics static.

Besides the above discussed criticisms, Robins definition seems to be related more to micro economic problems as he says "it is a study of human behaviour", which more implies individual behaviour. But economic problems are more social or aggregative rather than individual. In this context the scarcity definition on 'economics' given by Prof. P.Samuelson, the father of modern economics, who defines, "Economics is the study of how men and society choose, with or without the use of money, to employ scarce productive resources to produce various commodities over time and distribute them for consumption, how and in the future, among various people and groups in society", Seems more relevant. Thus samuelson has further extended the Robins definition to make our subject an aggregative and dynamic one. That's why we cannot discard his definition altogether rather can take it as an initiation towards the modern economic analysis.

SCOPE AND SUBJECT MATTER OF ECONOMICS

As 'economics' is a dynamic subject we cannot put a fence to determine its scope and subject matter. Yet, as it is customary to have a discussion on the scope and subject matter of any new subject so here we have tried to discuss on them both from traditional and modern view points.

From the traditional view point the scope and subject matter of economics can be determined from the very definitions of the subject discussed earlier. From the above discussed traditional definitions it is clear that economics is a study of human activities related to satisfaction of unlimited wants allocating limited resources, which are capable of alternative uses, on the basis of the choice of urgent wants so that the satisfaction is maximized. Thus want is the starting point of all economic activities and resources are needed to satisfy the wants. The resources can be acquired by effort i.e. by doing economic activities and with the use of acquired resources one can fulfill wants and get satisfaction. In this process every economic agent or unit tries to maximize its satisfaction for its economic welfare. This process is involved with various aspects of economics, discussed below, and constitute the subject matter of economics from traditional view point.

Want

Want is the starting point of all economic activities. Had there been no want there had not been any necessity of doing any economic activity. In economics want refers to the desire for any thing that can be made effective or actualized through effort. So all desires do not come with in the purview of economics. Only those desires which can be made effective are discussed in economics.

Consumption

Wants are fulfilled by means of consumption. In economics consumption means using up the utility of goods and services for the satisfaction of wants. It constitutes a significant part of the subject matter of economics as the level of satisfaction depends upon the level of consumption or the capacity to consume of the economic agents.

Production

For consumption there is the need for producing different goods and services having utility. In this sense production in economics is defined as "creation of utility'. This is possible with the help of factors of production such as land, labour, capital and organization including technology adopted in the production process. Use of factors of production and technology to produce goods and services involves costs. In this sense production means creation of utility having exchange value. Thus, production and factors involved in the process of production constitute a part of the subject matter of economics.

Distribution

Use of the factors of production, broadly classified under four heads such as land, labour, capital and organization involves their payments. These factor payments in the form of rent, wage, interest and profit respectively constitute a part of the subject matter of economics. In this part we study how the factor prices are determined. In this sense distribution refers to the allocation of the shares of different factor owners in the production venture.

Exchange

Exchange in economics refers to giving one thing for the purpose of getting an another thing. Exchange is involved in the process of consumption for satisfaction of wants as well as in the process of production. Wants of economic agents or units are so diversified that no agent or unit can produce everything to satisfy all its wants and hence exchange is necessitated. In economics exchange of goods and services takes place in markets. Market refers to the exchange of a commodity between two or more parties, usually called buyers and sellers. Again, on the basis of the nature of the commodity and number of sellers and buyers there are various types of market such as perfect competition, monopoly, monopolistic competition, oligopoly etc. and all these constitute a significant part of the subject matter of economics.

Welfare

Welfare as a subject matter of economics is related to the maximization of the satisfaction of the economic agents or units. Welfare, related to consumption means maximization of utility, related to production means maximization of profit or minimization of cost etc. All these require optimum and efficient use or allocation of resources, which is called 'economic efficiency'. Different theories developed my different economists to achieve economic efficiency also constitute a part of the subject matter of economics.

Besides the aboved discussed aspect of economics international trade, involving the export and import of goods and services for earning foreign exchange and for the satisfaction of domestic wants, among the countries of the globe, is also a part of the subject matter of economics. Moreover, the study of income and expenditure of the government and all the principles and policies underlying them are also included in the subject matter of economics from traditional view point.

MODERN APPROACH

From the modern view point the subject matter of economics is studied under two branches–micro economics and macro economics.

The Great Depression of 1930s made the economists to change their views on the analysis of economic problems. The failure of the European and American economies to revive from the state of depression characterized by fall in the price level, overproduction and glot, fall in profit, increasing unemployment etc., made the economists to look deep in to the problems. In this context the epoch making work was done by **J.M. Keynes**, an English economist, in the form of **The General Theory of Employment, Interest and Money'** which was published in the year 1936. It was then realized that the economic problems are to be studied at two levels–micro and macro levels, i.e. under two branches of economics–microeconomics and macroeconomics. **Prof Ragnar Frisch** of Olso University was the first to use terms 'Micro' and 'Macro' in economics in 1933.

The term 'Micro' is derived from the Greek word **'Mikros'** which means 'Small'. In this sense microeconomics refers to that branch of economics which studies and analyses the economic activities, problems and decision making of small or individual economic agents like an individual or household, a firm, an industry etc. not those of the economies as a whole. Such as how an individual will get maximum satisfaction from the consumption of various goods and services, how a firm will maximize its profit or minimize the cost of production etc.

From this it obviously implies that the subject matter of Microeconomics includes the concepts like–

1. The Theories of consumer's behaviour (consumption)
2. The Theories of Production (Production)
3. The Theories of Price determination (Pricing)
4. The Theories of factor Pricing (Distribution)
5. The Theories related to welfare of the economic agents. (Welfare Economics)

It is to be noted that the microeconomic theories are developed under the assumption of full employment and on the basis of the partial equilibrium technique. The economists like Alfred Marshall, A.C. Pigou, D. Ricardo, L. Robins and others have contributed significantly towards the studies of economic activities at the micro levels.

The term 'Macro' on the other hand is derived from the Greek word **'Makros'**, which means large or in aggregate. In this sense Macroeconomics refers to that branch of economics which studies the economic activities, Problems and their solutions of the economic agents as a whole or those of the economy as a whole. That's why macroeconomics is also called as the aggregative economics and its subject matter includes the theories related to –

1. National income and output.
2. General employment
3. General Price level
4. Economic development and growth
5. Macro distribution
6. Money, banking and international trade
7. Public Finance.

Broadly Speaking the economic affairs which are related to the economy of a country as a whole come with in the purview of macroeconomics. It is to be noted that the macroeconomic theories are developed on the assumption of underemployment and on the basis of general equilibrium technique. **J.M. Keynes** who brought out a revolutionary change in the economic thinking with his Publication of 'The General Theory of Employment, Interest and Money ' (1936) is considered as the father of macroeconomics. Other who contributed to the development of the Study of macroeconomics include K.E Boulding, Gardner Aekley and many more followers of Keynes.

CENTRAL PROBLEMS OF AN ECONOMY

WHAT IS AN ECONOMY ?

Before going to discuss on the Central Problems of an economy it is pertinent to know what is an economy ?

An economy refers to an organised system of production and distribution of goods and services in a country for the satisfaction of the wants of its people. In other words an economy refers to the arrangements in a country from which people earn their livelihood and get goods and services to satisfy their wants and achieve their welfare. Thus an economy is comprised of all economic agents like individuals, households, firms, industries and other sources of production, commercial organizations and the organizations and institutions including government that control and regulate the economic activities. Different countries have adopted different systems of organising production and distribution of goods and services and controlling other economic activities under different names such as capitalism, socialism, communism, mixed- economy etc.

Economic Problems

In almost all the economies, be it capitalist or socialist or communist or mixed-economy, all the economic problems are due to the facts that–

(i) Wants are unlimited.

(ii) Resources to satisfy the wants are limited and

(iii) Limited resources are capable of alternative uses.

These three facts have given rise to certain basic problems which are common to almost all the economies and hence and called the central problems of an economy. The important among them are discussed below.

1. What to produce and in what quantity ?

This is the most vital problem that every economy faces due to scarcity of resources and unlimited wants. In the light of scarcity of resources an economy has to decide what goods and services are to be produced and in what quantities . This involves the allocation of scarce resources in relation to the composition of total output in the economy. Simply speaking, this problem is related to the allocation of scarce resource for the production of varieties of goods and services out of which some are necessaries, some are comforts and some others are luxurious. This is a problem because, since the resources are scare, if one good, say a luxurious, is produced more, the production of other goods, say comforts or necessaries has to be reduced. That is, if a country decides to produce more of motor cars then the availability of resources to produce tractors will be less, which may affect the overall welfare of the country. So, the economy has to be careful in deciding what to produce.

Once the nature of goods, i.e. necessaries or comfort or luxuries, to be produced is decided, then their quantities are to be decided. Thus the economy has to decide how much of necessaries and how much of comforts and how much of luxurious goods have to be produced. This is to be decided on the priority basis keeping in view the status of the country.

2. How to produce ?

After deciding what to produce and in what quantity the next problem of an economy is to decide how to produce the decided goods and services, so that the cost of production of different goods and services will be minimum and there will be efficient allocation of resources. It simply implies the problem of how to produce is related to the choice of technique or method of production. The solution to this problem lies with the availability of resources, particularly labour and capital. If labour is available cheaply and in abundance, then the economy may adopt labour-intensive techniques, while in case of availability of capital in abundance it may adopt capital intensive technique. The technique to be used also depends upon the type and quantity of goods or services to be produced. For producing capital goods and large amount of output capital-intensive techniques can only do. On the other hand for simple consumer goods and to produce small amount of output labour-intensive technique may be adopted. Broadly speaking, in deciding how to produce goods and services, the economy should choose those combinations of factors and techniques of production which will minimize the cost of production of goods and services, ensure efficient allocation of resource and increase the productivity in the economy.

Labour-intensive Method *of production refers to that method in which more of labour and less of capital are used to produce goods. This method of production is adopted mostly by the underdeveloped countries where labour is available in plenty and cheaply and capital is scarce. However, in case of labour-intensive method the cost of production is high and the productivity is low.*

Capital-intensive Method *of Production refers to that method in which more of capital and less of labour are used to produce goods. This method of production is adopted mostly by the developed countries where capital is available in plenty and cheaply and supply of labour is scarce. In case of capital-intensive method the cost of production is low and productivity is high.*

3. For Whom to Produce ?

The problem of 'for whom to produce' is related to the distribution of national output or income among the people of different sections of the society. The distribution of income is determined by the quantity or resources contributed by a household in the form of services of labour, land and capital towards the generation of national output or national income, and the prices these services command in the market, i.e. wage, rent and interest. The larger the share of a factor on the national income large will be its share on the national output. Thus a rich person may have a larger share of goods due to higher income and a poor may have lesser quantities of the goods he needs. This may lead to inequalities in the distribution of income and wealth which is not conducive for the welfare of the economy as a whole. Here the government has to influence the income distribution pattern and to ensure equitable distribution of income as for as practicable through taxation and public expenditure policies.

4. Full Employment of Resources

To see whether the resources owned by them are fully utilized or employed or not is an another problem before almost all economies. Since the Great Depression of 1930s, which created mass unemployment in capitalist countries, full employment of resources has become a major problem for almost all economies. Because in case the resources of the economy are lying idle, the economy has to find out ways and means to utilize them fully. If the idleness of resources, say land or labour or capital is due to their malallocation, the economy has to adopt suitable monetory, fiscal and commercial policies to correct their idleness. Though full employment, according to Keynes is "a myth", the problem before the economies is to go ahead of what they have employed. In an economy, if the available resources are fully utilised, it is characterized by technical efficiency or full employment. Every economy tries to increase the output by employing more and more resources, i.e. factors of production to attain the level of full employment and to keep the growth process to continue.

5. Problem of Growth of Resources

An another important problem that an economy faces is to find out whether the resources are growing through time or not. If the resources are growing then we can say that economic development is taking place. For the developed countries, growth in their resources is required to maintain the already achieved growth. On the other hand if the economy is stagnant or growing slowly, its growth should be accelerated through a higher rate of capital formation. The rate of capital formation depends upon a number of factors which the economy has to deal with to keep the resources growing, either to achieve economic development or to maintain the already achieved growth.

6. Sustainable Development

Since last 40 to 50 years, each and every economy of the globe are confronting with an another major problem, i.e. the problem of how to achieve sustainable development, that is how to keep the development process to go on. This problem is related to the problems of environmental degradation. The economic development that the countries have achieved so far, is at the cost of natural environment. Man for his greed is exploitating natural resources indiscriminately in the name of economic development, but by this has endangered the environment for the present and the future generations. That's why the problem that every economy facing is how to achieve sustainable development, i.e. economic development along with the protection of environment. Now a days it has rather become a major problem for the globe as a whole.

***Sustainable development** refers to a situation of fulfilling the needs of the present generation without compromising with the needs of the future generations. Thus it is involved with the preservation of natural resources, exploring the new renewable natural resources etc. to protect the natural environment for the generations to come.*

The Central Problems of an economy discussed above are not independent of each other rather are inter-related and inter-dependent. The first three problems are related to microeconomics and the later three are related to macroeconomics.

PRODUCTION POSSIBILITY CURVE

The Central Problems of an economy, involving choice, such as what to produce, can be explained graphically with the help of production possibility curve or production possibility frontier. The production possibility curve is an analytical tool used to illustrate and explain the problem of choice or economizing process in a hypothetical economy. It represents various combinations of two goods, that can be produced by utilizing a given amount of resources and under the conditions of given technology, at a particular time.

The production possibility curve is drawn on the basis of following assumptions.

(i) Only two goods, say 'X' and 'Y', *i.e.* consumer goods and capital goods are produced in an economy in different proportions.

(ii) The given resources can be used to produce either or both of the goods and can be shifted freely between them. (Perfect mobility of factors)

(iii) Resources are given, but they can be re-allocated for the production of the two goods within limits.

(iv) Technique of production is given and constant.

(v) There is full employment of resources and utilised efficiently.

(vi) The economy works for a short-period.

With the above assumptions let us construct a hypothetical production possibility curve or Frontier (PPF) with help of a hypothetical production possibility schedule drawn below.

Combinations	Quantity of X	Quantity of Y
P	0	250
A	100	230
B	150	200
C	200	150
P_1	250	0

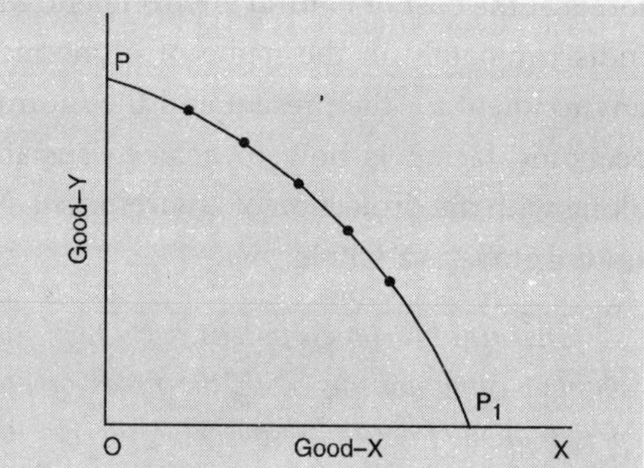

The schedule shows that using the given resources the economy can produce either 250 units of Y(zero of X) or 250 units of X (Zero of Y). But we have assume that the economy should produce both the goods.

We have shown other possible combinations of two goods that can be produced with the give resources. The combination 'A' represents that the economy can produce 100 units of X and 230 units of Y with the given resources. Similarly combination 'B' represents 150 units of X and 200 units of Y, which implies to produce 50 more units of X the economy has to sacrifice 30 units of Y. Combination 'C' represents 200 units of X and 150 units of Y, which implies for producing same more units (50) of X the economy has to scarcee more (50 units) of 'Y'.

Graphically, we have presented good-X on the horizontal axis and good-Y on the vertical axis. Presenting the pairs of goods X and Y the concave curve obtained PP_1 is the production possibility curve or frontier or the transformation curve. Each production possibility curve is the locus of output combinations which can be produced from given amount of resources or factor inputs. The production possibility curve shows not only the production possibilities but also the rate of transformation of one product into the other when the economy moves from one possible combination to an other possible combination. The rate of transformation on a production possibility curve increases as the economy moves down wards, i.e. from B to C and D.

The production possibility curve can also be applied to explain other basic facts of an economy like employment and unemployment, technological progress, economic growth and economic efficiency.

WHAT WE LEARNT

1. Economics is the oldest Social Science, which studies the prudent use of scarce resources having alternative uses, so as to get maximum satisfaction.
2. 'Want is the core of all economic activities.
3. Economics as a separate subject got its identity in 1776 with the publication of the book 'An Enquiry into the Nature and Causes of Wealth of Nations", written by Adam Smith.
4. Adam Smith is the Father of Economics.
5. Economics is the Father of all social sciences.
6. Adam Smith propounded the 'wealth definition' of economics.
7. Adam Smith considered the precious metals and material goods only as wealth, whose supply is scarce.
8. According to Adam Smith economics is a study of 'Nature and causes of wealth'.
9. Wealth definition of economics made our subject to be criticised as 'a dismal science', 'a Gospel of Mammon'.
10. Alfred Marshall systematically criticised Adam Smith's Wealth definition of economics in his book 'Principles of Economics', published in 1890.
11. Alfred Marshall Propounded the welfare definition of economics.
12. According to Marshall, 'Wealth is a means to an end and the end is welfare'.
13. In his definition on economics Marshall put emphasis on the welfare aspect of wealth.
14. Both Adam Smith and Alfred Marshall committed the same mistake of confining the meaning of wealth to material goods only.
15. In Marshall's definition of economics the concept of welfare is not clear.
16. Marshall and his followers tried to measure welfare in terms of money though 'Welfare' is a subjective concept.
17. Prof. Lionel Robins wrote the book, "An Essay on the Nature and Significance of Economic Science", which was published in 1932.
18. Robins propounded the Scarcity definition of economics.
19. According to Robins unlimited wants and limited resources capable of alternative uses are the causes of all economic problems.

20. 'Choice' of most urgent wants is the solution to all economic problems.
21. Robins has made economics a positive science ignoring its normative aspects.
22. Economic problems arise not only due to scarcity but also due to abundance of resources.
23. Economics is a dynamic subject.
24. Wants, consumption, production, distribution, exchange, welfare, money, banking, international trade, economic development and growth, public finance are the broad subject matters of economics.
25. Prof. Ragner Frisch introduced the terms 'Micro' and 'Macro' in economics in the year 1933.
26. The term 'micro' is derived from the Greek word 'Mikros' which means 'small' or 'individual'.
27. Microeconomics deals with the problems of small or individual economic units and their solutions.
28. The term 'Macro' is derived from the Greek word 'Makros' which means 'large' or 'aggregate'.
29. Macroeconomics studies the economic problems of an economy as a whole or in aggregate.
30. The subject matters of microeconomics are-consumption, production, distribution, pricing theories and economic welfare.
31. The subject matter of macroeconomics are National income or output, general employment, general price level, economic development and growth, macro distribution, money, banking, international trade, Public Finance and all other economic matters related to the economy as a whole.
32. An economy is an organized system of production and distribution of goods and services in a country for the satisfaction of the wants of its people.
33. The economic problems which are common to almost all the economies are called the Central Problems of an economy.
34. The Central problems of an economy are–What to produce ? How to produce ? For whom to Produce ?, how to achieve growth of resources ?, How to achieve full employment of resources ? and how to achieve sustainable development ?
35. The problem of 'What to produce' is related to the allocation of scarce resources.

36. The Problem of 'how to produce' is related to the choice of technique or method of production.

37. The problem of 'for whom to produce' is related to the distribution of national output or national income.

38. The method of production adopting more of capital and less of labour is called capital-intensive method.

39. The method of production adopting more of labour and less of capital is called labour-intensive method.

40. Sustainable development refers to keeping the development process to continue protecting the interest of the future generations, i.e. achieving economic development with the protection of environment.

41. The Central problems of an economy are not independent rather inter-related.

42. The Central Problems of an economy involving choice can be explained with the production possibility curve or frontier.

43. A production possibility curve is the locus of output combinations of two goods which can be produced from given amount of factor inputs.

44. The production possibility curve is also called 'transformation curve'.

45. A production possibility curve shows not only various output combinations of two goods but also the rate of transformation one product into the other, when the economy moves from one possible combination to an another.

QUESTIONS FOR REVIEW

A. *Choose the correct answer from the given alternatives in each question. (Each Carrying 1 Mark)*

1. What type of Science is Economics ?

(i) Natural (ii) Social

(iii) Physical (iv) Meta-physical

2. In which year 'Economics' as a discipline got its identity ?

(i) 1776 (ii) 1890

(iii) 1932 (iv) 1936

3. **who is the Father of Economics ?**

(i) Adam Smith (ii) Alfred Marshall

(iii) L. Robins (iv) P. Samuelson

4. **Who wrote 'The Wealth of Nations' ?**

(i) Marshall (ii) Robins

(iii) Adam Smith (iv) J.M. Keynes

5. **Who propounded the 'Wealth definition' of Economics ?**

(i) Adam Smith (ii) L. Robins

(iii) A. Marshall (iv) P. Samuelson.

6. **In his definition Adam Smith put much emphasis on –**

(i) Wants (ii) Wealth

(iii) Welfare (iv) All the above

7. **Who criticised economics as 'a dismal science' ?**

(i) Ruskin (ii) Marshall

(iii) Carlyle (iv) Maurice

8. **Who wrote 'The Principles of Economics' ?**

(i) Adam Smith (ii) Alfred Marshall

(iii) L. Robins (iv) P. Samuelson

9. **Who propounded the 'welfare definition' of Economics ?**

(i) A. Marshall (ii) J.S. Mill

(iii) J.B. Say (iv) N.W. Senior

10. **In his definition Marshall put emphasis on which aspect of wealth ?**

(i) Earning (ii) Spending

(iii) Welfare (iv) All the above

11. **Welfare is a ...... concept.**

(i) Subjective (ii) Objective

(iii) Stock (iv) Flow

12. **Who wrote 'An Essay on the Nature and Significance of Economic Science' ?**

(i) P. Samuelson (ii) Lionel Robins

(iii) A. Smith (iv) A. Marshall

13. **Robins's definition of economics is famous as ....**

(i) Wealth definition (ii) Scarcity definition

(iii) Welfare definition (iv) Growth definition

14. Which one according to Robins is the cause of all economic problems ?

(i) Unlimited wants

(ii) Limited resources

(iii) Alternative use capacity of resources

(iv) All the above

15. What according to Robins is the solution to all economic problems ?

(i) Choice (ii) Efficiency

(iii) Govt. Policy (iv) None of the above

16. Who is the father of modern economics ?

(i) A. Smith (ii) J. M. Keynes

(iii) P. Samuelson (iv) Lionel Robins

17. Who introduced the terms 'Micro' and 'Macro' in economics ?

(i) J.M. Keynes (ii) Ragner Frisch

(iii) P. Samuelson (iv) L. Robins.

18. Which one is not a subject matter of microeconomics ?

(i) Production (ii) Consumption

(iii) Development (iv) Distribution

19. Which one is a subject matter of macro economics ?

(i) National income (ii) Pricing theories

(iii) Theories of consumer's behaviour (iv) Production theories

20. The problem of 'What to produce' is related to ----

(i) Choice of technique (ii) Allocation of resources

(iii) Distribution of national income (iv) None of the above.

21. The problem of 'how to produce' is related to ......

(i) Allocation of resources (ii) Distribution of national income

(iii) Choice of method of production (iv) All the above

22. The problem of 'for whom to produce' is related to ......

(i) Distribution of national income (ii) Allocation of resources

(iii) Sustainable development (iv) Choice of technique

23. Development with the protection of environment is called......

(i) Steady development (ii) Sustainable development

(iii) Environmental development (iv) None of the above

24. The slope of the production possibility curve shows that the rate of transformation of one good into other.....

(i) Increases (ii) Decreases

(iii) Remains Constant (iv) None of the above

25. Who is the father of macroeconomics ?

(i) P. Samuelson (ii) Adam Smith

(iii) J.M. Keynes (iv) Ragner Frisch.

B. *Correct the statements, if necessary, without changing the underlined portions. (Each Carrying 1 Mark)*

1. Alfred Marshall propounded the wealth definition of economics.
2. Lionel Robins propounded the welfare definition of economics.
3. Adam Smith propounded the Scarcity definition of economics.
4. Marshall put emphasis on the welfare aspect of wealth.
5. Robins criticised economics as 'a Gospel of mammon'.
6. P. Samuelson is called as the father of economics.
7. According to Smith wealth is a means to welfare.
8. Microeconomics deals with aggregate economic problems.
9. General price level is a subject matter of microeconomics.
10. Macro distribution is included in macroeconomics.
11. J. M. Keynes introduced the terms 'micro' and 'macro' in economics.
12. Under developed countries mostly follow the capital intensive technique.
13. Capital-intensive technique increases the cost of production.
14. Pricing theories are included in the microeconomics.
15. Microeconomics theories are developed on underemployment assumption.

C. *Answer the following questions in 2-3 sentences each. (Each Carrying 2 Marks)*

1. What type of science is economics ?
2. How Adam Smith defined economics ?
3. Why Adam Smith is called as the Father of Economics ?
4. How Marshall defined economics?

5. How Marshall's definition of economics is an improvement over Adam Smith's definition ?
6. What common mistake both Adam Smith and Marshall committed while defining economics ?
7. How Lionel Robins defined economics ?
8. Point out the features of Robins's definition of economics.
9. What are the subject matters of economics from the traditional view point ?
10. What is microeconomics ?
11. What are the subject matters of microeconomics ?
12. What is macroeconomics ?
13. What are the subject matters of macroeconomics ?
14. What is an economy ?
15. Point out the central problems of an economy ?
16. What do you mean by the problem of 'What to produce ?'
17. What do you mean by the problem of 'how to produce' ?
18. What do you mean by the problem of 'For whom to produce' ?
19. What is sustainable development ?
20. What is production possibility curve ?

D. *Distinguish between the concepts in six sentences each. (Carrying 3 Marks)*

1. Wealth definition and welfare definition.
2. What to produce ? and How to produce ?
3. Labour-intensive method and capital intensive method.
4. Microeconomics and Macroeconomics.

E. *Long Answer Type Questions (Carrying 7½ Marks)*

1. Explain Adam Smith's definition of economics.
2. Explain Marshall's Welfare definition of economics.
3. Explain Robins's definition of economics.
4. Briefly discuss the scope and subject matters of economics.
5. Discuss the central problems of an economy.

Answer to Q. N. A

1.	(ii)	2.	(i)	3.	(i)	4.	(iii)	5.	(i)	6.	(ii)	7.	(iii)	8.	(ii)
9.	(i)	10.	(iii)	11.	(i)	12.	(ii)	13.	(ii)	14.	(iv)	15.	(i)	16.	(iii)
17.	(ii)	18.	(iii)	19.	(i)	20.	(ii)	21.	(iii)	22.	(i)	23.	(ii)	24.	(i)
25.	(iii)														

Answer to Q. N. B

1. Adam Smith	2. Alfred Marshall	3. Lionel Robins
4. Correct	5. Carlyle	6. Adam Smith
7. Alfred Marshall	8. Macroeconomics	9. Macroeconomics
10. Correct	11. Ranger Frisch	12. Developed countries
13. Labour-intensive	14. Correct	15. Full employment

❑❑❑

BASIC CONCEPTS

(WANTS, UTILITY, GOODS, VALUE, PRICE AND WEALTH)

In economics often we come across some basic concepts which are frequently used in analyzing and explaining various economic problems. These basic concepts have their specific meaning and characteristics which are not synonymous to what they are understood from the view point of a common man. So before going into the discussion on various economic analysis on the subject matters of economics, particularly of microeconomics. Let us first discuss on some of those basic concepts frequently used in economic science.

WANTS

For a layman want means the desire to have something. But in economics 'want' refers to the desire for a commodity or service which can be fulfilled or satisfied through continuous effort. Otherwise mere desire for a commodity cannot be considered as want if it cannot be satisfied. For example the desire to have 'the moon' cannot be treated as want because it can never be satisfied. In this sense only effective desires are considered as 'wants' in economics. Moreover, wants in economics are meant for human. So when we talk about wants, it obviously means human wants. In his economic life all the fuss that man is doing is only to satisfy his wants. That's why **Prof. Seligman** rightly remarks, *"Want is the starting point of all economic activities."* Had there been no want, there had not been any fuss.

Characteristics of Human Wants

Human wants have a number of characteristics. Important among them are discussed below :

1. **Human Wants are Unlimited.** Human wants have no limit. When his one want is satisfied another takes its place and thus the chain of wants continues in a never ending process. It is not possible to satisfy all his wants, but still man desires to fulfill more and more of his wants till his last. That's why man is said to a bundle of wants, a never satisfied animal. No man can ever say that he has no want or all his wants have been fulfilled.
2. **A Particular Want is Satiable.** Though wants are unlimited a particular want can be satisfied provided that one has the means. For example, if one is hungry and wants food, he can satisfy his hunger by taking food. As he starts taking food gradually his desire to have more food diminishes and finally a stage comes when he stops taking food. Because his want for food or hunger is satisfied. It is to be noted that the law of Diminishing Marginal Utility is developed on this characteristic of human wants.
3. **Wants Vary in Intensity.** Though our wants are unlimited, yet thank God that he has not made all our wants of same intensity. Because some of our wants are more urgent, some are less urgent and some others are least urgent or not urgent at all. On the basis of this characteristic wants have been broadly classified under three categories such as necessaries, comforts and luxuries. This characteristic of want helps man in choosing his wants which are to be fulfilled first and which are to be given up keeping in view the resources at his disposal.
4. **Some Wants are Competitive.** Some wants are competitive in the sense that they compete with each other in order to be satisfied first. This is because our wants are unlimited but means to satisfy them are limited and we want to get the maximum (satisfaction) using our limited resources which are capable of alternative uses.
5. **Some Wants are Complementary.** Some wants are complementary in the sense that the satisfaction of a particular want requires more than one good at a time. If one of the item of the group is not available then the want will remain unfulfilled. For example, want for tea means want for milk, sugar, tea-dust etc. If any of the items is missed then our want for tea will remain unsatisfied. Similarly our want for bike simultaneously involves want for petrol and mobile. Thus, there are so

many wants that man faces in his day to day life which are complementary to one another.

6. **Some Wants are both Competitive and Complementary.** There are some wants which first compete with each other to be satisfied but subsequently become complementary to each other. For example labour and capital compete with each other (man and machine) to be employed in the production process. But they are also complementary as both are required to carry out the production venture.
7. **Wants Vary with Person, Place and Time.** Wants of different persons are not same. It depends upon the attitude, social status, consumption patterns, level of income etc. For example to satisfy hunger some may want rice and some may prefer bread. Similarly, wants also differ from place to place. For example, the staple food in Northern India is bread where as it is rice in Southern India. People of cold countries want woolen cloth where as people of tropical climate prefer light clothes. Moreover, wants also vary with change in time. For example we want hot drinks like tea and coffee during winter where as we prefer cold drinks during summer. This is how wants vary with person, place and time.
8. **Some Wants are Recurring.** Some wants are recurring in nature in the sense that they occur again and again. In other words, there are some wants which once fulfilled do not mean that they will not be felt again. They occur again and again, either at regular or irregular intervals. For example, by taking food when we satisfy our hunger it does not mean we will never want food again. Hardly after 5 or 6 hours we will feel hungry and want food again. Similarly we want new cloth again and again at irregular intervals.
9. **Some Wants Turn into Habits.** Some wants turn into habits when they are fulfilled regularly and continuously. For example when the wants for intoxicants like betel, tobacco, cigarette, wine, tea etc. are fulfilled regularly, they turn into habits. They become so habitual that they become necessaries for their addicts.

Besides the above discussed characteristics there are also some other characteristics such as some wants are alternative in the sense that they can be satisfied by different types of substitute goods. Hunger can be satisfied by rice or bread or by any edible goods. Moreover, some wants are often influenced by advertisement and propaganda. Our wants for various semi-luxurious and luxurious commodities are mostly influenced by their advertisement and propaganda.

CLASSIFICATION OF WANTS

Human wants are unlimited. But resources to satisfy them are limited. So one cannot satisfy all his wants. What he can do is only to make a choice of his wants. The task of choosing which wants are to be fulfilled first is made easy by one of the characteristics of wants, i.e. 'Wants vary in their intensity'. This characteristic of wants implies that some wants are more urgent, some are less urgent and some yet are least urgent.

On the basis of this characteristic human wants are broadly classified into three categories :

(i) Necessaries

(ii) Comforts, and

(iii) Luxuries

Necessaries are further classified as :

(a) Necessaries for life,

(b) Necessaries for efficiency, and

(c) Conventional necessaries.

The classification of human wants is presented in the form of a tree-diagram drawn below :

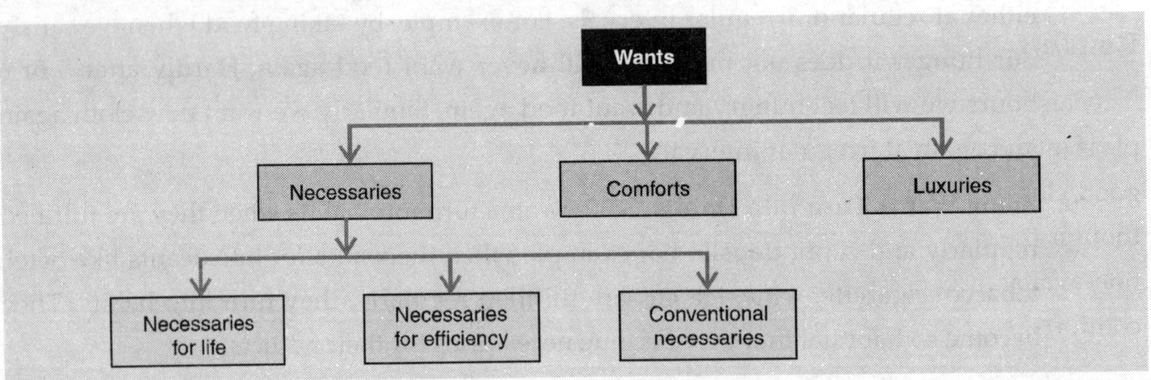

Necessaries

The basic requirements of life are kept under the necessaries category of wants. The most urgent wants of man come under this category. These wants are most urgent from different angles of life for which they are further classified as

(i) necessaries for life, (ii) necessaries for efficiency and (iii) conventional necessaries.

(i) **Necessaries for Life.** The wants, without the fulfillment of which man cannot survive come under the category of necessaries for life. In other words the goods and services which are required for the existence of life are called necessaries for life. Minimum food, clothing, shelter, medicines and the like things without which man cannot keep his body and soul together come under the category of necessaries for life.

(ii) **Necessaries for Efficiency.** Necessaries for efficiency refers to those goods and services which are required not for existence but to maintain the ability and efficiency to work. Nutritious foods like milk, egg, fish, meat etc., table and chair for a student, car for a busy doctor etc. are the examples of necessaries for efficiency.

(iii) **Conventional Necessaries.** Conventional necessaries refer to those things which are required neither for existence nor for maintaining efficiency but for either due to the pressure of social customs and traditions or due to the pressure of habits. The things required in marriages, funeral ceremonies, thread ceremony, birth day, for observing festivals, worshiping idols etc. are the examples of conventional necessaries. Moreover different intoxicants like wine, cigarette, betel etc. wants for tea and coffee as the matters of habit also come under the category of conventional necessaries.

Comforts

Comforts refer to the wants for those goods and services which make life easy, decent, pleasant and hence comfortable. Electric fan or cooler in summer, woolen clothes in winter, good clothes, well-furnished house etc. are the examples of comforts. It is to be noted that though the distinction between necessaries for efficiency and comforts is not clear as the non-availability of comforts may reduce the efficiency of man to work yet, it is a fact that comforts may increase efficiency to work but not necessarily.

Luxuries

Luxuries refer to those superfluous wants of life which are required neither for life nor for efficiency but to satisfy the desire of displaying the vaniety, showyness, social status and aristocracy. Expensive ornaments, luxury car, expensive clothes, palacial building, array of servants, etc. come under this category of wants. Broadly speaking, all goods which are meant for conspicuous consumption can be considered as luxurious goods.

To conclude on the classification of human wants, we can say that the above classification of wants in not like water-tight compartments or rigid and permanent. Because necessary, comfort and luxury are relative terms and hence cannot be generalized. What is luxury for one or in a particular situation may either be a matter of comfort for an another and may be a matter of necessary for an yet another. For example, car for a student is a matter of luxury, but the same for a professor or lawyer may be a matter of comfort. But the same car for a busy doctor becomes a matter of necessary for efficiency. Moreover, if the student is a lad of any dignitary person then also the car is no more a matter of luxury for him. Similarly, the urgency of different wants changes with time. What was a matter of luxury in the past, say cell phone, has now become a necessary. That's why the classification of want is not rigid.

UTILITY–MEANING, CHARACTERISTICS AND TYPES

Meaning

An another basic concept that is most widely used in economic analysis is 'utility'. A layman broadly understands utility as usefulness. But in economics utility refers to the wants satisfying capacity of goods and services, without the consideration of whether they are useful or not. In our day to day life we require different goods and services because they have the capacity or power to satisfy our wants. When we satisfy our hunger by taking bread or rice, then the power of bread or rice to satisfy our hunger is their utility. Unless a good or service has want satisfying capacity, i.e. utility it will not be required by anyone.

Characteristics

The sense in which the term 'utility' is used in economic analysis that clearly indicates towards the following four characteristics or features of the concept.

(i) Utility is not same as Usefulness. For a common man utility means usefulness. But technically utility is not same as usefulness. Because anything that has usefulness must have utility but anything that has utility may not have the usefulness. For example all intoxicants like wine, tobacco, opium etc. are not useful, rather they are harmful for human health, yet they are required by the people as they satisfy their want. So they have utility.

(ii) Utility is not same as Pleasure. Anything that has want satisfying capacity, i.e. utility may not give pleasure. Often we consume various goods for the sake of pleasure and anything that gives us pleasure must have utility. But anything that has utility may not be pleasant. For example medicines have utility but taking medicine is not a pleasant experience. We know pencilin injection is very painful and Quinine is extremely bitter in taste, yet they cure diseases and hence have utility.

(iii) **Utility is not Satisfaction.** Utility does not mean satisfaction in the sense that utility is expected satisfaction and satisfaction is the realised utility. We require anything because it has utility but we get satisfaction only after consuming it.

(iv) **Utility is a Subjective Concept.** Utility is a subjective concept in the sense that it can be felt only cannot be measured in terms of cardinal numbers. How much utility a person will derive from a particular commodity depends on his psychological conditions, his taste, prefence, habit etc. or how much importance he assigns to the commodity. In this sense, the same commodity may not have the same amount of utility for all, as psychology differs from person to person. Moreover, because of this subjective nature a consumer can say that he got more utility or satisfaction from the 1st unit of a commodity in comparison to the 2nd or 3rd units, but cannot say how much more.

Types of Utility

Broadly speaking there are four types of utility :

(i) From Utility, (ii) Place Utility, (iii) Time Utility, and (iv) Service Utility. Besides these four types, there are two more concepts of utility. They are marginal utility and total utility. But here we have discussed the first four concepts and later in the 'Consumption' chapter we will discuss the next two concepts of utility.

Form Utility. Form utility refers to the addition made to the existing utility of a good by changing its form or shape. In other words form utility is created when the shape of a commodity is given a new look to provide better satisfaction. In the process of changing the form or shape the increased utility is called the form utility. When a piece of log is transformed to timber, when a timber is transformed to a furniture, cotton is transformed into thread and thread is woven into cloth and cloth is transformed into dress etc. Form utility is created in every stages of transformation. This type of utility is created in every field of production. The artisans, craftsmen, carpenters, porters, tailors etc. all create form utility by changing the form or shape of an existing commodity.

Place Utility. Place utility refers to the addition made to the existing utility of a commodity by changing its place. In other words place utility is created when a thing is transferred from one place to another to provide increased utility. When a piece of log is transferred from forest areas to a saw-mill, when different manufactured goods are transferred from godown to the markets etc. place utility is created. Those who transfer and the means of transport help in creating place utility, such as the drivers of different freights vehicles.

Time Utility. When the utility of a good or service increases with the change in time, the increased utility is called time utility. During the harvesting time the supply of foodgrains is plenty, so their utility is low. By storing and preserving them their utility increases during the period of scarcity, like rainy season. This increase in utility is called time utility. Increase in the utility of cold drinks during summer and that of the hot drinks in winter are the examples of time utility.

Service Utility. Utility created by all types of personal services is called service utility. Personal services do not create any material goods but satisfy our wants and hence have utility, which are called service utility. Personal services are also sold and bought in the market. The services of teachers, doctors, lawyers, singers, dancers, nurses and such professions satisfy our wants rendering their services and hence are called service utility.

GOODS

In economics 'goods' refer to all those things which have utility or want satisfying capacity. They include both physical or material things and services. Physical things like book, Pen, Pencil, Car, TV, etc. and services of teachers, doctors etc. all have want satisfying capacity, i.e. utility and hence are called goods. Goods are available in different forms and with different characteristics.

On the basis of their distinctive nature and characteristics we usually classify them as discussed below :

1. Free Goods and Economic Goods

The goods which are available in plenty in relation to their demand and hence require no payment for their use or consumption are called free goods. These goods are free gifts of nature over whose supply man has no control. One can have as much as of these goods as he requires without making any payment. Thus these goods have no exchange value. All free gifts of nature except land, like air, water in the river, sand in the river bed, sunshine etc. are the examples of free goods.

The goods whose supply is scare in relation to their demand and hence we cannot have as much of them as we require without making any payment are called economic goods. These goods are bought and sold in the market. That means they have exchange value. All the goods which are the result of human effort like book, Pen, Car, TV etc. plus land (thought it is a free gift of nature) are the examples of economic goods. Economic goods are considered as wealth as they have utility, scarcity and marketability, the characteristics of wealth.

The distinction between the free goods and economic goods is not so rigid or fixed as it depends on place, person and time. For example, oxygen in the air is a free good but the same oxygen in a cylinder becomes economic good. Similarly water flowing in a river is free good but when the same water is supplied to the households through pipe becomes economic good. Air in an open space is free good but air of a fan inside a room becomes economic good.

2. Consumer Goods and Producer Goods

The goods which directly satisfy wants are called consumer goods. These goods directly enter into the consumption process and hence are called goods of first order. Consumer goods are of two types–durable consumer goods like car, TV, bike etc. which can be used for a longer period of time and perishable consumer goods like milk, fish, meat, fruits, vegetables etc. which can be used only for once. Consumer goods, be they perishable or durable, are used up sooner or later.

Producer goods are those goods which help in the further production of goods and thus indirectly satisfy human wants. That's why they are called goods of second order. These goods are otherwise called as capital. Producer goods are also of two types – Durable producer goods like machines, tools, factory, building etc. which can be used again and again in the production process, and perishable producer goods like fertilizer, raw material, coal, petrol, etc. which are of single use.

However, inspite of the above stated differences it is the use of the good which determines whether it is consumer good or producer good. For example, a car for personal use is a consumer good, but if it is used as taxi they it becomes a producer good. Similarly if milk is consumed by a person or household it is consumer good, but if it is used by a backery for making bread or cake then it becomes a producer good.

3. Intermediate Goods and Final Goods

Intermediate goods refer to those goods which are used up in the production process to produce other goods and lost their utility and identity. Raw materials, semi-finished goods etc. are the examples of intermediate goods. These goods are sold by one firm to another. Farmer sells wheat to flour mill, the miller sells flour to the backery to make bread, cotton is sold to textile industry and so on. It implies that the intermediate goods never cross production boundary. Similarly the raw materials like bricks, cement, sand, granite, wood etc. used in the construction of a building are the examples of intermediate goods. Moreover seeds, fertilizer, pesticide etc. used in the agricultural production are the examples of intermediate goods. It is to be noted that the value of intermediate goods are not taken into account while estimating the national income of a country to avoid double counting.

Final goods refers to those goods which are available in the market as the end-products or finished goods to be used by the consumers for their direct satisfaction of wants or by the producers as the producer, goods. TV, car, bike bread etc. are the examples of final goods. The value of the final goods are taken into account while estimating national income of a country.

However, the distinction between the intermediate goods and final goods is not clear cut. Because a same good can be treated as both final good and intermediate good on the basis of its use. For example sugar becomes a final good when it is directly consumed by a household, but when it is used by a backery or used for making sweets, it becomes an intermediate good.

4. Public Goods and Private Goods

Public goods refer to those goods which are owned, supplied and managed by the public authorities, i.e. by the governments. These goods are indivisible and once provided are equally available to all. The principle of exclusion is not applicable in case of public goods. It means no one can be excluded from enjoying the benefits of public goods, whether he or she contributes to their provision or not. Public goods are enjoyed not consumed. Pricing of public goods is not possible through market mechanism. It is determined by budgetary policy of the government. Marginal cost of producing a public good for an additional user is zero. Consumption of public goods is non-rival in the sense that consumption of public goods by one will not reduce the consumption of other(s). National defence, public road, public park, government schools and colleges, government hospitals etc. are the examples of public goods.

Private goods refer to those goods which are exclusively owned by private individuals or institutions or organizations. These goods are consumed by only those who pay for them. One who does not pay for a private good he is excluded from its consumption. Thus the principle of exclusion is applicable in case of private goods. The consumption of private goods is rival i.e. if one consumes more the consumption of other(s) will be less. The benefits of a private good accrue only to its owner or his keeth and kin, not to a stranger. It means the benefits of private goods are internalized. The pricing of the private goods is determined by the market mechanism. Pen, pencil, car, TV etc. owned by private individuals or institutions or organizations are the examples of private goods.

5. Material Goods and Non-material Goods

Material goods refer to those goods which can be seen and touched and have definite shape and existence. These goods are made up of certain matter. They are either natural or man-made. Rocks, buildings, books, car, TV, bed etc. including all liquid objects are the examples of material goods.

Non-material goods refer to those goods which cannot be seen or touched and have no shape. These goods are only felt. Though these goods are non-tangible they have exchange value and satisfy human wants. The services of teachers, doctors, lawyers, singers, dancers, actors etc. are the examples of non-material goods. There are also some non-material free goods such at air, sunshine, services of parents, brothers and sisters etc as they have no exchange value.

VALUE AND PRICE

The term 'value' is used in two different angles :

(i) Value-in-use or use value, and

(ii) Value-in-exchange, or exchange value

Value-in-use of a good refers to its usefulness. When we say nutritious foods have great value for a growing child, it implies the usefulness of the nutritious foods for the child. But this meaning of 'value' bears no significance in economics. In economics value is used in the sense of value-in-exchange or exchange value. It is the capacity of a good to command over an another commodity, i.e. the amount of other good(s) that can be exchanged for a good. For example if 3 pencils are available in exchange of a pen, then we say the exchange value of a pen is 3 pencils. There are some goods such as air, sunshine etc. which have use value but no value-in-exchange. On the other hand there are some goods which have value in-exchange but no use value, such as wine, tabacco etc. There are also innumerable goods like land, book, pen, car, TV etc. which have both exchange value and use value. All economic goods have value-in-exchange. So, value-in-exchange bears much significance in economics.

Price in economics is defined as the exchange value of a commodity expressed in terms of money. In other words the amount of money required to command over a unit of a commodity is called its price. For example if a pen is sold at ₹ 10, then we say the price of the pen is ₹ 10. If we know the prices of different goods then we can know their relative values. If the price of a pen is ₹ 10 and the price of pencil is ₹ 5 then we can say that the pen values more than the pencil.

It is to be noted that value and price do not mean the same thing. Because the prices of all goods may go in the same direction at the same time but the value of all goods may not move in the same direction at the same time. Rise in prices does not mean rise in the value of the goods, it may mean the fall in the value of money. Similarly fall in the price of a commodity may not mean fall in its value, it may mean the rise in the value of money. Thus the price of goods and value of money are inversely related.

WEALTH

Meaning

For a common man wealth means riches. In this sense, a man having a huge amount of cash, bank balance, immovable and movable properties like land, building, gold, vehicles and financial assets like shares, securities, debentures etc. is considered as a wealthy person. But in economics 'wealth' is used in a specific sense. In economics wealth refers to "stock of anything at a given time that has exchange value or money value." Thus wealth is a stock concept.

*According to **Prof. Hansen,** "Wealth is the stock of goods existing at a certain time which have utility, scarcity, money value and transferability."*

Characteristics of Wealth

From the above stated meaning and definition of wealth we can say that anything in order to be considered as wealth must have the characteristics discussed below. In the absense of any of the characteristics a thing cannot be considered as wealth in strict sense of the term. In that case it might be a personal or individual wealth or social or national wealth or cosmopolitan wealth.

1. **Utility.** Utility means the want satisfying capacity of goods and services. So anything in order to be considered as wealth must have the capacity to satisfy want, otherwise it would not be required by anyone. For example rotten eggs, rotten fruits have no utility and hence cannot be considered as wealth. We know

utility is not same as usefulness. So a good may not have usefulness but if it has utility, such as wine, it will be considered as wealth.

2. **Scarcity.** Things having utility cannot be considered as wealth unless they are scarce, i.e. their supply is not limited in relation to their demand. If a thing is not scarce then it will have no exchange value and if a thing has no exchange value it cannot be considered as wealth. For example air, sunshine etc. have utility but since they are not scarce in relation to their demand no payment is made for them, i.e. they have no exchange value and hence are not wealth. Only economic goods are wealth.

3. **Marketability (Transferability).** Utility and scarcity are not the sufficient conditions for a thing to be considered as wealth. Alongwith utility and scarcity it must have the characteristic of marketability. Marketability of a thing implies its transferability. Here transferability implies either physical or ownership transferability. In this sense land, building and other immovable properties are wealth as their ownership can be transferred or sold in the market. But any document or certificate showing the inherent qualities such as skill, degree, educational qualification etc. are not transferable and hence not wealth. Similarly good health, beauty etc. are not transferable and hence not wealth. However, good-will of a business is transferable and is considered as wealth.

4. **External Possession.** Any thing, in order to be called as wealth must be an external possession or part of man. In other words it should not be an inherent quality of man like talent, skill, voice (of a singer), efficiency etc. which are not transferable. So these are not wealth. Generally we say 'health is wealth', but this is not true is economics, as health is not an external possession of man and cannot be transferred, it is not wealth.

From the above discussion we can say that anything that has utility, scarcity, marketability and is an external possession of man is treated as wealth in true sense of the term. In this sense all economic goods are wealth.

TYPES OF WEALTH

There are a number of things which are not considered as wealth from the view point of economics in true sense of the term because of the absence of any of the characteristics of wealth discussed above.

Those things with different denotations are classified under the types of wealth discussed below :

1. Personal or Individual Wealth. All the material and non-material things owned by an individual or person are called personal or individual wealth. Material things include land, building, vehicle, furniture and other home appliances etc. owned by person. They also include all financial assets, copy right and patent right of a person. Non-material things included in personal wealth are the inherent qualities of a person such as the skill of a doctor, voice of a singer, beauty of a person, talent of a person in any field of action etc., which are not transferable.

It is to be noted that while calculating the personal wealth of an individual his debts and all other liabilities, which are called as negative wealth are subtracted from his gross possession of wealth.

National Wealth

National wealth, in the narrow sense, refers to the sum total of the wealth owned by all citizens and entities in a country minus the debts and the liabilities due to one another and the government during a given period.

However, in a broad sense it includes :

(i) The sum of the total wealth owned by all citizens and entities in a country.

(ii) All public properties-public land, public buildings, roads of all types, railways, public enterprises, dams, bridges etc.

(iii) According to Marshall, all free gifts of nature like rivers, mountains, forests, mineral deposits etc.

(iv) Non-material elements like scientific knowledge, art of production, findings of research, personal talent.

Cosmopolitan Wealth

The sum total of the wealth of all the nations of the world is called cosmopolitan or international wealth. It includes all free gifts of nature which do not come under any country's geographical territory and used by the whole human community like oceans, the Antaretica, the surface of the moon etc. Moreover it includes the scientific inventions, technological knowledge etc. being used and enjoyed by the whole human community, the properties of international organization and institutions like the UNO, the IBRD (World Bank), the IMF, the WTO etc.

COMPARISON OF WEALTH WITH SOME OTHER CONCEPTS

Discussion on wealth will remain incomplete if we do not compare wealth with certain other concepts widely used in relation to wealth. We have done this below :

(i) Wealth and Title to Wealth

Wealth	Title-to-Wealth
1. Wealth refers to the stock of anything that has utility, scarcity, marketability and is an external possession of man.	1. Title to wealth refers to those assets which are external possession and scarce but no utility of their own and are not always marketable or transferable.
2. Wealth satisfy wants directly as they have utility of their own.	2. Titles to wealth do not satisfy wants directly as they do not have utility of their own, but help in satisfying wants.
3. Land, building, car, TV, etc., i.e. all economic goods are the examples of wealth.	3. Currency notes and coins, all financial assets like shares, securities, debentures, cheques, bonds etc. are the examples of titles to wealth.
4. Wealth itself represents value.	4. A title to wealth is a claim or expression of value and hence is called representative wealth.

(ii) Wealth and Capital

Wealth	Capital
1. Wealth refers to the stock off anything that has exchange value.	1. Capital refers to that part of wealth which generates income or is used for further production of wealth.
2. Building of a person, his car for personal use, his other home appliances like TV, Furniture, ornaments etc. are the examples of wealth.	2. If building is let out on rent or car is used as taxi then they generate income and become capital. Tractor, machines and tools etc. which are used for further production and generate income are also capital.
3. All economic goods are wealth.	3. Only those economic goods are wealth which further produce wealth.
4. All wealth are not capital.	4. All capital are wealth.

(iii) Wealth and Income

Wealth	Income
1. Wealth is a stock concept.	1. Income is a flow concept.
2. Wealth refers to the stock of anything that has exchange value.	2. Income refers to the flow that is generated from wealth when used as capital.
3. A person's building is his wealth.	3. If he gets ₹ 5,000 per month by giving the building on rent, then that ₹ 5,000 p.m. is his income.
4. Wealth is static.	4. Income adds to wealth and hence dynamic.

(iv) Wealth and Money

Wealth	Money
1. Wealth refers to the stock of anything that has exchange value.	1. Money refers to anything that has the legal sanction to be accepted generally in business transactions and in setting other obligations.
2. Things having utility, scarcity, transferability and external possession are called wealth.	2. Money as a thing has scarcity, transferability and external possession, but it has no utility of its own.
3. Wealth can directly satisfy wants as it has utility of its own.	3. Money cannot directly satisfy wants, it can command over goods and services which satisfy want.
4. Wealth can never become useless.	4. Once the legal sanction behind money is withdrawn it becomes useless, so money is not wealth though it is considered so.

(v) Wealth and Welfare

Wealth	Welfare
1. Wealth refers to the stock of thing or things having the characteristics of utility, scarcity, transferability and external possession.	1. Welfare refers to a state of mind with the feelings of well-being which one attends with wealth and many other factors.
2. Wealth increases with the increase in the production of economic goods like car, TV, etc., intoxicants like wine, tobacco etc., war heads etc.	2. Increase in wealth may increase welfare but not necessarily, as increase in the production of intoxicants and war heads do not promote welfare.

3. Rapid industrialization and modernization of agriculture, rapid infrastructure development etc. increase wealth.	3. Environmental degradation caused by industria-lization modernization of agriculture, infra-structure development etc. retards welfare.
4. Wealth is an objective concept.	4. Welfare is a subjective concept.
5. Wealth is a means to welfare.	5. Welfare is the goal of wealth.

WHAT WE LEARNT

1. Want is the starting point of all economic activities.
2. In economics want refers to the desire for something which can be made effective through effort.
3. Human wants are unlimited.
4. A particular want can be satisfied, if we have means.
5. All wants are not of same intensity.
6. Some wants are competitive, some are complementary and some wants are both competitive and complementary.
7. Wants vary with person, place and time.
8. Some wants are recurring in nature.
9. Some wants turn into habit when fulfilled regularly.
10. Some wants are influenced by advertisement.
11. Wants are broadly classified as – Necessaries, Comforts and Luxuries.
12. Necessaries are classified as – Necessaries for life, Necessaries for efficiency and conventional necessaries.
13. Classification of wants is not rigid.
14. The want satisfying capacity of goods and services is called utility.
15. Utility is neither same as usefulness nor same as pleasure.
16. Utility does not mean satisfaction.
17. Addition made to the utility of a good by changing its form is called 'Form Utility'.
18. Addition made to the utility of a good by changing its place is called 'Place Utility'.
19. Increase in the utility of a good with the change in time is called 'Time Utility'.
20. Utility created from different services is called 'Service Utility'.

21. In economics anything which has utility or want satisfying capacity is called 'good'.
22. Goods may either be material or non-material.
23. Free goods have no exchange value.
24. Supply of free goods is greater than their demand.
25. Economic goods are scarce and hence have exchange value.
26. Though 'land' is a free gift of nature, it is an 'economic good'.
27. Man has no control over the supply of free goods.
28. Except land, economic goods are results of human efforts.
29. The economic goods are considered as wealth.
30. The distinction between free goods and economic goods are not so rigid or fixed.
31. The goods which directly satisfy wants are called consumer goods.
32. The consumer goods are called as the goods of first order.
33. Some consumer goods are perishable and some are durable.
34. Single use goods are called perishable goods.
35. The good which help in further production of goods and thus indirectly satisfy wants are called producer goods.
36. The producer goods are sold in the market as 'end-products'.
37. The producer goods are otherwise called as 'capital'.
38. The producer goods are called as the goods of second order.
39. The distinction between consumer goods are producer goods depends upon their use.
40. The goods which are used up in the production process of other goods and lost their utility and identity are called intermediate goods.
41. Intermediate goods never cross production boundary.
42. The value of intermediate goods are not taken into account white estimating national income.
43. The final goods are sold in the markets as the 'end-products.'
44. The value of final goods only are taken into account while estimating national income.
45. The distinction between final goods and intermediate goods is not clear-cut.

46. The goods which are owned, supplied and managed by the public authorities are called 'public goods'.
47. The public goods are equally enjoyed by all.
48. The consumption of public goods is non-rival.
49. The principle of exclusion is not applicable in case of public goods.
50. The marginal cost of producing a public good for an additional user is zero.
51. The goods which are exclusively owned by private individuals or institutions are called 'private goods'.
52. The consumption of private good is rival.
53. The principle of exclusion is applicable in case of 'private goods'.
54. The benefit of private goods is internalised.
55. The goods which are tangible, can be seen and have definite shape are called 'material goods'.
56. The goods which are intangible rather only felt are called non-material goods or services.
57. In economics value means value-in-exchange or exchange value.
58. All economic goods have exchange value.
59. Value expressed in terms of money is called price.
60. All prices may go together but not all values.
61. The stock of anything that has exchange value is called wealth.
62. Anything in order to be considered as wealth must have the characteristics of utility, scarcity, marketability and external possession.
63. Wealth is a stock concept.
64. All financial assets such as shares, bonds, securities, cheques, including currency notes and coins are title-to-wealth or representative wealth, not wealth.
65. Personal talent having national and international fame are considered as national wealth.
66. That part of wealth which generates income is called capital.
67. Income is a flow concept.
68. Money is a title-to-wealth, as it has no utility of its own.
69. Wealth is an objective concept.
70. Welfare is a subjective concept.

QUESTIONS FOR REVIEW

A. *Choose the correct answer from the given alternatives in each question. (Each Carrying 1 Mark)*

1. **In economics want means :**
   (i) Desire for a commodity
   (ii) Desire for a commodity which can be made effective
   (iii) Utility
   (iv) Satisfaction
2. **On which characteristic of want the law of Diminishing Marginal utility is developed ?**
   (i) Wants are competitive (ii) Wants are unlimited
   (iii) A particular want is satiable (iv) Wants vary in intensity
3. **What type of want is nutritious foods ?**
   (i) Necessary for efficiency (ii) Conventional necessary
   (iii) Necessary for life (iv) Luxury
4. **Car for a college student is :**
   (i) Necessary (ii) Comfort
   (iii) Luxury (iv) Necessary for efficiency
5. **Car for a busy doctor is :**
   (i) Necessary (ii) Comfort
   (iii) Luxury (iv) Necessary for efficiency
6. **What type of want is wine ?**
   (i) Necessary for life (ii) Luxury
   (iii) Necessary for efficiency (iv) Conventional necessary
7. **What type of want is electric fan in summer ?**
   (i) Necessary (ii) Comfort
   (iii) Luxuriy (iv) All the above
8. **Goods meant for conspicuous consumption are :**
   (i) Necessaries (ii) Comforts
   (iii) Luxuries (iv) All the above

9. What type of want is medicine for a patient ?

(i) Necessary for life (ii) Necessary for efficiency

(iii) Conventional necessary (iv) Comfort

10. Want satisfying capacity of goods and services is called ....

(i) Satisfaction (ii) Usefulness

(iii) Utility (iv) All the above

11. Utility is a ....

(i) Subjective concept (ii) Objective concept

(iii) Stock concept (iv) Flow concept

12. What type of utility is created by changing the shape a command ?

(i) Service utility (ii) Form utility

(iii) Place utility (iv) Time utility

13. What type of utility is created by a carpenter ?

(i) Form utility (ii) Place utility

(iii) Service utility (iv) Time utility

14. What type of utility is created when jute is transformed into gunny-bags ?

(i) Service utility (ii) Form utility

(iii) Time utility (iv) Place utility

15. What type of utility is created by a teacher ?

(i) Form utility (ii) Service utility

(iii) Place utility (iv) Time utility

16. What type of utility is created by a truck-driver ?

(i) Form utility (ii) Place utility

(iii) Service utility (iv) Time utility

17. What type of utility is created by storing goods to be used later ?

(i) Time utility (ii) Form utility

(iii) Place utility (iv) Service utility

18. What type of utility is created by transferring a piece of log from forest areas to a saw-mill ?

(i) Form utility (ii) Time utility

(iii) Place utility (iv) Service utility

19. Which goods have no exchange value ?

(i) Free goods (ii) Economic goods

(iii) Non-material goods (iv) Final goods

20. What type of goods is land ?

(i) Free good (ii) Public good

(iii) Economic good (iv) All the above

21. Water from the tap in your house is ....

(i) Free good (ii) Economic good

(iii) Public good (iv) None of the above

22. Only which goods are wealth ?

(i) Final goods (ii) Consumer goods

(iii) Economic goods (iv) Free goods

23. Which goods directly satisfy human wants ?

(i) Free goods (ii) Consumer goods

(iii) Producer goods (iv) Material goods

24. Which goods are called goods of first order ?

(i) Producer goods (ii) Final goods

(iii) Public goods (iv) Consumer goods

25. What type of good is a sewing machine ?

(i) Consumer good (ii) Producer good

(iii) Public good (iv) Intermediate good

26. What type of good is chemical fertiliser ?

(i) Free good (ii) Intermediate good

(iii) Public good (iv) None of the above

27. What type of good is an ornament ?

(i) Consumer good (ii) Economic good

(iii) Final good (iv) All the above

28. Which goods lost their utility in the production process ?

(i) Consumer goods (ii) Producer goods

(iii) Intermediate goods (iv) Final goods

29. Which goods are called the goods of second order ?

(i) Consumer goods (ii) Producer goods

(iii) Intermediate goods (iv) Final goods

30. Which goods never cross production boundary ?

(i) Intermediate goods (ii) Public goods

(iii) Final goods (iv) Economic goods

31. Which goods are sold in the markets as 'end-products' ?

(i) Intermediate goods (ii) Final goods

(iii) Public goods (iv) Material goods

32. The value of which goods are taken into account while estimating national income?

(i) Producer goods (ii) Intermediate goods

(iii) Final goods (iv) All the above

33. Which goods are equally available to all ?

(i) Economic goods (ii) Private goods

(iii) Public goods (iv) Final goods

34. Consumption of which goods is rival ?

(i) Private goods (ii) Free goods

(iii) Public goods (iv) None of the above.

35. The principle of exclusion is not applicable to which goods ?

(i) Private goods (ii) Public goods

(iii) Economic goods (iv) Final goods

36. Marginal cost of producing public good for an extra consumer is ......

(i) Positive (ii) Negative

(iii) Zero (iv) None of the above

37. A 100 rupee note is not wealth because it has no ......

(i)Utility (ii) Scarcity

(iii) Marketability (iv) External possession

38. Which of the following is wealth ?

(i) Your matriculation certificate (ii) Voice of a singer

(iii) Goodwill of a business (iv) Padmashri Award

39. What type of wealth is Kohli's batting talent ?

(i) Personal wealth (ii) National wealth

(iii) Cosmopolitan wealth (iv) None of the above

40. Good health is not wealth because it has no......

(i) Utility (ii) Scarcity

(iii) Marketability (iv) All the above

41. Which one of the following is not wealth ?

(i) Padma Award (ii) Wrist Watch

(iii) Goodwill of a business (iv) Motor car

42. Value expressed in terms of money is called......

(i) Exchange value (ii) Use value

(iii) Price (iv) Cost

43. The part of wealth which generates income is called......

(i) Capital (ii) Saving

(iii) Utility (iv) Stock

44. Which one of the following is a title to wealth ?

(i) 100 rupee note (ii) Sale deed

(iii) Cheque (iv) All the above

45. Which one is a flow concept ?

(i) Wealth (ii) Income

(iii) Stock (iv) None of the above

B. *Correct the statement, if necessary, without changing the underlined portions. (Each Carrying 1 Mark)*

1. Human wants are unlimited.
2. Wants are satiable.
3. The law of diminishing marginal utility is developed on 'human wants are unlimited' characteristics of wants.
4. Luxuries make our life easy, decent and pleasant.
5. Necessaries for efficiency increase our working ability.
6. The things that we need due to the pressure of habit are called necessaries for life.

7. Bike for a college teacher is luxury.
8. Table and chair for a college students is luxury.
9. Bread and butter is necessary for life.
10. Want satisfying capacity of a good is called usefulness.
11. By changing the shape of a commodity service utility is created.
12. Service utility is created by a doctor.
13. Free goods have exchange value only.
14. Free goods are the results of human efforts.
15. The goods which directly satisfy human wants are called producer goods.
16. Sugar used in making sweets is a final good.
17. Raw materials are the examples of consumer goods.
18. Final goods are sold in the market as the end-products.
19. Public goods are subject to the principle of exclusion.
20. Consumption of private good is non-rival.
21. The benefit of public goods is internalised.
22. Material goods have no definite shape.
23. Durable goods are of single-use.
24. In economics value is used in the sense of use value.
25. All capital are wealth, but all wealth are not capital.
26. Voice of a singer is wealth.
27. Title-to-wealth have no utility of their own.
28. Money is wealth.
29. Wealth refers to the stock of anything that has use value.
30. Wealth is a flow concept where as income is a stock concept.

C. *Answer the following questions in 2-3 sentences (Each Carrying 2 Marks)*

1. What is want in economics ?
2. How wants are classified ?
3. What is necessary ?

4. What is comfort ?
5. What is luxury ?
6. What is necessaries for life ?
7. What is necessaries for efficiency ?
8. What is conventional necessaries ?
9. Why classification of want is not rigid ?
10. What is utility ?
11. Is utility same as usefulness ?
12. What is form utility ?
13. What is place utility ?
14. What is time utility ?
15. What is service utility ?
16. What is free good ?
17. What is economic good ?
18. What is consumer good ?
19. What is producer good ?
20. What is intermediate good ?
21. What is final good ?
22. What is public good ?
23. What is private good ?
24. What is material good ?
25. What is non-material good ?
26. What is durable good ?
27. What is perishable good ?
28. What do you mean by value in economics ?
29. What is price ?
30. What is wealth in economics ?
31. What is personal wealth ?
32. What is national wealth ?
33. What is cosmopolitan wealth ?

D. Distinguish between the Concepts in Six Sentences each (Each Distinction Carries 3 Marks)

1. Necessaries and Comforts.
2. Comforts and Luxuries.
3. Necessaries for life and necessaries for efficiency.
4. Utility and usefulness.
5. Form utility and place utility.
6. Free goods and economic goods.
7. Consumer goods and producer goods.
8. Intermediate goods and final goods.
9. Public goods and private goods.
10. Material goods and non-material goods.
11. Value and price
12. Personal Wealth and National Wealth.
13. Wealth and Title-to-wealth (Representative Wealth).
14. Wealth and Capital.
15. Wealth and Income.
16. Wealth and Money.
17. Wealth and Welfare.
18. Value-in-Exchange and Value-in-use.

E. Long Answer Type Questions (Carrying 7½ Marks)

1. Define want. Discuss the characteristics of human wants.
2. Define want. Make a classification of human wants.
3. What is utility ? Discuss the characteristics of utility.
4. Define wealth. Discuss the characteristics of wealth.

Answer to Q. N. A															
1.	(ii)	2.	(iii)	3.	(i)	4.	(iii)	5.	(iv)	6.	(iv)	7.	(ii)	8.	(iii)
9.	(i)	10.	(iii)	11.	(i)	12.	(ii)	13.	(i)	14.	(ii)	15.	(ii)	16.	(ii)
17.	(i)	18.	(iii)	19.	(i)	20.	(iii)	21.	(ii)	22.	(iii)	23.	(ii)	24.	(iv)

25.	(ii)	26.	(ii)	27.	(iv)	28.	(iii)	29.	(ii)	30.	(i)	31.	(ii)	32.	(iii)
33.	(iii)	34.	(i)	35.	(ii)	36.	(iii)	37.	(i)	38.	(iii)	39.	(ii)	40.	(iii)
41.	(i)	42.	(iii)	43.	(i)	44.	(iv)	45.	(ii)						

Answer to Q. N. B

1. Correct	2. A Particular want is	3. a particular want is satiable
4. Comforts	5. Correct	6. Conventional necessaries
7. Necessary	8. Necessary for efficiency	9. Necessary for efficiency
10. Utility	11. Form utility	12. Correct
13. Use value	14. Economic goods	15. Consumer goods
16. An intermediate good	17. Intermediate goods	18. Correct
19. Private goods	20. Rival	21. Private goods
22. Non-material goods	23. Perishable goods	24. Exchange value
25. Correct	26. Personal wealth	27. Correct
28. Title-to-wealth	29. Exchange value	30. Stock, Flow

❑❑❑

UNIT – II

3. CONSUMPTION, DEMAND AND PRICE ELASTICITY OF DEMAND

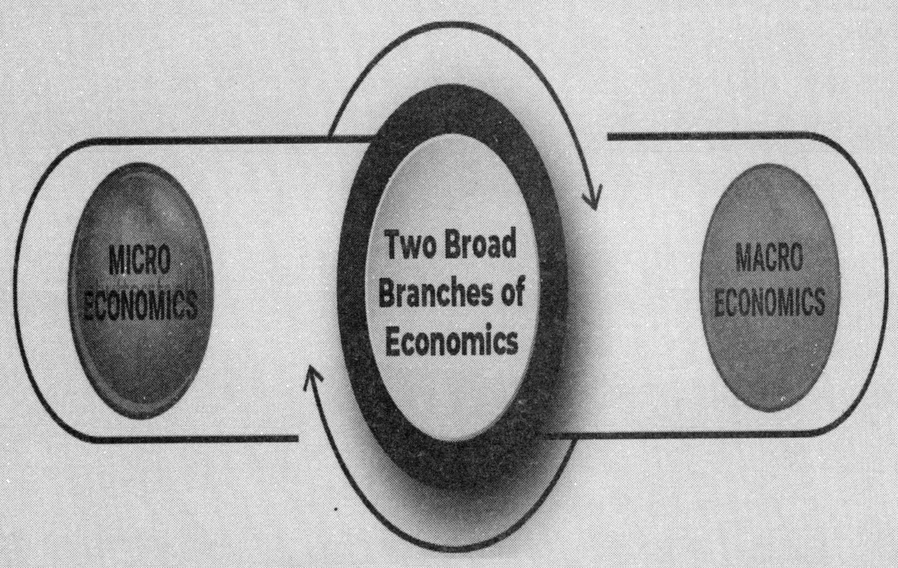

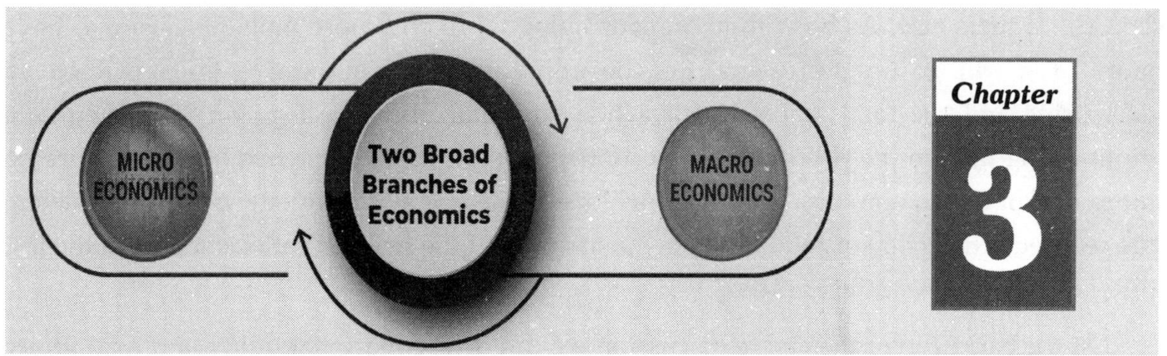

CONSUMPTION, DEMAND AND PRICE ELASTICITY OF DEMAND

We know want is the starting point of all economic activities. Man involves himself in various economic activities to satisfy his wants. The satisfaction of wants takes place by consumption. In this sense consumption means using up of wants satisfying capacity of goods for the satisfaction of wants, i.e. using up of utility of a commodity for the purpose of satisfaction of wants. This is also expressed as destruction of utility for the purpose of satisfying wants. So mere destruction of utility cannot be considered as consumption. For example, if a person drinks a glass of milk, the utility of milk is used up or destroyed. If the milk is poured down on the earth, its utility is also destroyed. The destruction of the utility of milk in the first case is considered as consumption where as in second case it is not consumption rather destruction.

Satisfaction of wants via destruction of utility of a commodity, i.e. consumption gives rise to two concepts of utility – **Marginal Utility** and **Total Utility.** We must have a clear cut idea about these two concepts to understand the manner in which a consumer behaves while satisfying his wants through consumption, which is studied in economics under the title 'consumer's behaviour'.

Marginal Utility and Total Utility

In the process of consumption when a consumer consumes the given amount of a commodity he expects some amount of satisfaction from each unit. Suppose he is given 5 units of a kind of sweet, say rasgolla. By consuming the 1st unit he will get some utility, which is nothing but 'realised satisfaction'. Similarly he will get some utility from the

2nd, 3rd, ... units also. As he will go on consuming more and more units his desire to have more of it will go on decreasing, i.e. the utility from the successive units will go on decreasing and the total realised satisfaction, i.e. total utility will go on increasing at a diminishing rate. In the process of consumption a stage will come when he will require no more unit of the commodity. That is he will reach the stage of complete satisfaction, where the realised satisfaction or total utility is maximum and the realised satisfaction from the last unit i.e. the marginal utility is zero.

On the backdrop of the above discussion we can define marginal utility and total utility as :

Marginal utility can be defined as the utility that a consumer gets from each successive unit of a given amount of a commodity. In other words, marginal utility refers to the addition made to the total utility, in the process of consumption, by consuming an additional unit of the given commodity.

For example, if the consumer is given 5 units of rasgollas and from 1st unit he gets 10 utils of utility (M.U. = 10), from the 2nd unit 8 utils of utility (MU = 8), from 3rd unit 5 utils of utility (MU = 5), from 4th, 1 utils (MU = 1) and from 5th unit '0' utility (MU = 0), this implies that his marginal utility from successive units are : 10, 8, 5, 1 and 0. It can also be known for a particular unit by deducting the total utility that he got upto previous units from the total utility that he is getting at the concerned unit. For example, if we are interested to know what is his marginal utility at 3rd unit then we can find it by deducting his total utility from 2 units (TU_{n-1}) from his total utility from 3 units (TU_n). Thus

$$\boxed{MU_{nth} = TU_n - TU_{n-1}}$$

In our example $TU_n = 10 + 8 + 5 = 23$

$$TU_{n-1} = 10 + 8 = 18$$

$$\therefore \quad MU_{3rd} = 23 - 18 = 5$$

Marginal utility is a function of change in the total utility with respect to change in the units consumed. So MU can be calculated using differential calculus as :

$$\boxed{MU = \frac{\partial TU}{\partial Q}}$$

∂ = Change w.r.t.

TU = Total utility

Q = Units consumed.

Total utility is defined as the sum of the marginal utilities or the sum of the utilities derived from all given units of a commodity symbolically :

$$TU_n = MU_1 + MU_2 + MU_3 + ... + MU_n$$

In our example given above $MU_1 = 10$, $MU_2 = 8$, $MU_3 = 5$, $MU_4 = 1$ and $MU_5 = 0$. So $TU_5 = 10 + 8 + 5 + 1 + 0 = 24$. i.e. the total utility from given 5 units of rasgollas is 24.

Relationship Between MU and TU

The relationship between the marginal utility (MU) and total utility (TU) is explained below with the help of a hypothetical MU and TU table drawn below :

M.U. & T.U. Schedule

Units	Marginal Utility	Total Utility
1	10	10
2	8	18
3	6	24
4	3	27
5	0	27
6	–2	25

The schedule drawn above shows that the consumer is getting 10 utils of utility from the consumption of the 1st unit of the given commodity. Since he has consumed only one unit his marginal and total utility are same (MU = TU), i.e. 10. When he consumes the subsequent units he is getting 8, 6, 3 ..... –2 utils of marginal utilities. The cumulative addition of the marginal utilities show his total utility from consuming subsequent units. It is to be noted that as he consumes the successive units his marginal utility is decreasing and total utility is increasing but at a diminishing rate. At the 5th unit the consumer has reached the complete satisfaction level as his marginal utility has become zero (0). This is shown by the highest total utility (27) at this level of consumption. After this, at the 6th unit the marginal utility has become negative (–2), showing a negative satisfaction as a result of which the total utility has decreased to 25.

Graphic Presentation :

The relationship between MU and TU is presented graphically below :

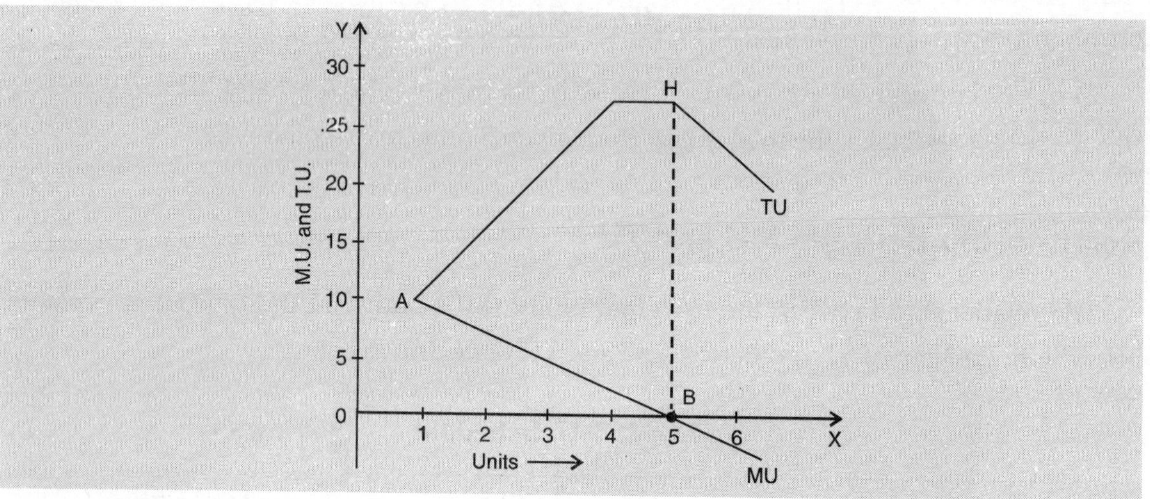

In the graph the units of good is presented on the OX-axis and OY-axis represents marginal and total utility. By plotting the marginal utilities from successive units and joining them we have obtained the MU curve which starts from point 'A' (utility –10) and gradually slopes downward to the right indicating decrease in the M.U. as the consumer consumes more and more units. The MU curve touches the base line (Ox-axis) at point 'B', i.e. at the 5th unit indicting zero (0) M.U. and then enters the negative zone.

Similarly by plotting the total utility at successive units, we have obtained the total utility curve TU. It starts from point A from where MU curve started, as at the 1st unit of consumption MU = TU. Then the TU curve has taken an upward slope to the right showing increase in the total utility with the increase in the units of consumption, but the slope in falling indicating increase in the total utility at a diminishing rate. The T.U. curve has reached at the highest point H, which is right above the point 'B' where MU curve touches the zero line. Then the TU curve turns downwards to the right indicating decrease in the total utility as marginal utility has become negative.

The relationship between the MU and TU can be summarised as :

(i) At the first unit of consumption MU = TU.

(ii) When MU decreases TU increases at a diminishing rate.

(iii) When MU becomes zero, T.U. becomes maximum.

(iv) When MU becomes negative, T.U. starts decreasing.

THE LAW OF DIMINISHING MARGINAL UTILITY

As one of the most fundamental law of consumption 'The Law of Diminishing Marginal Utility' is developed on a very common experience of day to day life that as we go on consuming more and more units of a commodity to satisfy a particular want then our desire for the commodity will gradually decrease and a stage will come when we do not want any more unit of that commodity. Because our that want is completely satisfied. This happens due to one of the characteristics of human want, **"a particular want is satiable".** The generalization of this characteristic of wants gives rise to the law of Diminishing Marginal Utility.

The law was originally formulated by Hermann Heinrich Gossen (H.H. Gossen) in 1854. However all credit goes to Alfred Marshall who developed it systematically and named it as **"Law of Diminishing Marginal Utility."** Yet, the law is also called as the Gossen's first law of consumption.

The Law

In the words of Gossen the law is :

> *"The magnitude of one and the same satisfaction, when we continue to enjoy it without interruption, continually decreases until satisfaction is reached."* ***– H.H. Gossen***

Alfred Marshall systematically presenting the law defined the law using technical terms. According to him the law is :

> *"The additional benefit which a person derives from a given increase of his stock of a thing diminishes with every increase in the stock that he already has."* ***– A. Marshall***

Simply speaking the law of diminishing marginal utility states that in the process of consumption of some given units of a commodity to satisfy a particular want the utility that the consumer gets from successive units diminishes.

Assumptions

As a law of consumer's behaviour under the utility approaches the law of diminishing marginal utility is developed on the following assumptions.

1. Rational Consumer

The consumer for whom the law is intended is assumed to be a rational or normal human being. In other words the consumer is not an abnormal person such as mad, drunkard, miser etc. The persons like thinkers, philosophens, poets etc. also behave irrationally when they are merged into deep thoughts and the law may not operate in that state of mind.

2. Homogeneous Units

All the units of the commodity being consumed are homogeneous, i.e. alike from all aspects-size, weight, quality etc. otherwise the law will not operate.

3. Reasonable Size

The units of the commodity are of reasonable size. For example to quench thirst the reasonable size of water is 'a glass of water'. If we give some one water spoon by spoon to quench his thirst then the utility from successive spoon of water will not diminish, i.e. the law will not operate.

4. No Time-Gap

There is no time-gap in between the consumption of any two units of the commodity. That is, consumption is continuous or in quick succession. If any time interval is allowed in between the consumption of two units then the law will not operate.

5. No Change in Taste, Preference and Income

The law assumes that the taste, preference and income of the consumer remain constant through out the consumption process. If his taste and preference are allowed to change in between the consumption process then his M.U. may increase. Similarly, after consuming some units if he gets to know that his income has increased then the utility from the subsequent unit(s) may increase.

6. Cardinal Measurement

The utility approach of consumer's behaviour and hence the law of diminishing utility assumes that the utility derived from different units of a commodity can be measured in terms of cardinal numbers. It also assumes 'money' as a measuring rod of utility.

Explanation of the Law

The law of diminishing marginal utility can be explained with the help of the utility table of a hypothetical consumer consuming some units of a commodity, say rasgolla, drawn follow :

M.U. and T.U. Table

Units	Marginal Utility	Total Utility
1	12	12
2	10	22
3	7	29
4	4	33
5	1	34
6	0	34
7	–2	32

The table shows that the consumer is getting 12 utils of utility from the 1st unit. From the successive 2nd, 3rd ....units he is getting 10, 7, ... Utils of utility respectively. As he consumes more and more units, his total utility is gradually increasing indicating decrease in the intensity of his desire for more rasgolla. That's why the marginal utility is gradually decreasing. At the 6th unit his marginal utility has become zero (0) indicating the level of complete satisfaction and at this level of consumption the total utility is maximum (34) If he will consume further, i.e. the 7th unit. M.U. will further fall (–2), indicating negative satisfaction which may come in the form of vomiting, and decrease in the T.U.

Graphic Presentation

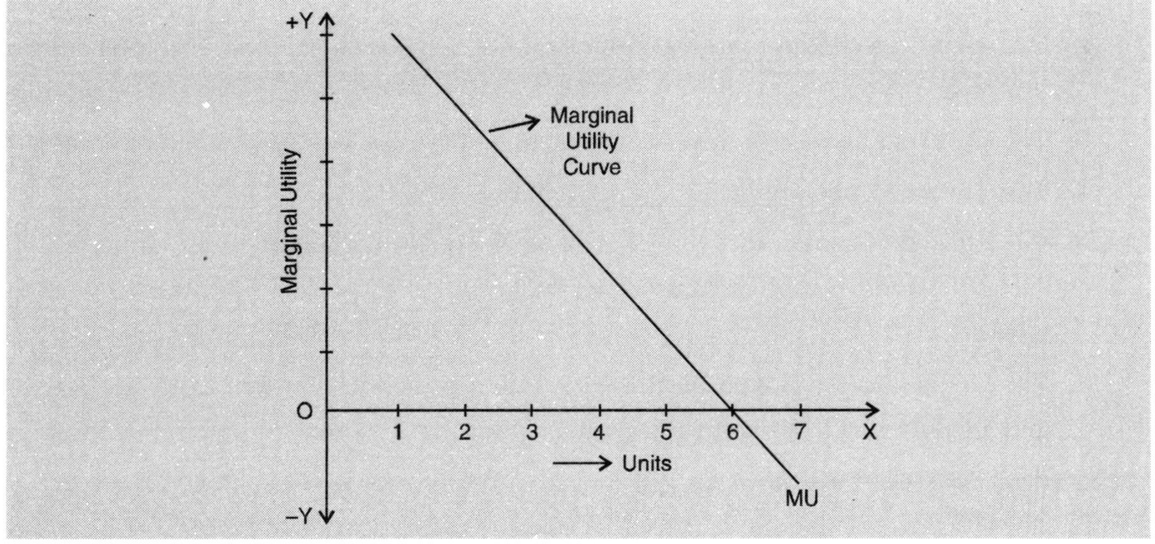

Graphically, the units of the commodity are presented on the horizontal axis and marginal utility from the successive units are presented on the vertical axis. By plotting the corresponding units and marginal utility derived from them and joining them successively we have obtained the marginal utility curve MU. The negative slope of the MU curve, i.e. downwards to the right indicates decrease in the marginal utility from successive units. The MU cure intersects the horizontal line at 6th unit of consumption indicating zero (0) MU from this unit. Then it enters the negative zone of the graph indicating negative marginal utility.

Two factors can be held responsible for the operation of the law of diminishing marginal utility. They are :

(i) A particular want is satiable.

(ii) Goods are not perfect substitutes of one another.

Limitations of the Law

The law of diminishing marginal utility is subject to a number of limitations. The important among them are :

1. The law is developed upon the unrealistic assumption of cardinal measurement of utility. Utility being a subjective concept cannot be measured in terms of cardinal numbers.
2. The law is not applicable in case of abnormal persons like misers, drunkards, mad persons, even in case of poets, philosophers, thinkers etc. It implies that the tendency of declining marginal utility cannot be generalize. If so, then how it can be a law.
3. The law is not applicable in case of collection of rare articles, stamp and old coins.
4. The law is not fully applicable in case of money.
5. the utility of a commodity does not depend on its own supply only, rather on its substitutes and complementary goods also. But the law has not taken this in to account.
6. The law is also developed on the wrong assumption of constant taste, preference and income making a consumer's behaviour static when the subject economics itself is dynamic.
7. The law may not operate in the initial stage of consumption.
8. The law is not applicable in case of indivisible material goods and non-material goods.

Importance

Inspite of the above limitations the law of diminishing marginal utility bears much significance in the sense that it forms the basis of other laws of consumption like the law of equi-marginal utility and the law of demand. That's why the law is called as the first law of consumption. The law helps on explaining why more is demanded at a lower price and vice versa. This law also helps in solving the paradox of value like why water having high use value commands a low price and diamond having low use value commands a very high price. (Which you will come across in higher studies in economics). Moreover, the law also helps in understanding the concept of consumer's surplus, which is included in the syllabus of higher classes. Above all, the law provided a way to the later economists to bring further improvement in the study of consumer's behaviour.

LAW OF EQUI-MARGINAL UTILITY (LAW OF SUBSTITUTION OR CONSUMER'S EQUILIBRIUM)

The law of Equi-marginal utility is an extension of the law off diminishing marginal utility. The law of diminishing marginal utility deals with a single commodity. But in real life, a consumer needs a variety of goods. But his money income being limited the problem is how he will allocate his limited money among different goods so that he will get maximum satisfaction. The law of equi-marginal utility provides solution to this problem, for which this law is also know as the 'Law of maximum satisfaction'. This law was also initially developed by H.H. Gossen and hence known as Gossen's Second Law of Consumption. However, it was Marshall who developed it systematically and popularized it in explaining consumer's behaviour.

The Law

*According to **Marshall** the law is, "If a person has a thing which he can put to several uses, he will distribute it between these uses in such a way that it has the same marginal utility in all."*

While purchasing different goods with a given amount of money a consumer will compare the marginal utilities of different commodities he wants to purchase and also the marginal utility of each commodity to its price. If he finds that the marginal utility of good 'X' (MU_X) is higher than that of good 'Y' (MU_Y) he will substitute good 'X' for good 'Y' till their marginal utilities are equalized ($MU_X = MU_Y$). Moreover, each good has a price of its own. So the consumer will allocate his given money in such a way that the last rupee spent on each good gives him the same marginal utility. If the last rupee spent on 'X' gives him less marginal utility he will withdraw this amount from 'X' and spend it on 'Y', if it gives him more marginal utility. The consumer will go on substituting his purchase till the marginal utility and price ratio of all goods is equal, i.e. :

$$\frac{MU_X}{P_X} = \frac{MU_Y}{P_Y}$$

P_X = Price of good-X

P_Y = Price of good-Y

Simply speaking the law states that the consumer will get maximum satisfaction when he allocates his given money among different goods in such a way that the marginal utility of last unit of money spent on each good becomes equal. This is possible when :

$$\frac{MU_X}{P_X} = \frac{MU_Y}{P_Y} = \ldots\ldots = \frac{MU_n}{P_n} = MU_m \text{ (Marginal Utility of Money)}$$

Till this equality, which is called 'Proportion Rule', is not reached the consumer will go on substituting his purchase of different goods. That's why the law is also called as the law of substitution. At this equality, the consumer will be in equilibrium *i.e.* in a state of changelessness in respect of his purchase.

Explanation of the Law

To explain the law let us take a concrete examples.

Suppose our hypothetical consumer has ₹ 9 to spend on two goods, 'X' and 'Y' and price of both the goods is ₹ 1 (we have assumed this for the sake of simplicity of the analysis). The supposed marginal utilities from both the goods is presented in the table drawn below :

Marginal Utility of Good 'X' and Good 'Y'

Units	M.U. of Good-X	M.U. of Good-Y
1	12	10
2	10	8
3	8	6
4	6	4
5	4	2
6	2	1
7	1	0
8	0	–1
9	–2	–2

The table clearly shows that our consumer being a rational man will not spend his money on 9th unit of 'X' or on 8th and 9th units of 'Y' as they yield negative marginal utility. Rather he will spend those units of money on other units of the either yielding positive marginal utilities. On this ground the possible combinations of two goods that he may consider and the sum of the utilities from those combinations are presented in the table given below :

Combinations	Sum of MU_X	Sum of MU_Y	Total Utility	Explanation
8x + y	43	10	53	T.U. is increasing.
7x + 2y	43	18	61	So substitution of X
6x + 3y	42	24	66	for Y will continue
5x + 4y	40	28	68	State of Equilibrium
4x + 5y	36	30	66	T.U. is decreasing.

The table shows that from combination 8x + y the total utility that the consumer getting is 43 + 10 = 53, at this combination $MU_X < MU_Y$ (0 < 10) so he will substitute X for Y and try combination 7x + 2y. The total utility from this combination 43 + 18 = 61 is increasing but still $MU_X < MU_Y$ (1 < 8). So he will again substitute X for Y and try the subsequent combinations till $MU_X = MU_Y$ combination is arrived at, so that his total utility will be maximum. This is reached at the combination 5x + 4y, where the total utility, 40 + 28 = 68, is maximum and at this combination, as is shown in table-1, the $MU_X = MU_Y$, i.e. 4. As the prices of both the goods are same (₹ 1) here the rationality rule is also satisfied, that is :

$$\frac{MU_X}{P_X} = \frac{MU_Y}{P_Y} \Rightarrow \frac{4}{1} = \frac{4}{1}$$

Graphical Presentation : This law is presented graphically below. Below we have drawn the figure in two panels. Panel-A represents Good-X and Panel-B represents good-Y. In both the panels we have presented units of goods on the OX-axis and their respective marginal utilities on the OY-axis. The curve MU_X is the marginal utility curve of good-X obtained by plotting the marginal utilities derived from successive units of 'X'. MU_Y is the marginal utility curve of good-Y obtained by plotting the marginal utilities derived from successive units of 'Y'. The horizontal line EM drawn at the '4' utils of utility is the 'Line of Equi-marginal Utility', representing $MU_X = MU_Y = 4$ at the combination 5x + 4y, i.e. 5 units of good 'X' and 4 units of good 'Y'. This combination also yields the highest total utility. So our hypothetical consumer is said to be in equilibrium at this combination.

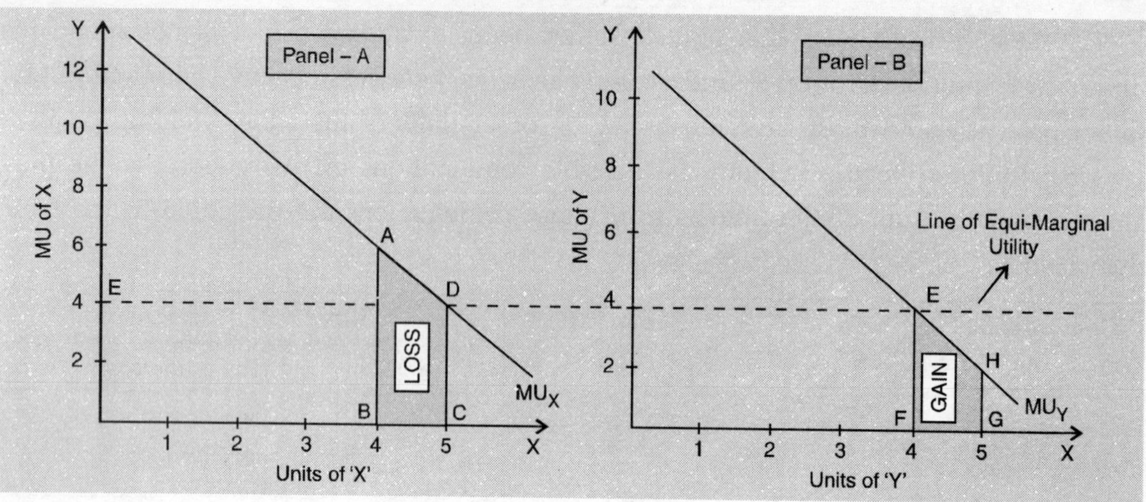

Now let us see what will happen if he changes his purchase. For example, if he will opt for the combination 4x + 5y, i.e. give up one unit of X for an additional unit of Y then as shown in the figure (Panel-A) he is losing ABCD amount of utility from good X and gaining EFGH amount of utility from good 'Y'. But geometrically the loss is more than the gain as Area ABCD > area EFGH and hence his total utility will decrease. So a rational consumer will not do that. He will choose the combination 5x + 4y.

Assumptions

From the above explanation we can say that the law of equi-marginal utility is developed on the following assumptions.

1. The consumer is rational one.
2. The goods he wishes to purchase are divisible.
3. The units of goods are homogeneous.
4. The prices of the goods and the money at the disposal of the consumer are given and constant.
5. Utility can be measured in terms of cardinal numbers.
6. Money is the measuring rod of utility.
7. Marginal utility of money remains constant.

Limitations of the Law

Like the law of diminishing marginal utility this law is also subject to several limitations. Important among them are :

1. Utility is a subjective concept. So measurement of utility by cardinal numbers is unrealistic.

2. Marginal utility of money is assumed to be constant which is unrealistic. Like any other commodity when the stock of money decreases its utility (importance) rather increases. Hence it can't be a measuring rod of utility.
3. How much rational a man may be he cannot be a calculating machine to calculate the marginal utility from different units accurately before his purchase. Practically it is neither possible nor happens.
4. In case of durable goods the law is not applicable.
5. The law is also not applicable in case of indivisible goods.
6. The law is not applicable in case of goods which are required due to the pressure of social customs and traditions.

Importance of the Law

In spite of the above limitations the law of equimarginal utility certainly bears some theoretical and practical significance. It is true that exact equalization of utilities from different goods is not possible, yet a consumer makes a rough measurement in his mind while making his purchase of more than one good. In the field of production the law helps the producer in choosing the optimum combination of factors to minimize the cost of production and to maximize profit. Likewise in case of public finance it helps the public authorities to maximize social welfare by choosing the optimum combination of public expenditure. Hence the practical importance of this law cannot be ruled out completely.

CONDITIONS OF CONSUMER'S EQUILIBRIUM

From the above discussion on the consumer's behaviour under cardinal utility analysis we can draw the conditions of consumers equilibrium as :

(i) In case of a single commodity the consumer will be in equilibrium when the marginal utility of the commodity is equal to its price. That is :

$$MU_X = P_X$$

(ii) In case of more than one commodity with same price the consumer will be in equilibrium when the marginal utilities of all the commodities are equal. That is :

$$MU_X = MU_Y = \ldots\ldots = MU_n$$

(iii) In case of more than one commodity with different prices the consumer will be in equilibrium when the ratio of MU of all commodities to their corresponding prices are equal or the proportionality rule is satisfied. That is :

$$\frac{MU_X}{P_X} = \frac{MU_Y}{P_Y} = \ldots\ldots\ldots = \frac{MU_n}{P_n} = MU_n$$

DEMAND

In economics after 'want', most probably the widely used term is 'demand'. In our day-to-day life often we come across the term 'demand', which implies 'desire for some thing'. But in economics it is used not in the sense of mere desire. In economics the term 'demand' is used in the sense of 'effective desire' or the desire for something which can be made effective. A desire can be made effective only when one has the ability and willingness to pay for the desired commodity at a given time knowing its price. In this sense the desire of a beggar cannot be 'demand' since he has no ability to pay, the desire of a miser also cannot be 'demand' since he has no willingness to pay. Even one's desire for a commodity having the ability to pay and willingness to pay for it cannot be considered as demand unless the price of the commodity at the time of desire is known. Because the price is an important factor affecting the ability of a person to desire for a commodity. This implies that the concept of demand is meaningless without reference to price and time.

Definition

From the above stated meaning of demand we can define 'demand' as :

"Desire for a commodity backed by ability and willingness to pay for it at a given price at a given time."

According to ***Benham,*** *"The demand for anything at a price is the amount of it which will be bought per unit of time at that price."*

Features of Demand

(i) Desire for a commodity.

(ii) Ability to pay for it.

(iii) Willingness to pay for it.

(iv) Price must be known

(v) Time must be mentioned.

Demand Function

Demand is a relative concept. Because demand for a commodity depends upon a number of factors. It varies with the change in price of the commodity, changes in the prices of the relative goods–either substitutes or complementary goods, changes in the ability and willingness a person to pay-which again is affected by a number of factors, changes in time and so on. The functional relationship between the quantity demanded of a commodity and the factors affecting its demand in technical term is called 'demand function'. In equation form it is written as :

$$D_X = f(P_x, P_r, Y, T, P, C, G.....)$$

Where :

D_X = Demand for 'X', P_x = Price of 'X', P_r = Price of a related good,

Y = Income of the consumer, T = Taste, preference and habit of the consumer,

P = Population, C = Climate, G = Government policy and so on.

DETERMINANTS OF DEMAND

The concept of demand is a relative concept. Because demand for a commodity is influenced by several factors. Some of these factors may be economic some may be socio-cultural and some of them may be psychological relating to the person(s) demanding a commodity. All these factors affecting the demand for any commodity are called as the determinants of demand.

Some of these determinants are discussed below :

1. **Price of the Commodity.** Price of the concerned commodity is one of the most important determinants of the demand for the commodity. Normally, there is an inverse relationship between the price of a commodity and its quantity demanded, other factors affecting its demand remaining constant. That is, the demand for a commodity normally increases when its price decreases and vice versa. This inverse relationship between the price and quantity demanded is studied under the law of demand. However, in case of inferior goods called 'Giffen's goods' the relationship between price and quantity demanded is direct.

2. **Prices of Related Goods.** Demand for a good is also influenced by the prices of its related goods. Related goods may either be its substitutes or its complementaries. For example tea and coffee are substitutes. Any change in the price of tea will affect the demand for coffee and the reverse. That is, the price of coffee remaining constant if the price of tea increases, some marginal consumer may substitute tea for coffee. As a result of which the demand for coffee will increase. Similarly tea dust, milk and sugar and complementaries. The price of tea dust remaining constant if the price of milk or sugar or both increases it will adversely affect the demand for tea dust.

3. **Income of the Consumer.** Income of the consumer determines his purchasing power or ability to pay for a commodity and hence his demand. Larger income implies greater purchasing power and more demand and the reverse. Other factors affecting demand remaining constant if the income of a person increases then his demand will increase and the reverse. Thus the income of the consumer and his demand for a normal commodity are directly related, i.e. demand is a direct function of income.

4. **Price Expectation.** The demand for a commodity is determined not only by its current or prevailing price but also by its expected future price. Because if people will expect the price of a commodity to rise in near future then its demand at prevailing price will increase. Similarly, if people will expect the price of a commodity to fall in near future then its demand at the prevailing price will fall. Even, if the price of a commodity is falling and is further expected to fall in near future its demand will fall and reverse will happen in case when price is rising. For example, when the price of gold falls people stop purchasing jewellary with the exception of further fall in the price of gold and the reverse.

5. **Taste and Preference of the Consumer.** Changes in the taste and preference of the consumer for different goods also affect the demand for different goods and services irrespective of their prices. For example, demand for traditional food is decreasing where as the demand for junk foods is constantly increasing due to change in the taste and preference of the people. Similarly changes in the fashion in the dynamic world is also affecting the demand pattern of the people.

6. **Population.** The demand for different goods and services is also influenced by the size and composition of the population. If there is increase in the population, other factors affecting demand remaining constant, demand for different goods and services will increase and vice versa. Demand for different goods and services also changes with the composition of population, i.e. in age-structure or sex-composition.

7. **State of Economic Activities.** Demand for various goods and services is also affected by the state of economic activities. For example during the period of boom or prosperity of the economy demand for various goods and services increases due to rise in income irrespective of rise in prices. On the other hand, during depression or falling tendency of economic activities demand for goods and services decreases despite the fall in prices of goods and services.

8. **Income Distribution.** Over all demand for various goods and services in an economy is also influenced by the income distribution pattern. An equitable distribution of income will increase the over all demand for goods and services in the economy. On the other hand inequalities in the distribution of income will create an imbalance in the demand pattern. Greater the inequality in the distribution of income lower will be the over all demand for goods and services in the economy.

9. **Demonstration Effect.** Demand for various goods and services is also affected by their advertisement and propagonda and the desire of the people to imitate the consumption pattern of their rich neighbours. This is called the demonstration effect on demand. Often the demand for various semi-luxurious and luxurious goods and services increases due to demonstration effect.

10. **Weather and Climate.** Demand for some goods and services is also influenced by the changes in the weather and climate of a region. For example demand for woolen clothes, hot drinks like tea and coffee increases during winter season, where as the demand for cotton clothes, cold drinks, fan, air conditioner etc. increases during the summer.

11. **Government Policy.** Fiscal policy of the government of a country, i.e., policy on taxation, subsidy, public expenditure, public borrowing, trade policy etc. also influence the demand for various goods and services via their redistributive effects on income and business activities.

Besides the above discussed determinants the demand for various goods and services are also influenced by a number of socio-cultural and political factors. Demand for various goods and services increases during various festive occasions and political activities like strikes, gheraos, elections etc.

THE LAW OF DEMAND

The law of demand is an important law of consumption. We know demand is a function of multi-variable factors. That is the demand for a commodity depends upon a number of factors which we have already discussed above as the determinants of demand. The law of demand, however, seeks to explain the functional relationship between the price and quantity demanded of a commodity, assuming other factors affecting its demand remaining constant.

Common experience shows that there is an inverse relationship between the price of a commodity and its quantity demanded, other factors affecting its demand remaining constant. Alfred Marshall explained this inverse relationship as :

> *Under ceteris paribus condition, "amount demanded increases with a fall in price and diminishes when price increases."*

Simply speaking the law of demand states that, other factors affecting the demand for a commodity remaining constant, more will be its demand when its price is low and vice versa. Thus there is an inverse relationship between price and quantity demanded of a commodity.

This inverse relationship can be presented as :

$$D_X \propto \frac{1}{P_X}$$

$\Rightarrow$ If $P_X \downarrow \rightarrow D_X \uparrow$

and, If $P_X \uparrow \rightarrow D_X \uparrow$

Where, D_X = Demand for X

P_X = Price of X

$1/P_X$ = inverse of P_X

$\propto$ = Functional relation

$\downarrow$ = Fall, $\uparrow$ = Rise

Assumptions

Marshall, developed the law on the 'ceteris paribus' assumption. 'Ceteris Paribus' means other things remaining constant. It implies :

1. The income of the consumer, his taste and preference are constant.
2. The prices of related goods – the substitute and complementary goods, are constant.
3. The size of population, climate, fashion etc. are constant.
4. The income distribution pattern in the economy is constant.
5. There is no expectation of any change in the price of the concerned commodity in near future.
6. There is no change in the government policy.
7. The commodity concerned is a normal commodity.

Explanation of the Law

The law of demand can be explained with the help of an individual demand schedule drawn below.

Individual Demand Schedule

An individual demand schedule is a list of various quantities of a commodity which a consumer is willing to purchase at different possible prices. The schedule drawn below shows that when the price of the commodity, say 'X' is ₹ 40 the consumer is willing to purchase 5 units of it, i.e. the quantity demanded is 5 units. As the price of 'X' falls to ₹ 35, ₹ 30 and so on, his willingness to purchase or quantity demanded increases to 10 units, 15 units and so on respectively. Reverse will be the case if we take the relationship between the price and quantity demand from the bottom of the table to upwards. Thus a demand schedule is a tabular presentation of the law of demand.

Individual Demand Schedule For 'X'

Price/Unit (in ₹)	Quantity Demanded (in Units)
40	5
35	10
30	15
25	18
20	20

Graphic Presentation (Individual Demand Curve)

The law of demand can be presented graphically in the form of a demand curve. Below we have presented the individual demand schedule drawn above in the form of a graph to get an individual demand curve.

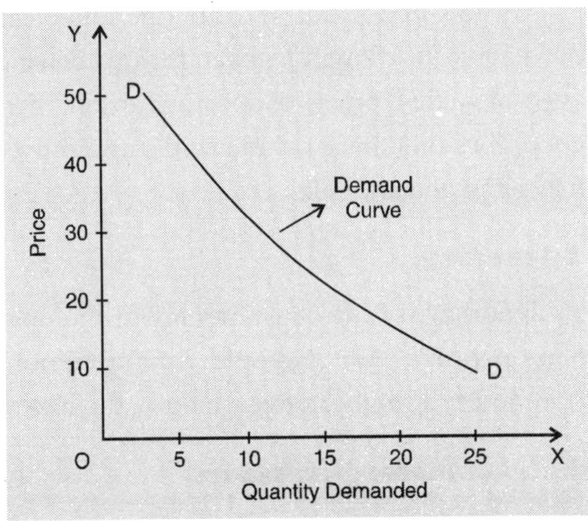

In the figure we have presented quantity demanded of the commodity on the OX-axis and its price on the OY-axis. Plotting the corresponding figures of price and quantity demanded on the graph we get some points and by joining the points the curve that we have got (DD) is the demand curve. The slope of the curve is negative, i.e. downwards sloping to the right, representing the inverse relationship between the price and quantity demanded. Thus a demand curve is the graphic presentation of the law of demand.

Exceptions to the Law

The law of demand does not operate in certain cases which are called exceptions to the law.

Some of those exceptions are :

1. Prestigious goods and Goods for Conspicuous Consumption

The law of demand does not operate in case of prestigious goods inspiring high respect and status in the society. These goods are demanded by the richer section of the society only for the sake of vanity not for their intrinsic value. Gold and diamond ornaments, expensive electronics devices etc. are the examples of these goods. Goods for conspicuous consumption also come under this category. Demand for these goods increases with the rise in their prices.

2. Highly Essential Goods

The law of demand does not work in case of the goods which are highly essential either for life or for maintaining working efficiency or to keep update according to the changing life style etc. Essential food items, medicine, cell phone as the necessity of modern life etc. are the example of goods.

3. Price Expectation

The law of demand will not operate in case of those goods whose prices are expected by the people to change in near future. During marriage season people demand more gold even at higher prices expecting further increase in prices. Similarly, when the price of a good goes on falling people stop purchasing that good anticipating further fall in price and hence the demand falls.

4. Ignorance

Ignorance of the consumer about the market conditions often makes the law of demand non-operative. For example due to ignorance a consumer may purchase more of a commodity at higher prices making the law of demand inoperative.

5. Conventional Necessaries

The law of demand also does not operate in cage of goods which are demanded for conventional necessities such as due to the social or traditional or religious or habitual pressures.

6. Giffen's Goods

The law of demand also does not operate in case of inferior goods which are called as Giffen's goods, named so after the name of Sor Robert Giffenn of Ireland. He proved that while comparing two goods – meat and potato, the law of demand does not work in case of potato, it being inferior to meat, when the price of both the goods change in the same direction.

CAUSES OF THE OPERATION OF THE LAW (WHY DEMAND CURVE TAKES A NEGATIVE SLOPE ?)

The law of demand states that other things affecting demand remaining constant, quantity demanded of a commodity rises with the fall in its price and vice versa. It implies that there is an inverse or negative relationship between the price and quantity demanded of a commodity.

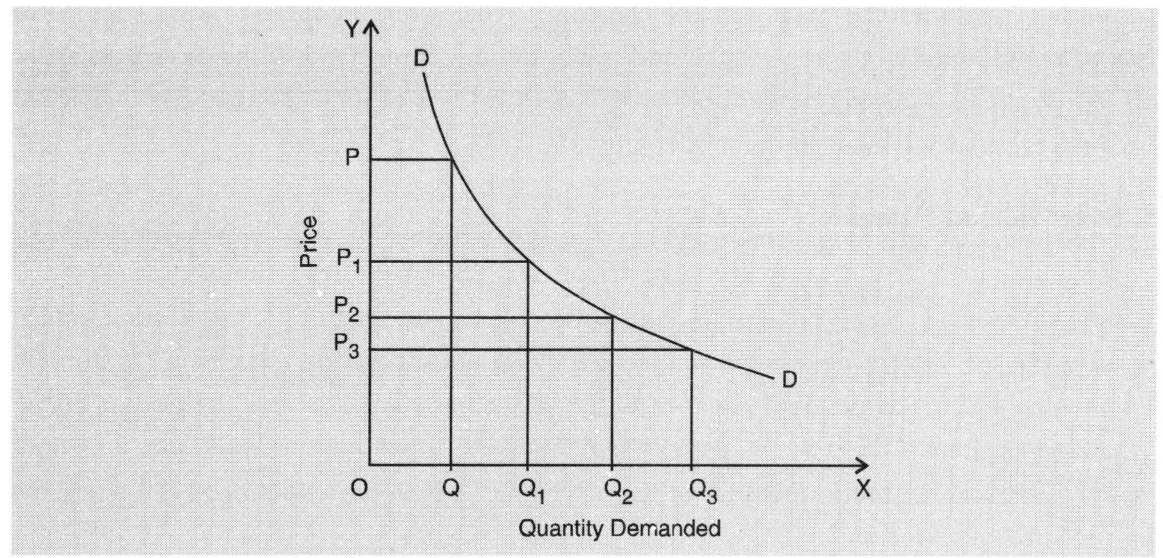

When we present this negative relationship between price and quantity demanded of a commodity in a graph the curve that we obtain is called demand curve. The shape of the demand curve for a normal commodity is downward sloping to the right. This negative slop of the demand curve implies more is demanded at a lower price and vice versa and is the graphical presentation of the law of demand.

Now the question is why the law of demand operates ? or why more is demanded at a lower price and vice versa ? or why a demand curve takes a negative slope ? Four major causes can be held responsible for this.

They are discussed below :

1. Application of the Law of Diminishing Marginal Utility

The law of diminishing marginal utility states that as a consumer consumes more and more units of a commodity the utility derived from each successive units falls. So he will value each successive unit less than the previous one and will purchase more of a commodity only when its price falls. That is, comparing the marginal utility with the price of the commodity he will demand more at a lower price which makes the law of demand to operate and give the demand curve a negative slope.

2. Income Effect

Money income remaining constant, as the price of a commodity changes the real income of a consumer will also change to affect his demand for the commodity. If the price of a commodity falls the real income of the consumes will increase and he will be capable of purchasing more of it, i.e. he will demand more. On the other hand, if the price goes up it will reduce his purchasing power and he will demand less of it. Thus the income effect of price change causes the law of demand to operate.

3. Substitution Effect

When the price of a commodity falls, the price of its substitutes remaining the same, it becomes relatively cheaper than its substitutes. This will result in substitution effect. Because the consumers have a normal tendency to substitute the cheaper good for the dearer good and the demand for cheaper good will increase. For example, the price of coffee remaining constant if the price of tea falls some marginal consumer of coffee will substitute tea for coffee and hence the demand for tea will be more. Reverse will happen if the price of tea rises that of coffee remaining constant. Thus the substitution effect of price change also contributes towards the operation of the law of demand.

4. Entry of New Consumers

When the price of a commodity comes down its demand rises because some marginal consumers or new consumers, who could not afford it earlier when price was high, enter into the market. Consequently the demand for the commodity will rise on the other hand when the price goes up those marginal consumers leave the market or stop purchasing the commodity and hence the quantity demanded decreases.

In fact, all the above reasons working simultaneously result in the working of the law of demand or lead to more demand at a lower price and vice versa and give the demand curve of a commodity a negative slope.

SOME OTHER CONCEPTS RELATED TO DEMAND ANALYSIS

Giffen's Goods

Earlier, in the exceptions of the law of demand, we have stated that the law of demand does not operate in case of a Giffen's good. Now the question may arise what is Giffen's good ? In economics Giffen's good is used as a relative concept. When we compare two goods from their qualitative aspects, the inferior one is called 'Giffen's good'. This is so named after the name of an Irish economist Sir Robert Giffen who tested the operation of the law of demand in an Irish market and found a paradoxical situation. Taking two goods – meat and potato, in to account he found that when the prices of meat and potato changing in the same direction the law of demand is working in case of meat but not in case of potato. Rather the demand for potato was changing in the direction of change in price, establishing a positive relationship between the price and quantity demanded of potato. In economics this finding of Giffen is known as 'Giffen's Paradox'.

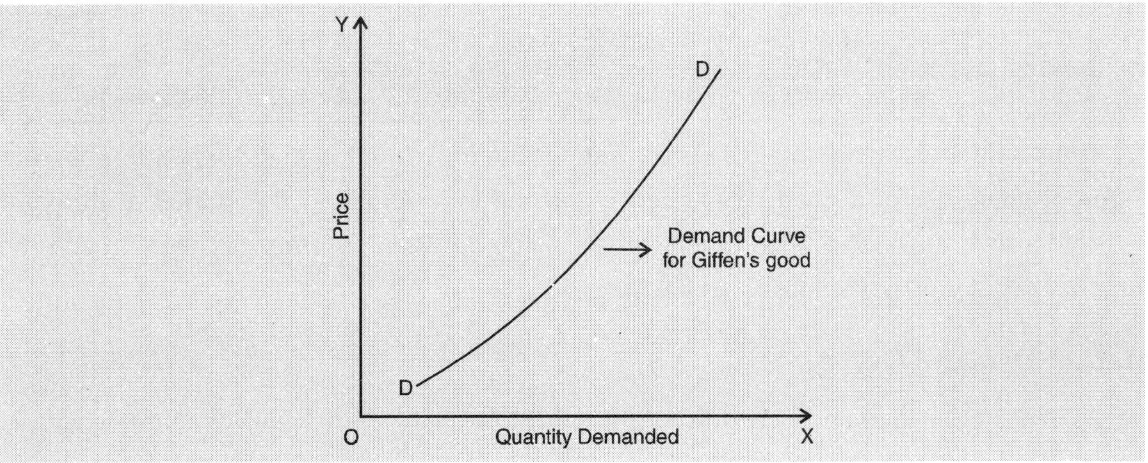

Since then it is assumed that the law of demand does not work in case of inferior goods, termed as Giffen's goods as it works in case of superior goods. So in case of Giffen's good the prices and quantity demanded are positively related and in case of Giffen's goods the demand curve takes a positive slope, i.e. upward sloping to the right as shown in the figure drawn above.

Market Demand Schedule

White explaining the law of demand we had taken the demand schedule of an individual for a commodity showing his willingness to purchase different quantities of a commodity at different possible prices. But in a market there is not one consumer of a commodity rather many consumers having different capacity to purchase the commodity at the same possible pries. In this sense market demand schedule refers to the list or table showing the sum of various quantities of a good that all the consumers present in the market taken together are willing to purchase at different possible prices. Suppose there are 3 consumers in the market demanding different amount of the good, say 'X' at different possible prices.

Their individual demand and the market demand of good 'X' is shown in the schedule drawn below :

Market Demand Schedule

Price (₹)	Quantity Demanded by – A	Quantity Demand ed by – B	Quantity Demand ed by – C	Market Demand
6	15	20	30	15 + 20 + 30 = 65
5	20	25	40	20 + 25 + 40 = 85
4	25	28	50	25 + 28 + 50 = 103
3	30	32	55	30 + 32 + 55 = 117
2	35	38	58	35 + 38 + 58 = 131
1	40	45	60	40 + 45 + 60 = 145

Thus, market demand schedule is the sum of the individual demand schedule showing different quantities of a good demanded by all the individuals in the market at different possible prices. It also shows an inverse relationship between the price of the good and the quantity demanded in the market as a whole.

Market Demand Curve

As the market demand schedule is the addition of the individual demand schedule, market demand curve is also the graphical addition of the individual demand curves of the consumer present in the market. Graphically we can obtain it directly plotting the pairs of prices and quantity of market demand or by horizontal addition of individual demand curves or by their lateral addition. For the sake of simplicity we have drawn the market demand curve below by lateral addition.

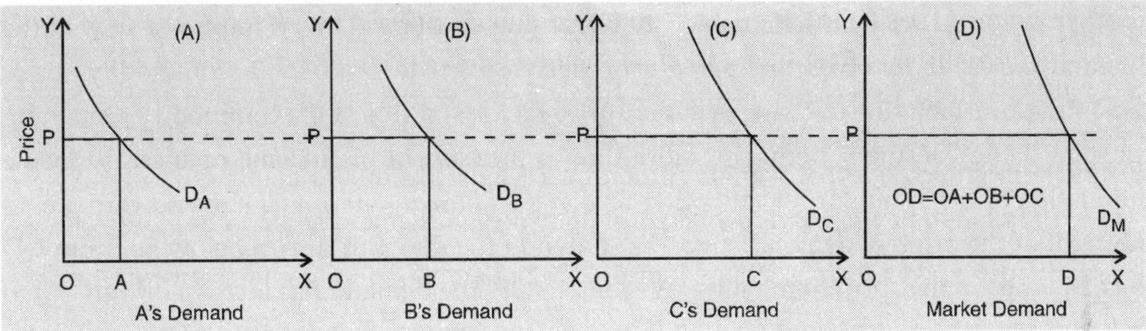

In the figure drawn above the market demand curve D_M is shown in panel (D). It is obtained by the lateral addition of the individual demand curves D_A, D_B and D_C of individual A, B and C respectively. In the figure it is shown that at price 'OC' the demand of A is OA, that of 'B' and 'C' are OB and 'OC'. By adding 'OA', 'OB' and 'OC' we have obtained the market demand 'OD'. Like individual demand curve the market demand curve also slopes downwards to the right indicating market demand will be more at lower price and vice-versa.

Change in Demand (Shift in the Demand Curve)

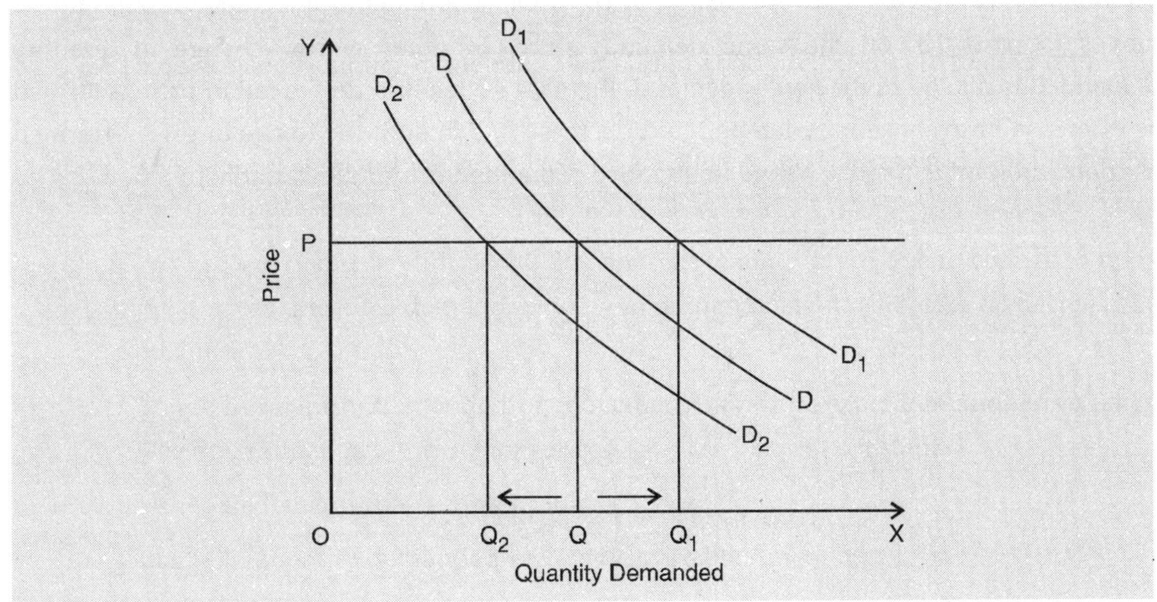

We know the demand for a commodity is influenced by a number of factors such as price of the concerned commodity, prices of its related goods, income of the consumer, his taste, preference, habit, population etc. change in demand takes place when there is change in other factor(s), price of the commodity remaining constant. Thus it implies a shift in the demand curve. It involves an increase or decrease in demand for a commodity, price remaining constant, due to changes in non-price factor(s). Price of the commodity remaining constant if the consumer demands more due to increase in his income or increase in the population of his family or for any other reason his demand curve will shift upward, i.e. to the right of the original demand curve, as shown in the diagram drawn below i.e. from DD to D_1D_1. This implies price remaining constant at 'OP' the demand has increased from OQ to OQ_1. On the other hand, price remaining the same, if the consumer demands less, say OQ_2, then his demand curve shifts to the left of the original demand curve, i.e. to D_2D_2. Thus change in demand is a multi-variable function.

Change in Quantity Demanded (Movement Along the Demand Curve)

Change in quantity demanded of a commodity takes place where there is a change in demand due to change in its price, other factors affecting its demand remaining constant. Thus, in case of change in quantity demanded there is movement along the same demand curve from one point to another. As shown in the figure drawn below when the price is 'OP' the consumer is demanding 'OQ' of the commodity. At this purchase he is at point 'A' on the demand curve DD. With the fall in price to OP_1 his demand increases to OQ_1 and he moves to point 'B' on the same demand curve. In other words, change in quantity demanded is related to the law of demand. Increase in demand due to fall in price is termed as extension or expansion in demand and decrease in demand due to rise in price is termed as contraction in demand. Change in quantity demanded is a single-variable function.

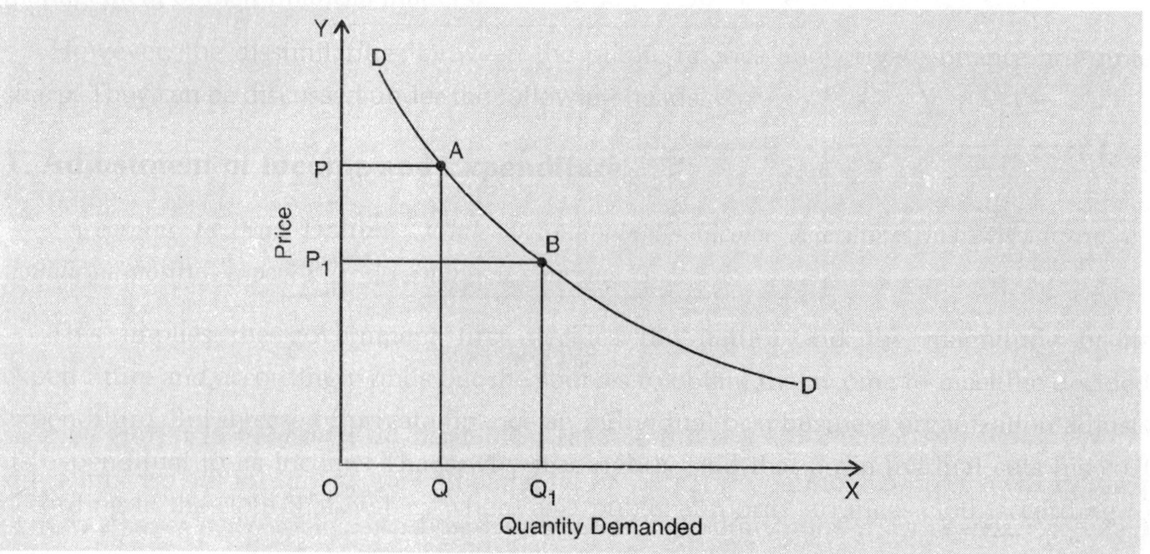

PRICE ELASTICITY OF DEMAND

The law of demand only states about the existence of an inverse relationship between the price of a commodity and its quantity demanded, other factors affecting its demand remaining constant. Thus it only states about the direction of change in quantity demand due to change in price, not the magnitude of change which bears much significance in decision taking process. For this we need a different study called 'elasticity of demand'. The term 'elasticity' mean the feature of expansion and contraction. To what extent a thing will expand or contract or what will be the elasticity of a thing that depends upon the physical feature of the thing, force applied to it etc. Likewise to what extent the demand for a commodity will expand or contract that also depends upon change in the factors) affecting its demand. In this sense 'elasticity of demand can be defined as :

"the degree of responsiveness in quantity demanded of a commodity due to a given change in any of the factors affecting its demand."

However, most of the factors affecting the demand for a commodity are subjective. So the measurement of any change in those subjective factors is not possible. That's why to measure the degree of change in quantity demanded i.e. the elasticity of demand we mostly take into account the objective factors such as the price of the commodity, income of the consumer and the prices of the related goods and accordingly measure three types of elasticity of demand :

(i) Price elasticity of demand.

(ii) Income elasticity of demand and

(iii) Cross elasticity of demand.

Price Elasticity of Demand

Price elasticity of demand can be defined as "the degree of responsiveness in quantity demanded of a commodity due to a given change in its price."

*According to **Marshall**, "The elasticity or responsiveness of demand in a market is great or small accordingly as the amount demanded increases much or little for a given fall in price and diminishes much or little for a given rise in price."*

*In the words of **Prof. Boulding**, "Elasticity of demand measures the responsiveness of demand to change in price."*

However, Mrs. Joan Robinson presented the definition of price elasticity of demand on mathematical terms. According to her price elasticity of demand for a commodity is "the ratio of the proportionate change in its quantity demanded and the proportionate change in its price."

Thus, $$E_P = \frac{\text{Proportionate Change in Quantity Demanded}}{\text{Proportionate Change in Price}}$$

$$= \frac{\text{Change in Q.D.}}{\text{Original Q.D.}} / \frac{\text{Change in Price}}{\text{Original Price}}$$

Symbolically,

$$E_P = \frac{\Delta Q}{Q} / \frac{\Delta P}{P} = \frac{\Delta Q}{Q} \times \frac{P}{\Delta P} = \frac{\Delta Q}{\Delta P} \times \frac{P}{Q}$$

Where, E_P = Price elasticity of demand

ΔQ = Changing in quantity demanded

$\Delta Q = Q \sim Q_1$ (Q = original demand, Q_1 = New demand, ~ = Difference)

ΔP = Change in Price

$\Delta P = P \sim P_1$ (P = Original Price, P_1 = New Price, ~ = Difference)

Q = Original quantity demanded

P = Original price

Numerical Example

When the price of a commodity changes from ₹ 10 to ₹ 8 per unit the quantity demanded changes from 80 units to 100 units. What is the price elasticity of demand ?

Solution

We are given $P = 10$, $P_1 = 8$, $Q = 80$ and $Q_1 = 100$

So, $\Delta P = P \sim P_1 = 10 \sim 8 = 2$ and

$\Delta Q = Q \sim Q_1 = 80 \sim 100 = 20$

$$E_P = \frac{\Delta Q}{\Delta P} \times \frac{P}{Q} = \frac{20}{2} \times \frac{10}{80} = \frac{5}{4} = 1.25$$

(In percentage form it is 1.25 × 100 = 125 ; Which implies there is a 25% change in the quantity demanded)

TYPES OF PRICE ELASTICITY OF DEMAND

Though the relationship between price and quantity demanded of a commodity is inverse the price elasticity of demand is always taken as positive and the numerical value of the price elasticity of demand ranges from zero to infinite (0 to do). The price elasticity of demand is different for different goods. Basing upon the sensitiveness of demand of different goods to change in price, economists have divided the price elasticity of demand in to following five types :

1. Perfectly Inelastic Demand
2. Relatively Inelastic Demand
3. Unitary Elastic Demand
4. Relatively Elastic Demand
5. Perfectly Elastic Demand

Perfectly Inelastic Demand

Demand for a commodity is said to be perfectly inelastic if any change in its price has no effect on its quantity demanded. For example, if the price of the commodity changes by 20% (ΔP = 20%) leading to no change in quantity demanded (ΔQ = 0), then $E_P = \frac{\Delta Q}{\Delta P} = \frac{0}{20\%} = 0$.

Thus in case of perfectly inelastic demanded the numerical value of price elasticity of demand is zero (E_P = 0). Elasticity of demand of the goods whose consumption cannot be postponed due to rise in prices or cannot be consumed more due to fall in prices come under this category. For example – medicine, salt etc.

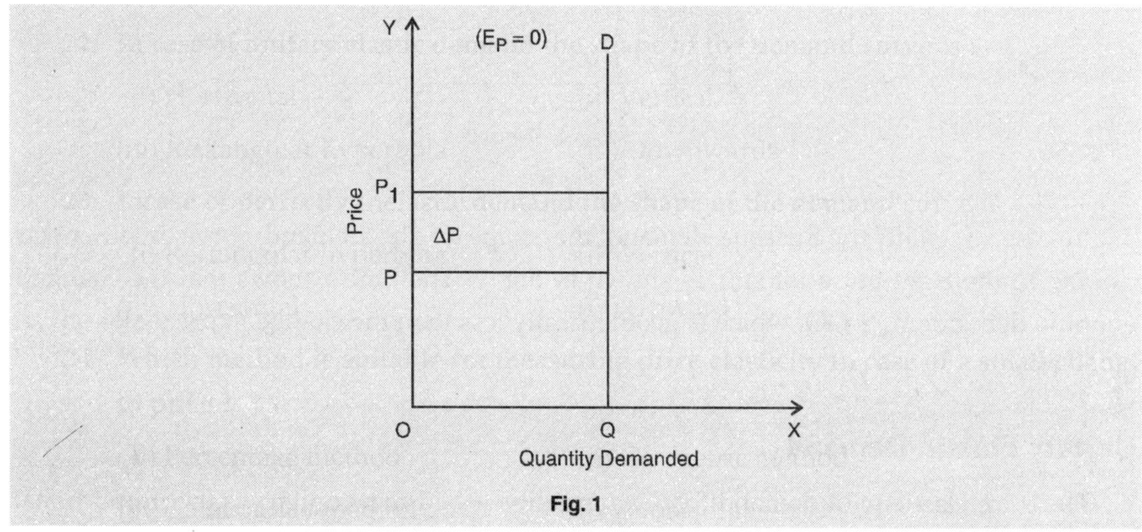

Fig. 1

In case of perfectly inelastic demand, the shape of the demand curve is vertical as shown in Fig. 1. The figure shows, when the price is 'OP', the quantity demanded is OQ. Change in price from 'OP' to OP_1, has no effect on the quantity demanded which has remained unchanged at OQ.

Relatively Inelastic Demand

Demand for a commodity is said to be relatively inelastic if the proportionate change in quantity demanded $\left(\frac{\Delta Q}{Q}\right)$ is less than the proportionate change in price $\left(\frac{\Delta P}{P}\right)$. That is $\frac{\Delta Q}{Q} < \frac{\Delta P}{P}$. Numerically if a 10% change in price ($\Delta P = 10\%$) leads to less than 10% change in quantity demanded, say by 5%, then the numerical value of price elasticity will be $E_P = \frac{\Delta Q}{\Delta P} = \frac{5\%}{10\%} = 0.5$. Thus in case of relatively inelastic demand $E_P < 1$. It is to be noted that the numerical value of price elasticity in case of relatively inelastic demand lies in between 0 and 1, i.e. $E_P > 0$ and < 1.

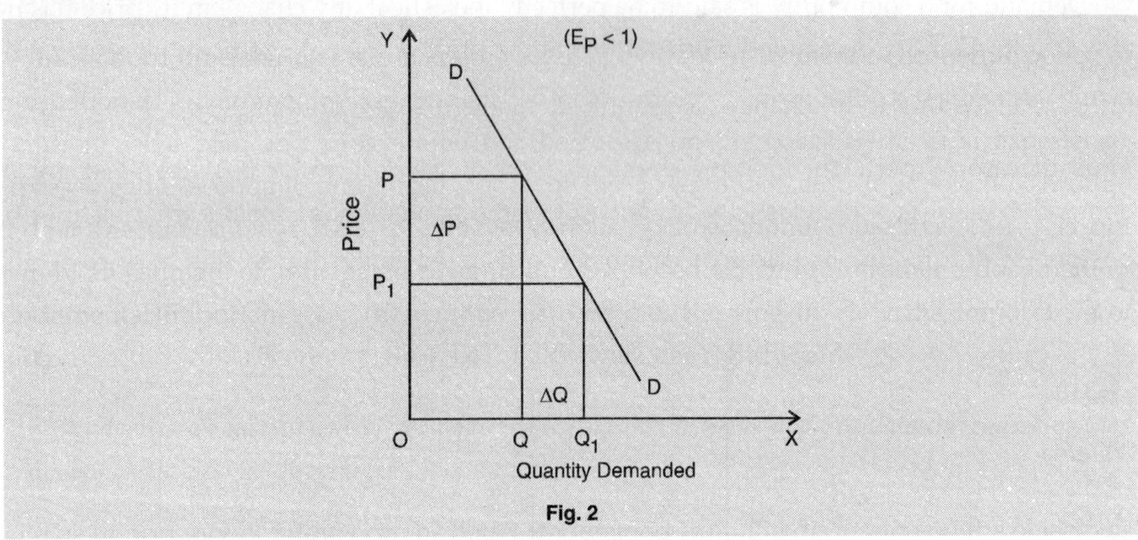

Fig. 2

In case of relatively inelastic demand the shape of the demand curve is downward sloping to the right but a bit stiff as shown in Fig. 2. The figure shows that the change in quantity demand $\Delta Q = QQ_1$ which is geometrically less than the change in price $\Delta P = PP_1$, *i.e.* $QQ_1 < PP_1$

Unitary Elastic Demand

The price elasticity of demand for a commodity is said to be unitary is the proportionate change in quantity demanded $\left(\frac{\Delta Q}{Q}\right)$ is exactly equal to the proportionate change in it price $\left(\frac{\Delta P}{P}\right)$. For example if a 10% change in price (ΔP = 10%) leads to exact 10% change in quantity demanded (ΔQ = 10%), then the price elasticity of demand would be $E_P = \frac{\Delta Q}{\Delta P} = \frac{10\%}{10\%} = 1$. Thus in case of unitary elastic demand the numerical value of price elasticity is 1 ($E_P = 1$).

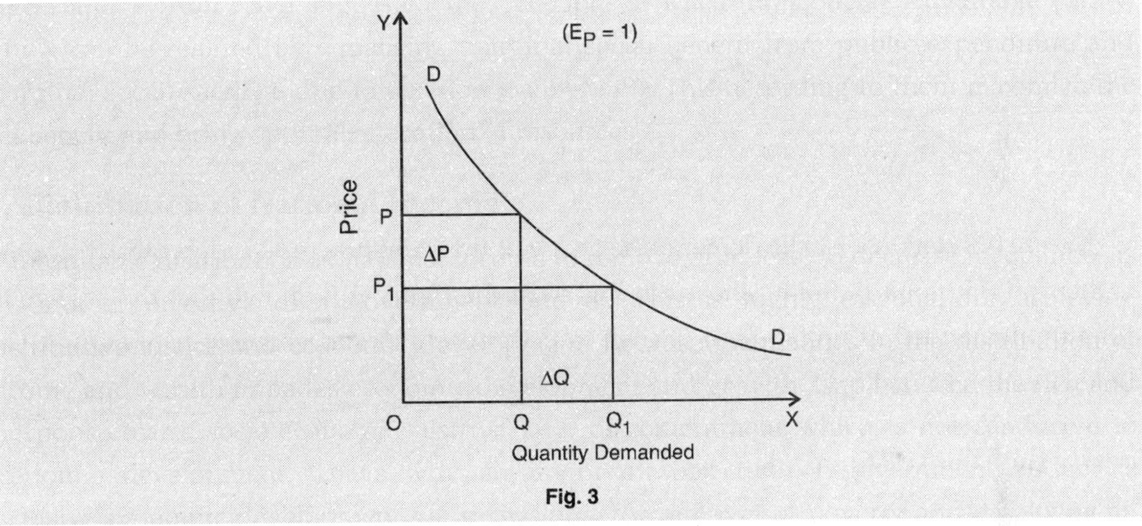

Fig. 3

In case of unitary elastic demand the demand curve takes the shape of a rectangular hyperbola as shown in Fig. 3. In the figure it as shown that the change in quantity demanded QQ_1 is exactly equal to the change in price by PP_1, *i.e.* $QQ_1 = PP_1$

Relatively Elastic Demand

Demand for a commodity is said to be relatively elastic if the proportionate change in quantity demanded $\left(\frac{\Delta Q}{Q}\right)$ is greater than the proportionate change in Price $\left(\frac{\Delta P}{P}\right)$, i.e. $\frac{\Delta Q}{Q} > \frac{\Delta P}{P}$. Numerically, if a 10% change in price leads to a more than 10% change in quantity demanded, say by 15% then the price elasticity of demand is $E_P = \frac{\Delta Q}{\Delta P} = \frac{15\%}{10\%} = 1.5$. Thus the numerical value of price elasticity in case of relatively elastic demand is greater than 1 ($E_P > 1$) but less than infinite ($E_P < \infty$).

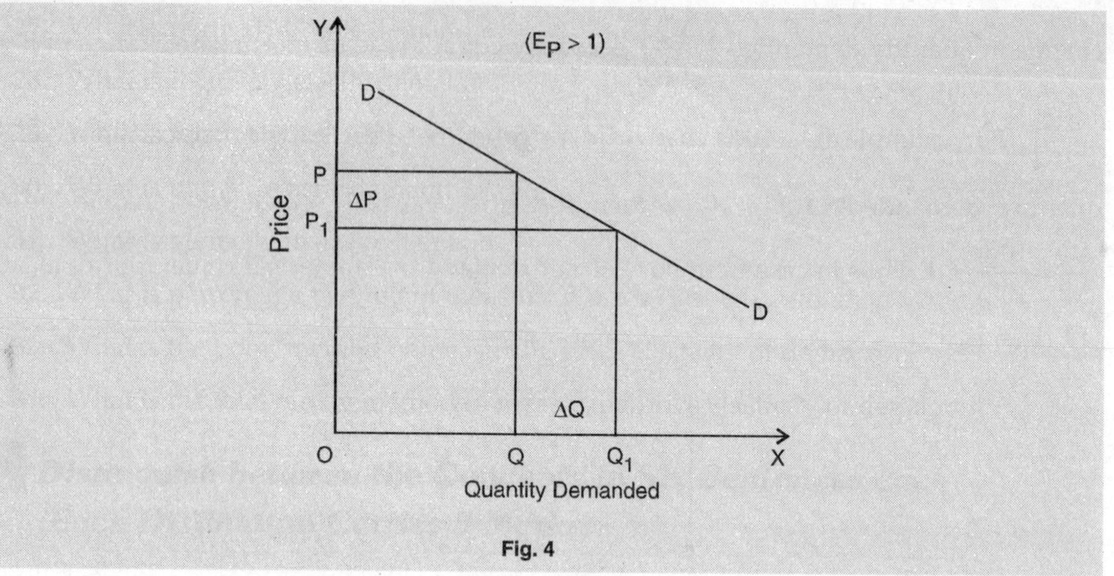

Fig. 4

In case of relatively elastic demand the shape of the demand curve is downward sloping to the right but a bit flatter as shown in Fig. 4. In the figure it is shown that the change in quantity demanded $\Delta Q = QQ_1$ and change in price $\Delta P = PP_1$ and geometrically $\Delta Q > \Delta P$ or $QQ_1 > PP_1$.

Perfectly Elastic Demand

Demand for a commodity said to be perfectly elastic if a very negligible or even no change in price leads to an infinite change in its quantity demanded. In case of perfectly elastic demand the price elasticity of demand is said to be infinite ($E_P = \infty$). Because here $\Delta Q = \infty$ and $\Delta P = 0$. So, $E_P = \frac{\Delta Q}{\Delta P} = \frac{\infty}{0} = \infty$. The shape of the demand curve in case of perfectly elastic demand is horizontal straight line parallel to OX-axis as shown is Fig. 5, indicating infinite change in quantity demanded with even no change in price.

However, in real world the demand for no commodity can either be perfectly inelastic ($E_P = 0$) or be perfectly elastic ($E_P = \infty$). When we say the demand for a commodity is elastic we really mean relatively elastic and when we say the demand is inelastic it really means relatively inelastic. In this sense the price elasticity of demand usually refers to either relatively inelastic ($E_P < 1$) or relatively elastic ($E_P > 1$) or unitary elastic ($E_P = 1$). For the exact measurement of the numerical value of the price elasticity of demand economists have developed different methods, that we have discussed later in this chapter.

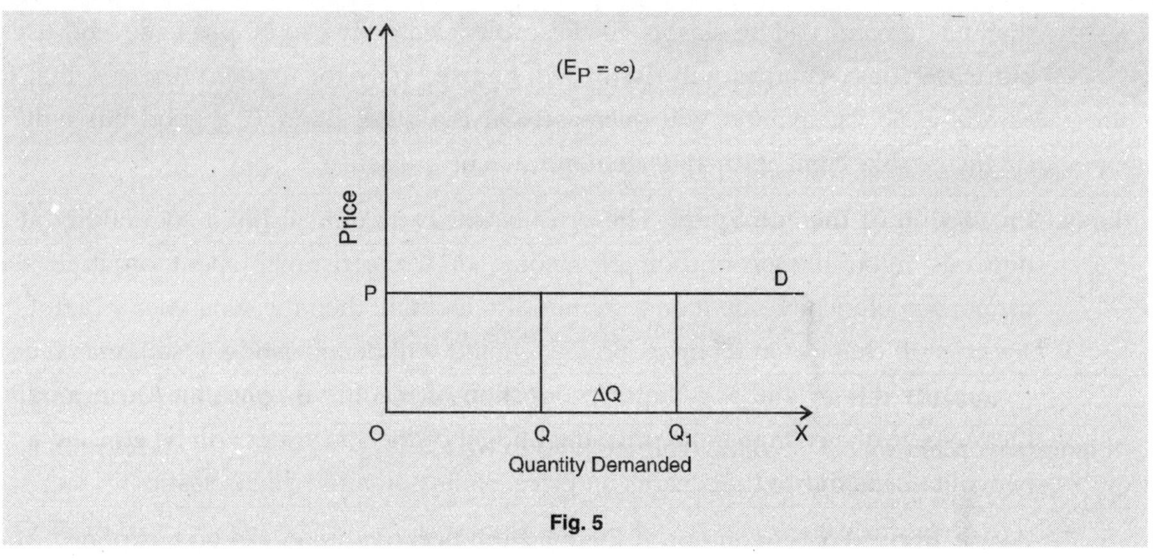

Fig. 5

FACTORS AFFECTING PRICE ELASTICITY OF DEMAND

The price elasticity of demand of different goods is not the same. There are several factors which bear significance in determining the price elasticity of demand of a commodity.

Some of those factors are discussed below :

1. **Nature of the Commodity.** We know, on the basis of urgency goods are classified as necessaries, comforts and luxuries, on this consideration the demand for necessaries are inelastic. Because some of them are indispensable for life, some are to maintaining efficiency and some are in dispensable due to conventional reasons on the other hand the demand for comforts and luxuries are elastic, as they are less or not indispensable and demanded more or less according to the ability of a person.

2. **Availability of Substitutes.** The elasticity of demand for a commodity is also influenced by the availability of its substitutes. If a commodity has substitutes then its demand will be relatively elastic, e.g. tea and coffee are substitutes. If price of coffee will increase some marginal consumer of coffee will substitute it for tea and vice versa. There are also commodities like salt, cement etc. which have no close substitute. So their demand will be inelastic. However, the degree of substitution will determine the degree of price elasticity of demand.

3. **Alternative Uses.** The degree of price elasticity of demand of a commodity is also influenced by the variety of its use. If a commodity has alternative or several uses,

then its demand will be elastic. For example, electricity can be put to several uses, but if electricity charges will rise, it will be used only for urgent purposes, that to carefully. So its demand will decrease. On the other hand, if a good has only a single use, like cement, then its demand will be inelastic.

4. **Proportion of Income Spent.** The price elasticity of demand of a commodity also depends upon the proportion of income of the consumer spent on it. If the proportion of income spent on a commodity is small, then the consumer will not be sensitive to changes in its price. So its demand will be inelastic e.g. salt, match box etc. on the other hand if a larger proportion of income is spent on a commodity then in case of a change in its price the budget of the consumer will be affected and he will be sensitive to that change in price. So its demand will be elastic.

5. **Possibility of Postponement.** If the consumption of a good can be portponed due to the rise in its price, it implies that the good is not urgent and hence its demand will be elastic. For example semi-luxurious and luxurious goods. On the other hand if the consumption of a good cannot be postponed, in spite of the rise in its price, like the necessaries for life, then its demand will be inelastic.

6. **Price Range**. The degree of price elasticity of demand of a commodity also depends upon its price range. Elasticity of demand tends to be low when prices are very high or very low. Because high priced goods are demanded by the rich and a change in prices of these goods does not affect their demand similarly a low-priced commodity like salt or match box, does not have a significant change in its price and hence its demand is not much affected.

7. **Durability of the Good.** If a good is durable one, i.e. can be used again and again for a long period of time then people will be sensitive to its price change. That is, its demand will be elastic. On the other hand the demand for perishable goods or single use goods will be less elastic or inelastic.

8. **Habit.** If the consumption of a good has turned into habit as a result of regular consumption then its demand will be inelastic. Because one becomes so accustomed to the good that it becomes a necessary one (conventional necessary) for him. So its price change will have no effect on its demand.

Besides the above discussed factors there also factors like the time or period of demand for a good, joint demand, income distribution pattern, changes in the fashion etc. which also affect the degree of price elasticity of demand of a good.

MEASUREMENT OF PRICE-ELASTICITY OF DEMAND

Price elasticity of demand refers to the degree of responsiveness in quantity demanded of a good due to a given change in its price, other factors affecting its demand remaining constant. In economic analysis the measurement of this degree or magnitude of responsiveness in quantity demanded or the price-elasticity of demand bears much significance in the decision taking process.

For this economists have developed different methods. Some of them are discussed below :

1. Percentage or Proportionate Method

The percentage or proportionate method of measuring price elasticity of demand was developed by Mrs. Joan Robinson. According to this method 'Price elasticity of demand is the ratio of percentage change in quantity demanded of a commodity to the percentage change in its price'. In other words, the price elasticity of demand of a commodity is the ratio of the proportionate change in quantity demanded to the proportionate change in its price.

This can be presented as :

$$E_P = \frac{\text{Percentage Change in Quantity Demanded}}{\text{Percentage Change in Price}} \times 100$$

Or,

$$E_P = \frac{\text{Proportionate Change in Quantity Demanded}}{\text{Proportionate Change in Price}}$$

Symbolically,

$$E_P = \frac{\Delta Q}{Q} / \frac{\Delta P}{P} = \frac{\Delta Q}{Q} \times \frac{P}{\Delta P}$$

Or,

$$\boxed{E_P = \frac{\Delta Q}{\Delta P} \times \frac{P}{Q}}$$

Where,

E_P = Price elasticity of demand

ΔQ = Change in quantity demanded

(Difference between original and new quantity demand)

ΔP = Change in Price (Difference between original price and new price)

P = Original Price

Q = Original quantity demanded

(**N.B.** 1. Though the relationship between the price and quantity demanded is negative, the price elasticity is taken as positive.

2. While taking the difference between the original and new q.d./price sign is ignored)

2. Geometric or Point Method

The geometric method of measuring price elasticity of demand was developed by Alfred Marshall. This method is useful for measuring price elasticity in case of a small change in the prices of the commodities. Under this method the price elasticity of demand is measured at a point on the demand curve by drawing a tangent to the point. That's why this method is also called point method of measuring price elasticity of demand.

Under this method the tangent drawn at the point of a demand curve is taken as a straight line demand curve and the elasticity of demand is measured at any point by taking the ratio of the distance of the lower segment and the upper segment of the straight line demand curve as shown in the diagram drawn below.

That is :

$$E_P = \frac{\text{Distance of the Lower Segment of the Demand Curve}}{\text{Distance of the Upper Segment of the Demand Curve}}$$

In the figure 'RN' is the straight line demand curve. We have to measure the price elasticity at any point on the demand curve as the ratio of the distances of the lower segment and the upper segment, i.e. at point say 'D' $E_P = \frac{DN}{RD}$ and so on.

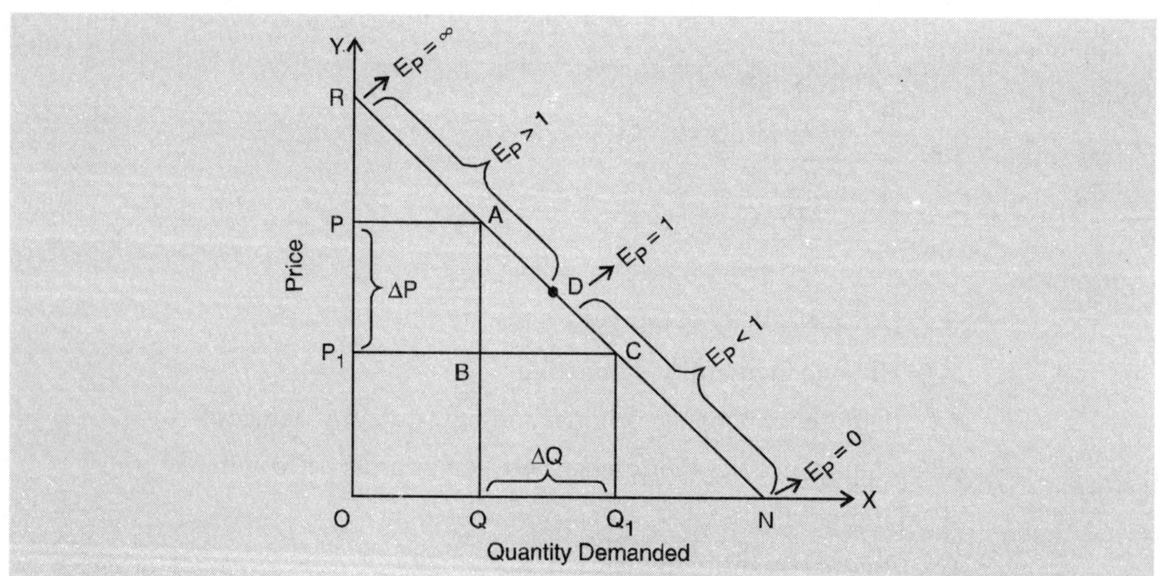

Let us prove this geometrically. From the proportionate method of measuring price elasticity of demand we know :

$$E_P = \frac{\Delta Q}{\Delta P} \times \frac{P}{Q}$$

Putting the figure in the formula :

$$E_P = \frac{\Delta Q}{\Delta P} \times \frac{P}{Q} = \frac{QQ_1}{PP_1} \times \frac{OP}{OQ} = \frac{BC}{AB} \times \frac{AQ}{PA} \left(\text{as } \begin{matrix} QQ_1 = BC, PP_1 = AB, \\ OP = AQ, OQ = PA \end{matrix} \right) \qquad \ldots\text{(i)}$$

Now in ΔABC and ΔAQN :

(i) $\angle A$ is common

(ii) $\angle ABC = \angle AQN$, Right angles

(iii) $\angle ACB = \angle ANQ$, Resemble angles

$\therefore \Delta ABC \cong \Delta AQN$ (AAA)

So, the ratio of their sides must be equal, i.e. $\frac{BC}{AB} = \frac{QN}{AQ}$ substituting this in Eq. (i)

$$E_P = \frac{BC}{AB} \times \frac{AQ}{PA} = \frac{QN}{AQ} \times \frac{AQ}{PA} = \frac{QN}{PA} \qquad \ldots\text{(ii)}$$

Similarly we can prove that $\Delta RPA \cong \Delta AQN$ and so the ratio of their sides are equal, that is : $\frac{QN}{PA} = \frac{AN}{AR}$.

From eq. (ii) we got $E_P = \frac{QN}{PA}$ and $\frac{QN}{PA} = \frac{AN}{AR}$.

So, $E_P = \frac{AN}{AR} = \frac{\text{Distance of the Lower Segment}}{\text{Distance of the Upper Segment}}$

This implies that, at the mid point of the straight line demand curve, i.e. at point D, $E_P = \frac{DN}{RD} = 1$, in between points R and D, E_P, say at point A is $\frac{AN}{AR} > 1$, in between points D and N, E_P, say at point 'C' is $\frac{CN}{RC} < 1$. At point R, $E_P = \frac{RN}{0} = \infty$ and at point 'N' $E_P = \frac{0}{RN} = 0$.

3. Total Outlay Method

The total outlay method of measuring price elasticity of demand was developed by Marshall. Under this method the price elasticity of demand (E_P) is measured taking into account the total expenditure made on a commodity before and after the change in its price.

On this basis we can trace out three separate cases of price elasticity of demand which is shown in the total expenditure table drawn below :

Total Expenditure Table

Price (₹)	Quantity Demanded (Units)	Total Expenditure (₹)	Price Elasticity
10	10	100	
9	20	180	$E_P > 1$
8	30	240	
7	40	280	
6	50	300	$E_P = 1$
5	60	300	
4	70	280	
3	80	240	$E_P < 1$
2	90	180	
1	100	100	

Greater than 1 ($E_P > 1$)

If with the fall in the price of a commodity the total expenditure on the purchase of the commodity increases or with the rise in the price the total expenditure on the commodity decreases, then the price elasticity of demand for the commodity is said to be greater than unity, i.e. $E_P > 1$. In the table it is shown upto price ₹ 6. The table shows that with the fall in price from ₹ 10 to ₹ 9 and so on upto price ₹ 6 the total expenditure spent is increasing, i.e. from ₹ 100 to ₹ 180, ... upto ₹ 300 on the other hand with the rise in price from ₹ 6 to ₹ 7 ..... the total expenditure is decreasing from ₹300 to ₹ 280, ₹ 240 ..... respectively. So the price elasticity is greater than unity ($E_P > 1$).

Unitary Elastic

If with the fall or rise in the price of a commodity the total expenditure on the purchase of it remains constant, then the price elasticity of demand is said to be unitary, i.e. $E_P = 1$. As shown in the total expenditure table, when the price of the commodity is ₹ 6 the total expenditure made on the commodity is ₹ 300, but with the fall in the price to ₹ 5 the total expenditure has remain unchanged i.e. at ₹ 300. Similarly, when price rises from ₹ 5 to ₹ 6 the total expenditure remains unchanged. This represents $E_P = 1$.

Less than 1 ($E_P < 1$)

If with the fall in the price of a commodity the total expenditure made on the purchase of the commodity decreases or with the rise in the price of a commodity total expenditure on the commodity increases, then the price elasticity of demand of the commodity is said to be less than unity, i.e. $E_P < 1$. As shown in the total expenditure table, with the fall in the price from ₹ 5 to ₹ 4 the total expenditure has decreased from ₹ 300 to ₹ 280, ₹ 240 ….. and so on, and represents less than unitary elastic demand, i.e., $E_P < 1$.

Graphical Presentation

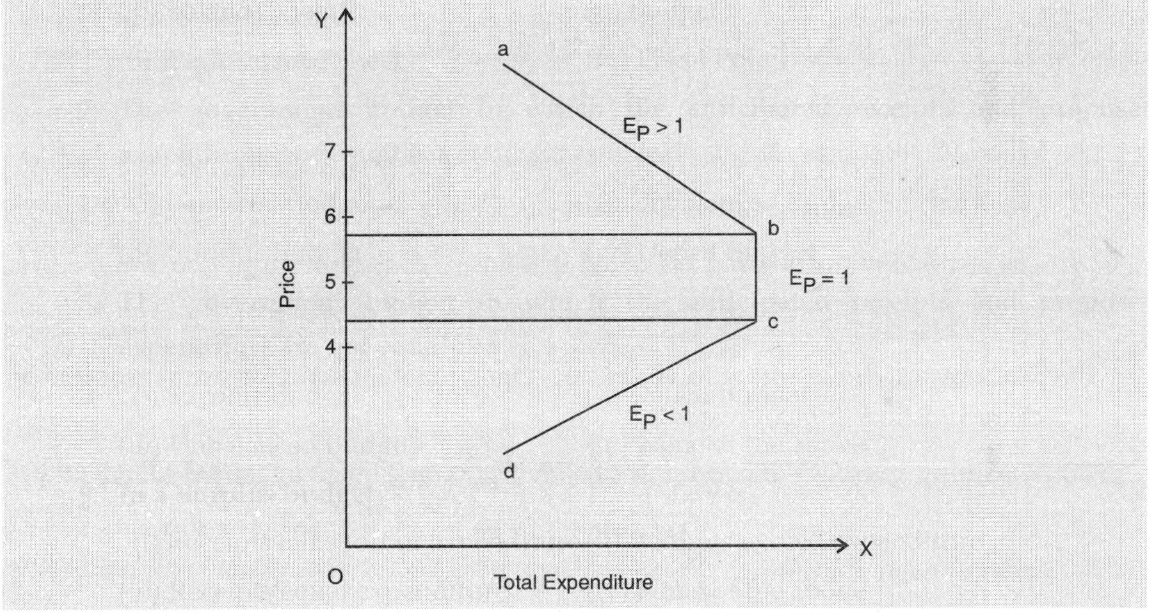

The above stated three cases of price elasticity of demand is presented graphically as shown in the diagram drawn above. In the figure 'abcd' is the total expenditure curve obtained by plotting the total expenditure made on the purchase of different units of the commodity at different price. The 'ab' portion of the curve sloping downwards to the right implies that total expenditure is increasing with the fall in prices. The 'bc' segment of the total expenditure curve is verticle, showing total expenditure is unchanged with the fall in price from ₹ 6 to ₹ 5. The 'cd' segment of the curve with a backward slope towards the origin implies that total expenditure is decreasing with a further fall in price. Thus the 'ab' segment of the total expenditure curve 'abcd' represents $E_P > 1$, 'bc' segment represents $E_P = 1$ and the 'cd' segment represents $E_P < 1$.

WHAT WE LEARNT

1. Consumption means using up of utility of a commodity for the purpose of satisfaction of want.
2. Utility derived from an additional unit of a commodity or addition made to the total utility by consuming an extra unit of a commodity is called marginal utility. ($MU = TU_n - TU_{n-1}$).
3. Sum of the marginal utilities from the given units of a commodity is called total utility. ($TU_1 = MU_1 + MU_2 + \ldots\ldots MU_n$).
4. At the 1st unit of consumption of a good MU = TU.
5. When MU decreases TU increases at a diminishing rate.
6. When MU becomes zero, TU becomes maximum.
7. When MU becomes negative, TU starts decreasing.
8. The law of diminishing M.U. is called first law of consumption.
9. The law of diminishing M.U. was originally propounded by H.H. Gossen.
10. The law of diminishing M.U. is developed on 'a particular want is satiable' characteristic of human wants.
11. The utility approach of consumer's behaviour is developed by Alfred Marshall.
12. The utility approach of consumer's behaviour is based on the cardinal measurement of utility.
13. The law of Equi-marginal utility is called as 'the second law of consumption', 'the law of substitution'.
14. The law of equi-marginal utility explains consumer's equilibrium.
15. Under utility approach the condition for consumer's equilibrium is : $\frac{MU_X}{P_X} = \frac{MU_X}{P_Y} = \ldots \frac{MU_n}{P_n} = MU_M$.
16. Demand means desire for a commodity backed by ability and willingness to pay for it at a given price and at a given time, i.e. the desire which can be made effective.

17. The functional relationship between the quantity demanded of a commodity and the factors affecting its semand is called demand function. It is written as :

    $D_X = f(P_X, P_r, Y, T, P, C, G.....)$

18. The functional relationship between quantity demanded of a commodity, and its price, other factors remaining constant, is explained in the law of demand.
19. The price and quantity demanded of a normal good are inversely related.
20. The table showing the quantity demanded of a commodity at different possible prices is called 'demand schedule'.
21. The normal shape of a demand curve is downward sloping to the right (negative slope).
22. The sum of individual demand schedules is called market demand schedule.
23. The horizontal or lateral addition of the individual demand curves gives rise to market demand curve.
24. Giffen's good is a relative concept which refers to the inferior good when two or more goods are compared.
25. Law of demand is not applicable to Giffen goods.
26. The price and quantity demanded of a Giffen good are positively related (move in the same direction).
27. The shape of demand curve in case of a Giffen's good is upward sloping to the right (positive slope).
28. Change in demand or shift in the demand curve takes place due to change in non-price factors affecting demand, price remaining constant. (Increase or decrease in demand).
29. Change in quantity demanded or movement along the same demand curve takes place due to change in price, non-price factors remaining constant.
30. Change in demand is a multi-variable function.
31. Change in quantity demanded is a single-variable function.
32. Degree of responsiveness in quantity demanded of a commodity due to a given change in its price, other non-price factors remaining constant is called price elasticity of demand.

33. The formula to calculate price elasticity of demand is :

$$E_P = \frac{\Delta Q}{\Delta P} \times \frac{P}{Q}$$

34. If change in quantity demanded (ΔQ) is greater than the change in price (ΔP), i.e. $\Delta Q > \Delta P$, the demand is relatively elastic.

35. If change in quantity demanded (ΔQ) is less than the change in price (ΔP), i.e. $\Delta Q < \Delta P$, the demand is relatively inelastic.

36. If change is quantity demanded (ΔQ) is exactly equal to the change is price (ΔP), i.e. $\Delta Q = \Delta P$, the demand is unitary elastic.

37. If any change in price has no effect on quantity demanded then the demand is said to be perfectly inelastic.

38. If a negligible or even no change in price causes an infinite change in quantity demanded the demand is said to be perfectly elastic.

39. In case of unitary elastic demand the demand curve takes the shape of a rectangular hyperbola.

40. In case of perfectly inelastic demand the shape of the demand curve is vertical.

41. In case of perfectly elastic demand the shape of the demand curve is horizontal.

42. The demand for necessaries are inelastic.

43. The demand for luxuries are elastic.

44. The demand for high-priced and low-priced goods are inelastic.

45. The demand for goods having alternative or several uses are elastic.

46. The demand for perishable and single use goods are inelastic.

47. The demand for durable goods are elastic.

48. The percentage method of measuring price elasticity of demand was developed by Mrs. Joan Robinson.

49. The geometric method or point method and total outlay method of measuring price elasticity of demand was developed by Alfred Marshall.

50. In geometric method the price elasticity of demand is measured on a straight-line demand curve.

51. Geometric or point method of measuring price elasticity of demand is useful to measure elasticity in case of a small change in price.
52. At the mid-point of a straight line demand curve the $E_P = 1$.
53. If the total expenditure on a commodity increases after the fall in price, then $E_P > 1$.
54. If the total expenditure on a commodity remains unchanged after the change in price, then $E_P = 1$.
55. If the total expenditure on a commodity decreases after the fall in price, then $E_P < 1$.

QUESTIONS FOR REVIEW

A. Choose the correct answer from the given alternatives in each question. (Each Carrying 1 Mark)

1. Using up the utility of a commodity for satisfaction of want is called :

(i) Satisfaction (ii) Consumption

(iii) Destruction (iv) None of these.

2. Who developed the utility approach of consumer's behaviour ?

(i) Marshall (ii) Adam Smith

(iii) Joan Robinson (iv) Benham

3. Addition made to total utility by consuming an extra unit of a commodity is called:

(i) Equi-marginal utility (ii) Total utility

(iii) Marginal utility (iv) Satisfaction

4. Which one is the sum of the marginal utilities ?

(i) Total utility (ii) Marginal utilities

(iii) Equi-marginal utility (iv) Complete satisfaction

5. What happens to total utility when marginal utility decreases ?

(i) Remains constant (ii) Decreases

(iii) Increases (iv) Increases at a diminishing rate

6. What happens to Marginal utility when total utility maximizes ?

(i) Decreases (ii) Becomes zero

(iii) Maximizes (iv) Increases

7. What happens to Marginal utility when total utility decreases ?

(i) Maximizes (ii) Becomes negative

(iii) Becomes zero (iv) Increases

8. The law of diminishing marginal utility is developed on which one ?

(i) Wants are unlimited (ii) Wants are competitive

(iii) A particular want is satiable (iv) Wants vary in intensity

9. Originally who propounded the law of diminishing marginal utility ?

(i) Alfred Marshall (ii) H.H. Gossen

(iii) Robins (iv) Adam Smith

10. Which law is known as the second law of consumption ?

(i) Law of demand (ii) Law of Diminishing Marginal Utility

(iii) Law of Equi-marginal Utility (iv) None of these

11. Which law is also called 'the law of substitution' ?

(i) Law of Equi-marginal Utility (ii) Law of Diminishing Marginal Utility

(iii) Law of Demand (iv) First Law of Consumption

12. What is the shape of the marginal utility curve ?

(i) Horizontal (ii) Downward sloping to the right

(iii) Vertical (iv) Upward sloping to the right

13. In economics demand means :

(i) Desire for a commodity (ii) Ability to buy

(iii) Desire which can be made effective (iv) None of these

14. The functional relationship between quantity demanded of a good and factors affecting its demand is called :

(i) Law of demand (ii) Change in demand

(iii) Change in quantity demand (iv) Demand function

15. Price and quantity demanded of a commodity are related :

(i) Inversely (ii) Proportionally

(iii) Directly (iv) Linearly

16. **The table showing various quantity demanded at different possible prices is called:**

    (i) Demand function (ii) Demand schedule

    (iii) Demand curve (iv) Law of demand

17. **What is the shape of a normal demand curve ?**

    (i) Downwards sloping to the right (ii) Horizontal

    (iii) Upward sloping to the right (iv) Vertical

18. **If there is the expectation of a rise in price of a commodity in near future, then its demand will :**

    (i) Decrease (ii) Remain constant

    (iii) Increase (iv) None of these.

19. **The law of demand does not operate in case of :**

    (i) Giffen goods (ii) Prestigious goods

    (iii) Habitual goods (iv) All the above

20. **A market demand curve :**

    (i) Slopes upward to the right (ii) Slopes downward to the right

    (iii) Takes horizontal shape (iv) None of these

21. **In case of perfectly elastic demand the shape of the demand curve is :**

    (i) Vertical (ii) Horizontal

    (iii) Downward (iv) Upward

22. **In case of unitary elastic demand the shape of the demand curve is :**

    (i) Horizontal (ii) Vertical

    (iii) Rectangular hyperbola (iv) Downwards

23. **Incase of perfectly inelastic demand the shape of the demand curve is -**

    (i) Rectangular hyperbola (ii) Vertical

    (iii) Horizontal (iv) Upward

24. **Which method is suitable for measuring price elasticity in case of a small change in price ?**

    (i) Percentage method (ii) Geometric method

    (iii) Total outlay method (iv) None of these

25. When price is ₹ 10, Q.D. is 80 kgs. with the fall in price by ₹ 2 Q.D. increases to 100 kgs. what is the price elasticity of demand ?

(i) 1 (ii) 1.25

(iii) 1.5 (iv) 0.75

B. Correct the statement, if necessary, without changing the underlined portions. (Each Carrying 1 Mark)

1. Consumption means creation of utility for satisfaction.
2. At the first unit of a commodity Marginal Utility is greater than total utility.
3. Marshall originally propounded the first law of consumption.
4. Law of Diminishing Marginal Utility is the first law of consumption.
5. Law of Diminishing Marginal Utility is based on proportionality rule.
6. Consumer's equilibrium is explained by the law of D.M.U.
7. Total utility maximizes when marginal utility becomes negative.
8. Marginal utility from successive units increases.
9. Demand function is a multi-variable function.
10. Demand curve in case of Giffen goods slopes downwards to the right.
11. Giffen's good is an absolute concept.
12. In case of change in demand Consumer moves along the demand curve.
13. Demand curve shifts in case of change in quantity demanded.
14. Price and quantity demanded are normally related directly.
15. Law of demand measures the degree of responsiveness in q.d.
16. Marshall propounded the point method of measuring elasticity of demand.
17. Demand for necessaries are perfectly elastic.
18. At the mid-point of a straight line demand curve $E_P = 0$.
19. If the total expenditure increases with the fall in price, the price elasticity is said to be less than unity.
20. If the total expenditure remains unchanged after the change in price of a commodity the price elasticity is said to be zero.

C. Answer the following questions in 2-3 sentences each. (Each Carrying 2 Marks)

1. What is Consumption ?
2. What is Marginal Utility ?
3. What is total utility ?
4. How marginal utility and total utility are related ?
5. State the law of Diminishing Marginal Utility.
6. What is cardinal measurement of utility ?
7. Point out the assumptions of the law of DMU.
8. Point out the importance of the Law of DMU.
9. What is the Law of Equi-marginal Utility ?
10. Point out the assumptions of the Law of Equi-marginal Utility.
11. What are the Conditions of Consumer's equilibrium ?
12. What is equilibrium of a consumer ?
13. What is demand in economics ?
14. What is demand function ?
15. Point out the features of demand.
16. What is the law of demand ?
17. Point out the assumptions of the law of demand.
18. What is demand schedule ?
19. What is demand curve ?
20. Point out the reasons of the working of the law of demand.
21. What is Giffen's good ?
22. What is market demand schedule ?
23. What is market demand curve ?
24. What is change in demand ?
25. What is change in quantity demanded ?
26. What is price elasticity of demand ?

27. What is perfectly elastic demand ?
28. What is relatively elastic demand ?
29. What is relatively inelastic demand ?
30. What is unitary elastic demand ?
31. What is perfectly inelastic demand ?
32. What is percentage method of measuring price elasticity of demand ?
33. What is the point method of measuring price elasticity of demand ?
34. What is the total outlay method of measuring price elasticity of demand ?

D. Distinguish between the Concepts in Six Sentences each (Each Distinction Carries 3 Marks)

1. Marginal utility and total utility.
2. Demand schedule and demand curve.
3. Change in demand and change in quantity demanded.
4. Individual demand and market demand.
5. Perfectly elastic demand and perfectly inelastic demand.
6. Relatively elastic demand and relatively inelastic demand.

E. Long Answer Type Questions (Carrying 7½ Marks)

1. Explain the Law of Diminishing marginal utility with its limitations.
2. Explain the law of Equi-marginal utility with its limitations.
3. Explain the relationship between marginal and total utility.
4. Discuss the factors affecting the demand for a commodity.
5. Explain the law of demand with its limitations.
6. What is price elasticity of demand ? Explain the types of price elasticity of demand.
7. Discuss the determinants of the price elasticity of demand.
8. Briefly discuss the methods of measuring price elasticity of demand.
9. Explain the Geometric method of measuring price elasticity of demand.
10. Explain the total-outlay method of measuring price elasticity of demand.
11. Explain why does a demand curve has negative slope.

Answer to Q. N. A

1.	(ii)	2.	(i)	3.	(iii)	4.	(i)	5.	(iv)	6.	(ii)	7.	(ii)	8.	(iii)
9.	(ii)	10.	(iii)	11.	(i)	12.	(ii)	13.	(iii)	14.	(iv)	15.	(i)	16.	(ii)
17.	(i)	18.	(iii)	19.	(i)	20.	(ii)	21.	(ii)	22.	(iii)	23.	(ii)	24.	(ii)
25.	(ii)														

Answer to Q. N. B

1. Destruction/using up	2. Equal to	3. H.H. Gossen
4. Correct	5. Law of Equimarginal utility	6. Law of Equimarginal utility
7. Zero	8. Decreases	9. Correct
10. Upwards to the right	11. Relative concept	12. Change in quantity demanded
13. Change in demand	14. Inversely	15. Elasticity of demand
16. Correct	17. Perfectly inelastic	18. $E_P = 1$
19. Greater than unity ($E_P > 1$)	20. Equal to 1 (Unitary)	

❑❑❑

UNIT – III

4. PRODUCTION

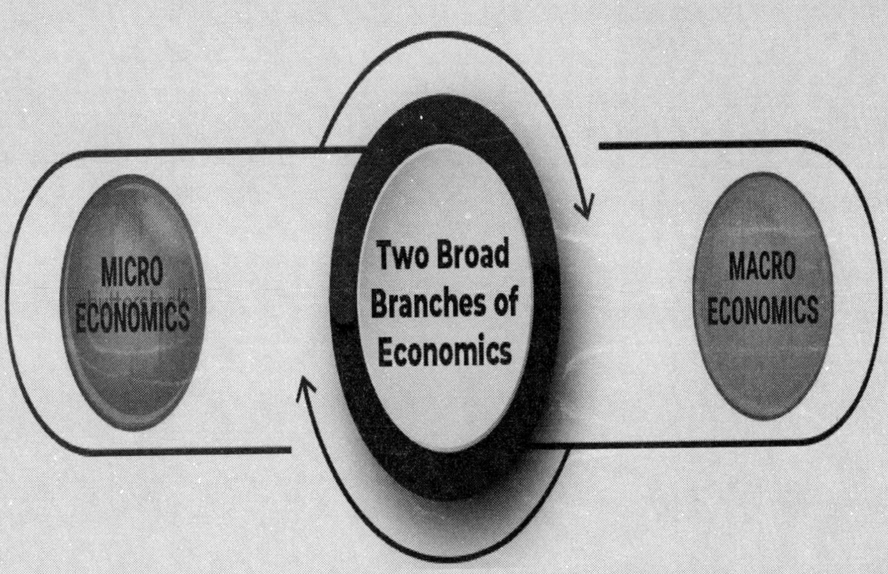

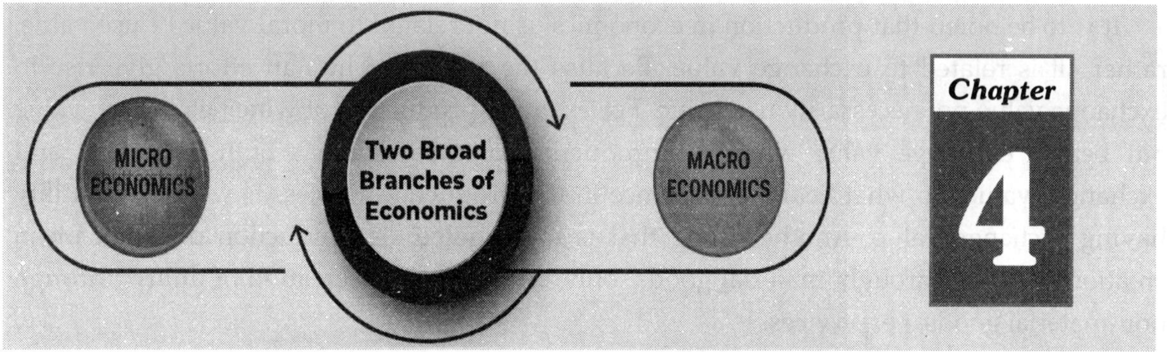

PRODUCTION

Man in his day-to-day life requires several goods to satisfy his different types of wants. Some of these goods are free gifts of nature and some are the results of his own effort, some of them are material and some are non-material. Truely speaking man has no capacity to create any thing new. Yes, he has the capacity to convert or to give a new shape or new look to an already existing thing provided by nature. The origin of each and every object that we see and use to satisfy our wants lies in the nature in the form of soil, air, water, mineral deposits, vegetation and all the living and non-living organisms. Man only gives shapes and converts the natural objects in to different goods in accordance with his necessities. By this, the efforts that he makes or the activities that he undertakes, is used in economics in the sense of production. Thus when man changes the form or adds to the usefulness of an existing object or adds to the wants satisfying capacity of an object, we call his efforts as 'Production'. In this sense production in economics means any activity that creates utility or adds utility to an existing object. Production takes place for the purpose of exchange or transaction. In this sense production in economics can be defined as –**'creation of utility having exchange value'.**

Definitions

"Production is any activity that results in goods or services intended for exchange." **–Meyers**

"Production is the creation of value in a commodity". **–Prof. Thomas**

"Production is the making of goods for sale or the rendering of paid services". **–Cairncross**

"Production means creation of economic utility." **–Prof. Ely**

It is to be noted that production in economics is not related to moral value or use value, rather it is related to exchange value. Because the results of human efforts give rise to exchange value not necessarily use value. For example production of wine has no use value but bears exchange value where as production of medicine has both use value and exchange value. So what bears significance in the production process is creation of utility having exchange value. Another thing that is to be noted is production does not mean creation of utility through material goods only, it also includes creation of utility through non-material goods, i.e. services.

In the production process utility is created in four broad forms, such as–

(i) ***Form utility,*** which is created by changing the form or shape of a commodity.

(ii) ***Place utility,*** which is created by changing the place of a commodity.

(iii) ***Time utility,*** which is created in a commodity with the change in time.

(iv) ***Service utility,*** which is created by different services.

We have already discussed all these four types of utility earlier in this book. We have mentioned about them here as they are related to the act of production.

FACTORS OF PRODUCTION

Factors of production refers to all those inputs which are used in the process of production of a commodity or in creation of utility having exchange value. Factor inputs or factors of production include various material and non-material goods and what results from their joint efforts is called output. However, for the sake of simplicity of our analysis we classify the factor inputs required in the process of production of a commodity under four broad categories, known as four factors of production, such as –

(i) Land

(ii) Labour

(iii) Capital, and

(iv) Organization

Out of these four factors land and labour are considered as Primary Factors, Capital is a Secondary or man-made factor and the act of organization is a special type of labour. Let us discuss in which sense four factors are used in the production analysis.

1. Land

For a common man 'land' means the surface of the earth. But in economics, as a factor of production the term 'land' is used in a wider sense. In economics land refers to the surface of the earth and any things that is permanently attached to it. Those anything include the natural resources like mineral deposits, Forests, rivers, streams etc. over whose supply man has no control and the man made things like building and all other immobile objects. Land is a primary factor of production. It is to be noted that any thing which is permanently attached to the earth like building, tree, mineral deposits etc. one considered as land. But. If a tree is cut down or detached from the earth is no more land. Similarly when the mineral deposits are under the earth, are included in land . But once they are excavated, they are no more land, rather become capital. Payment made for the use of land is called rent.

2. Labour

Generally labour means any physical activity. But in economics labour means any physical or mental exertion which is undergone for the purpose of any reward either in cash or in kind or in both, other than the mental pleasure derived from the work. Thus, in economics any physical or mental work performed partly or whole with a view to earn something is considered as labour. Any physical or mental work performed for mental pleasure only, e.g. the work of a social worker or for social responsibility, e.g. a mother's care for her baby or the work of housewife etc. are not considered as labour in economics. Because no formal payment is made in such cases. Labour is inseparable from the labourer. Labourer sells his labour for wage, not himself.

3. Capital

Capital refers to those man-made factors which help in further production of goods and services. That's why capital is called 'Produced means of production. It includes machines, Plants, tools, semi-finished goods or inventories, raw materials etc. capital can be divided into different types such as fixed capital, floating capital, working capital, Financial capital etc., Payment made for the use of capital is called interest. Broadly Speaking, capital is that part of wealth which helps in further production or generates income.

4. Organization

The act of organising the factor inputs to carry out the process of production is called organization. It includes planning of production, collection of factor inputs i.e. land, labour and capital and to combine them in appropriate proportion, decisions regarding what to produce and how much to produce etc. One who does all these is called the organizer or the entrepreneur. An organizer or entrepreneur is a special type of labour with top business skill and foresight. He takes all possible measures in the production process and bears all risks involved there in. For his acts he is rewarded by profit which may either be positive or negative, i.e. loss.

Production Function

The functional relation that exists between the factors of production or factor inputs is called production function. The relation described in the production function is a technical relation. It presents how much output can be produced using how much of which factor input. In other words it indicates the minimum quantity of factor inputs required to produce a given amount of output. It can be expressed in the form of graph or table or mathematical equation.

In the form of equation production function is written as-

$Q = f(L, K)$ Where, Q = Amount of output

L = Labour , K = Capital

It explains that the amount or quantity of output to be produced depends upon the amount of labour and capital, other factors affecting production assuming constant.

In the production process time is an important factor. On the basis of time period required to carryout a production venture, production function can be as–

(i) Short-run production Function

(ii) Long-run Production Function

Short-run or short period refers to that time period in the production venture in which some factors of production can be varied to adjust the volume of output and some other factor inputs cannot be changed. Thus in short-run production venture some factors of production are fixed and some are variable. If there are two factors of production–Labour (L) and capital (K) out of which capital is fixed factor, as it cannot be changed in short-run, then the short-run production function can be written as–

$Q = f(L, \bar{K})$ Where, L = Labour , Variable factor

$\bar{K}$ = Capital, Fixed factor

Q = Amount of output

Thus, in short-run variable factor(s) play significant role in the adjustment of the level of output.

Long-run or long-period refers to that time period in the production venture in which all factor inputs can be adjusted or varied to fully adjust the level of output. This is a time period in which all factors of production are variable and hence can be adjusted to increase or decrease the level of output. In other words in long-run the scale of production can be changed by varying all factor inputs.

The long-run production function is written as-

$$Q = f(L, K) \quad \text{(L and K both are variable)}$$

Remember : Short-run production function is explained through the **Law of variable proportion** and the long-run production function is explained through the **Laws of Returns to scale.** (Explained later in this chapter)

- **Fixed and Variable Factors**

On the basis of the time period required in the production process the factors of production are broadly classified as–

(i) Fixed factors and

(ii) Variable factors

Fixed Factors refer to those factors of production which cannot be changed during the production process. Fixed factors are related to short-run only. They remain unchanged for all levels of production. In other words Fixed Factors are independent of the level of output. They have no role to play in the adjustment of the level of output. In short-run land, building, plant, machineries, permanent employees etc. are the examples of Fixed Factors.

Variable Factors refer to those factors of production which can be changed or varied during the production process to adjust the level of output. Variable factors are related to both short-run and long-run production venture. In short-run the level of output depends upon the amount of variable factors. In short-run labour, raw-materials, power, fuel etc. are the examples of variable factors. However in long-run all factors are variable. Thus the distinction between the fixed and variable factors is related to short-run only.

CONCEPTS OF TOTAL, AVERAGE AND MARGINAL PRODUCTS

In the analysis of production theories three concepts of production bear significance in taking decision regarding production. They are –total product, average product and marginal product.

Total Product

Total product may be defined as the amount of aggregate output produced by a given amount of all factor inputs in a stipulated time period. In short-run total product (TP) is a direct function of the variable factor (V), i.e. TP = *f*(V). Because in short-run variable factor plays all important role in determining the volume of total product. In short-run fixed factor remaining constant, the volume of output increases with the increase in the units of variable factor and decreases with the decrease in the units of variable factor. But in long-run since all factors are variable the volume of total product is a function of all factor inputs, i.e. Q= *f*(L, K).

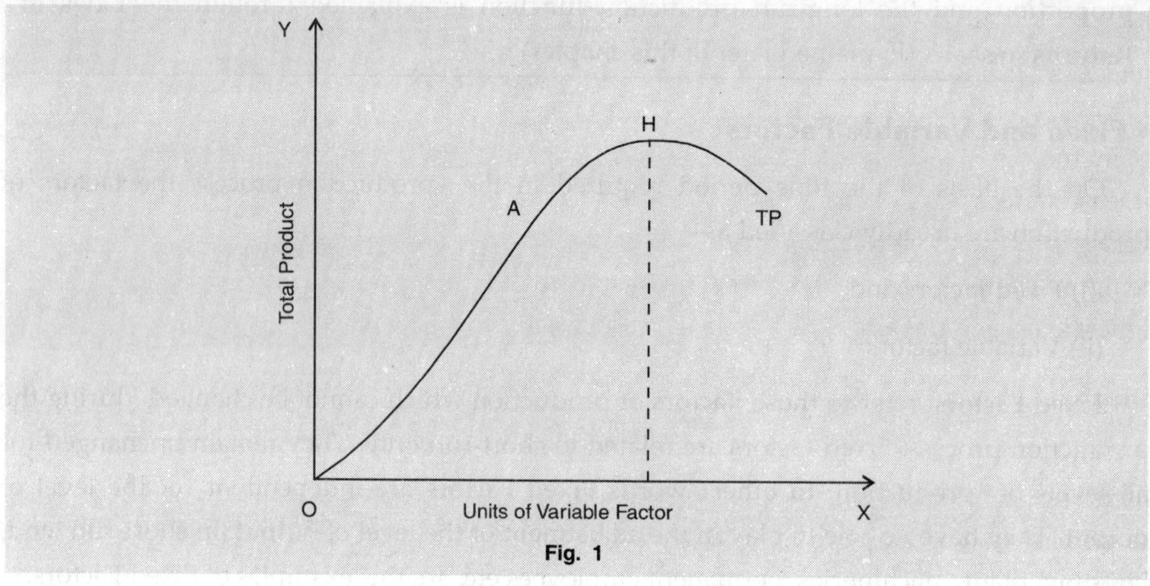

Fig. 1

The total product curve, TP, as shown in the figure drawn above starts from the origin and at the initial stages moves upward to the right at an increasing rate upto point 'A', representing increasing returns. Then rises up-ward to the right at a diminishing rate upto point H, where it reaches the highest point. This stage represents diminishing return. After this, the TP curve turns downward representing relative returns from the variable factors.

Average Product

Average product can be defined as the amount of output produced per unit of the variable factor employed in producing a given amount of output. Average product (AP) is obtained by dividing the total product (TP) by the quantity of variable factor (V) employed.

That is $$AP = \frac{TP}{V}$$

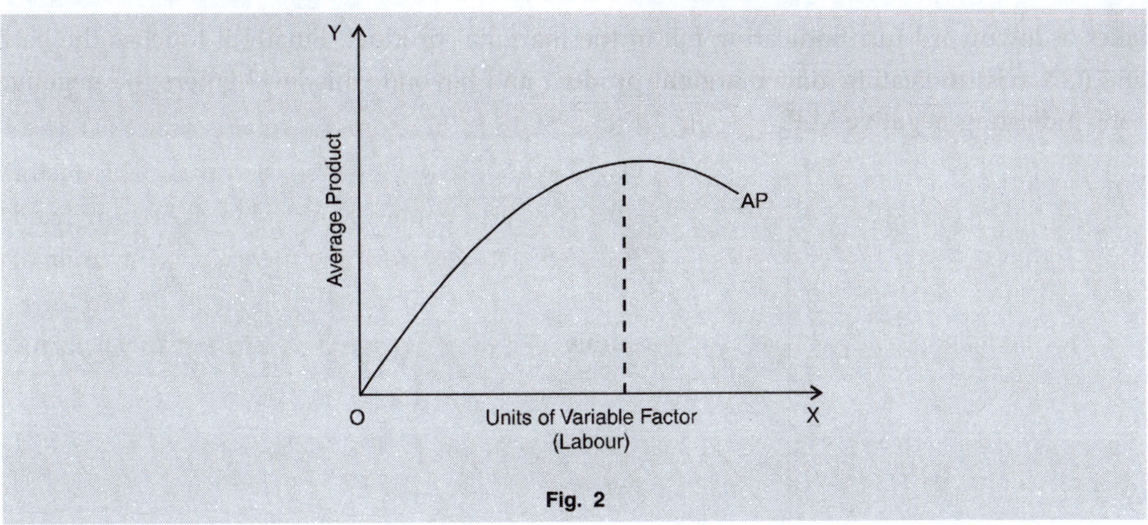

Fig. 2

In the process of production as the units of variable factor increases total product increases and average product also increases but at a diminishing rate. In the later stages average product reaches a maximum and then starts decreasing. The AP curve, as shown in the figure, starts from the origin then rises upward at a diminishing rate then reaching at its highest starts moving downwards. AP, however, can never be zero.

Marginal Product

Marginal product can be defined as the addition made to the total product by employing one more unit of the variable factor, say labour. In other words marginal product (MP) is the increase in the total product (TP) by employing an additional unit of the variable factor. Symbolically.

$$MP = TP_n - TP_{n-1}$$

N = number of variable-factor (Labour)

Marginal product can also be expresses as the change in the total product with respect to a change in the total product with respect to change in the variable factor, say labour.

Symbolically-

$$MP = \frac{\partial TP}{\partial L}$$ Where ∂ = change

L = variable factor, Labour.

The marginal product curve (MP) as shown in the fig. 3 starts from the origin, then increases upto a certain stage with the increase in the units of labour employed. Then it takes a downward turn indicating fall in the marginal product. Finally it touches the base line (OX-axis) indicating zero marginal product and beyond this level enters the negative zone indicating negative M.P.

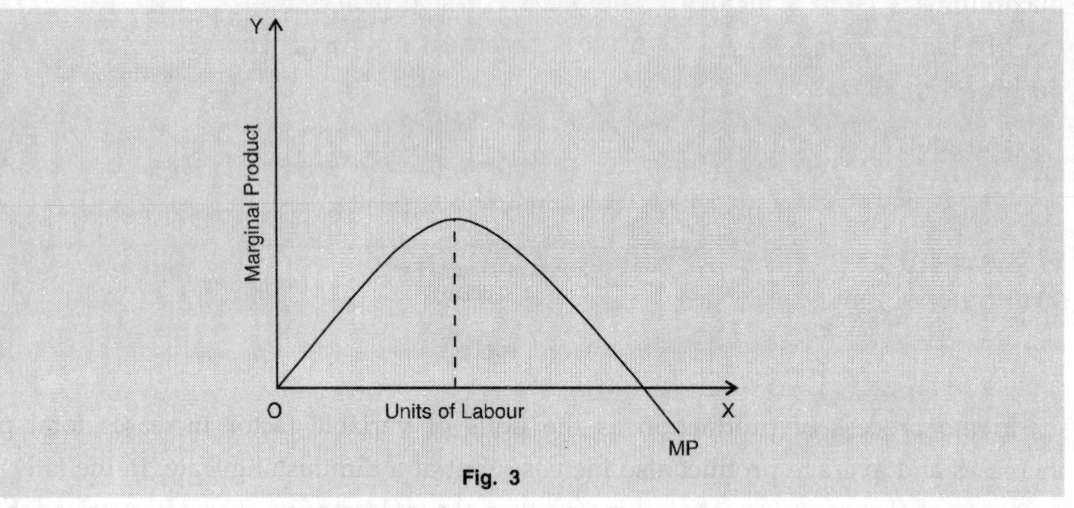

Fig. 3

Relationship between TP, AP and MP

Since both average product (AP) and marginal product (MP) are calculated from the total product (TP) there exist a close relationship between AP and MP. This is shown with the help of the hypothetical table of TP, AP and MP drawn below.

The table shows with a given amount of fixed factor when the 1st unit of variable factor, labour, is employment the total product is 10. At this stage the average product (AP= TP/L) and marginal product (MP = $\frac{\partial TP}{\partial L}$) both are same, i.e., 10. Then with employing 2nd, 3rd.... unit of variable factor, i.e., labour, the total product has increased to 22, 36 ..... units respectively. Accordingly the AP has increased to 11, 12,....units and MP has increased to 12, 14 ....units.

Units of Labour	Total Product (TP)	Average Product (AP)	Marginal Product (MP)
1	10	10	10
2	22	11	12
3	36	12	14
4	48	12	12
5	55	11	7
6	50	10	5
7	50	7.14	0
8	48	6	–2
9	45	5	–3

Upto 5th unit of labour the AP has increased and then has started decreasing. However the M.P. has started decreasing earlier from 4th unit of variable factor. TP has become maximum at 7th unit of labour where the MP has become zero. Then from 8th unit onwards the MP has become negative resulting decrease in the TP. However, AP has remained positive throughout.

Thus the relationship can be summerised as -

1. At the 1st unit of variable factor TP = AP = MP.
2. In the initial stages of employing more and more variable factors TP, AP and MP increases more than proportionately and MP > AP.
3. In the subsequent levels of variable factors TP increases at a diminishing rate.
4. MP Falls prior to Fall in the AP and MP < AP.
5. When MP = 0, TP becomes maximum.
6. When MP becomes negative, TP starts decreasing.
7. AP remains positive throughout.

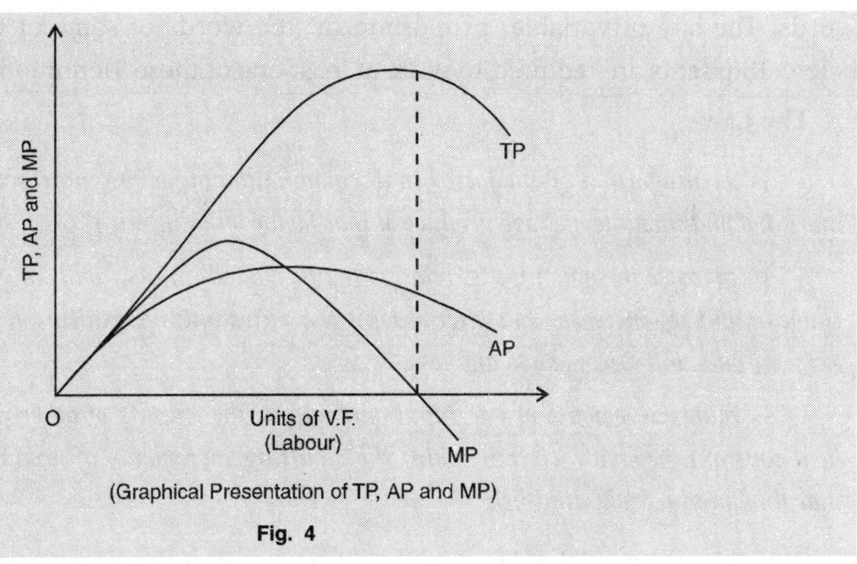

(Graphical Presentation of TP, AP and MP)

Fig. 4

• THE LAW OF VARIABLE PROPORTION

In short-run production venture we know some factors of production are fixed and some others are variable. In this sense, when with a fixed factor of production more and more units of a variable factor are employed factor proportion changes. The effect of changes in factor proportion on output is the matter of discussion under the law of variable proportion. Thus the law of variable proportion examines the behaviour of short-run production function.

The law of variable proportion in fact is the new name given to the classical law of diminishing return propounded by Alfred Marshall. Of course he confined the law to the field of agriculture only saying, *"An increase in the capital and labour applied in the cultivation of land causes, in general, a less than proportionate increase in the amount of product raised unless it happens to coincide with an improvement in the art of agriculture."*

Thus assuming land as a fixed factor, capital and labour as variable factor with the given technology, Marshall explained in the law of diminishing return that as more and more variable facts are applied, the marginal product of the successive variable factor units will go on diminishing.

However, the modern economists like samuelson, Benham, Boulding, Stigler and others have extended the application of the law to all fields of production where at least one-factor is variable and others are fixed. To them, when with a fixed factor more and more units of a variable factor will be applied it will lead to variation in factor proportion. So they named the effect of variable factor proportion on the total product as the law of variable proportion. They defined the law more or less in the same sense in different words. The law of variable proportion in the words of some of the economists is given below. (Students are required to write at least one of these definitions).

The Law–

"As the proportion of one factor in a combination of factors increased, after a point, first the marginal and then the average product of that factor will diminish". **–Benham**

"An increase in some inputs, relative to other fixed inputs, will, in given state of technology, cause output to increase, but after a point the extra output resulting from the same additions of extra inputs will become less and less." **–Samuelson**

"As equal increments of one inputs are added, the inputs of other productive services being held constant, beyond a certain point the resulting increments of product will diminish, i.e. the marginal product will diminish." **–Stigler**

Simply speaking the law says that state of technology remaining constant when increasing units of variable factor are added to a given fixed factor, the average and marginal product of the variable factor will eventually diminish.

Assumptions :

The law is developed on the following assumptions-

(i) The state of technology or technique of production is given and constant.

(ii) At least one factor is variable and others are constant.

(iii) The units of variable factor are homogeneous.

(iv) The factor proportion can be varied.

Explanation of the Law

Assuming land as the Fixed Factor and labour as the variable factor the law of variable proportion can be explained with the help of the table drawn below.

Input-output Table with One Factor Variable

Fixed Factor (Land)	Variable Factor (Labour)	Factor Proportion	Total Product (TP)	Average Product (MP)	Marginal Product (MF)	Stages of Return
2 Acres	1	2 :1	10	10	10	Stage–I Stage of Increasing Return
2 Acres	2	2:2	22	11	12	
2 Acres	3	2:3	36	12	14	
2 Acres	4	2 : 4	48	12	12	Stage–II Stage of Diminishing Return
2 Acres	5	2 : 5	55	11	7	
2 Acres	6	2 : 6	60	10	5	
2 Acres	7	2 : 7	60	8.57	0	
2 Acres	8	2 : 8	56	7	–4	Stage–III Stage of Negative Return
2 Acres	9	2 : 9	50	$5.\overline{5}$	–6	

In the table it is shown that with a fixed amount of land, 2 acres, when more and more units of labour are employed the factor proportions are varying, i.e. from 2:1 to 2:2, 2:3 .... and so on. With the change in factor proportion the total product is increasing from 10 to 22, 36, i.e. at an increasing rate up to the 3rd unit of the variable factor. So up to the 3rd unit of the variable factor the stage of production is marked as stage–I, i.e. the stage of increasing return. But with the addition of the 4th unit of the variable factor the marginal product of the variable factor starts declining and from here the stage–II, i.e. the stage of diminishing return starts. In this stage the total product is increasing but at a diminishing rate till the addition of the 7th unit of the variable factor where the marginal product becomes zero(0) and total product becomes maximum and the stage of diminishing return ends. A rational producer will stop employing any more unit of variable factor at the end of this stage. Because beyond this stage the marginal product of the variable factor becomes negative in stage–III, i.e. the stage of negative return which will decrease the total product.

So far as the average product is concerned it increases upto 4th unit of variable factor and starts declining from 5th unit but remains positive in the subsequent stages.

Remember : The stage of increasing return implies diminishing cost, the stage of diminishing return implies increasing cost and the stage of negative return implies loss.

Graphic Presentation

The law is presented graphically below.

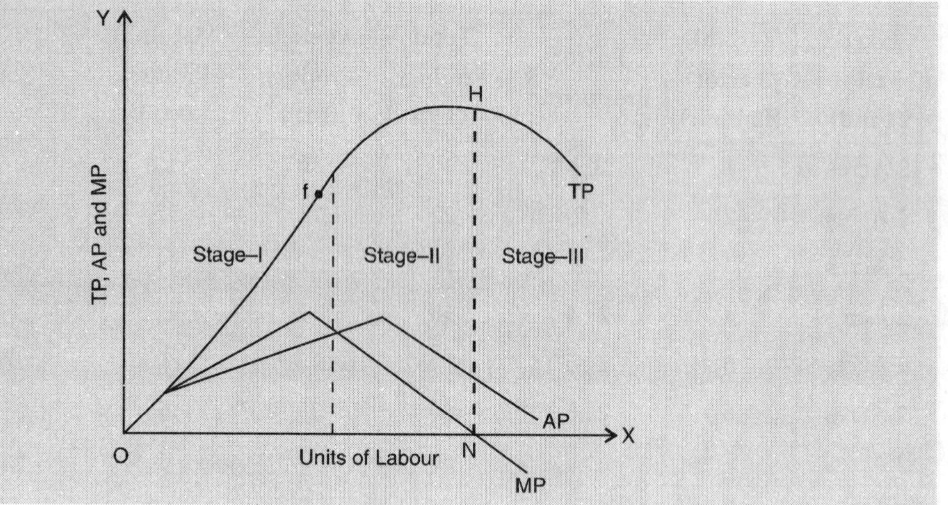

In the figure the units of variable factor (Labour) is preseated on the horizontal axis and TP, AP and MP are presented on the vertical axis. As shown in the figure with the application of more and more units of labour the total product curve TP, average product curve AP and marginal product curve MP are rising upward in Stage–I. The MP curve in this stage is rising right upto below point 'F' on the TP curve indicating increase in the TP at an increasing rate. In stage–II both AP and MP curves have taken a negative slope indicating fall in the average and marginal product of the labour. But the TP curve is rising upward but at a diminishing rate up to point 'H', *i.e.* the point H of highest total product and right below the point 'H' the MP curve has touch the base line 'OX' indicating zero marginal product. The stage–II, i.e. the stage of diminishing return ends here. This Stage–II is crucial as rational producer will stop employing more labour units here. Beyond this the MP curve enters the negative zone indicating negative marginal product from where stage–III, i.e. the stage of negative return starts. In this stage the TP curve takes a downward turn indicating decrease in the total product. However, the AP curve is falling through out the second and third stages, indicating fall in the average product but still positive.

Causes of Increasing Returns

Economists have held the following causes responsible for the operation of the increasing return in the early stages (stage–I) of production.

1. **Indivisibility of the Fixed Factor :** Fixed factors are mostly indivisible. In the initial stage they have to be installed in complete, but are not fully utilised. Gradually when more and more units of variable factor are employed the fuller utilization becomes possible which causes the total product to increase in an increasing rate or causes the increasing return to operate.
2. **Division of Labour :** As more and more units of labour are employed there takes place division of labour which promotes specialization and increase in the efficiency of labour. As a result of which the marginal productivity of labour increase and causes the increasing return to operate.
3. **Economies of scale :** Economies of scale refer to the benefits of increasing the size of a firm. When the size of the firm, in the initial stage starts realising certain benefits in the form of internal and external economies which lead decreasing cost or increasing return to operate.

Causes of Diminishing Returns

In short-run production venture diminishing returns is a logical necessity due to the reasons like-

1. **Imperfect Substitutability of Factors :** Fixed factors and variables factors of production are not perfect substitutes. When the fixed factors are fully utilised in the later stages of production the level of output mostly becomes dependent on the variable factors. But the variable factors are not the substitutes of the fixed factors so in the later stages of production the deficiency of the fixed factors, after their fuller utilization in the presence of more variable factors causes the marginal product of the variable factor to decrease or causes the diminsing returns to operate.
2. **Inefficiency in Factor Proportion :** In short-run fixed factor can't be increased. So factor proportion changes as more units of variable factor are employed. But in the later stages of production the units of variable factor becomes too much for the given Fixed factor. As a result the factor proportion become inefficient and total product starts declining due to fall in the marginal product of the variable factor units.

3. **Diseconomics of Scale :** In the later stages of Production by employing more and more units of variable factor the firm realizes certain disadvantages which are called diseconomics of scale. It includes lack of co-operation, lack of responsibility, lack of co-ordination among different section of workers and management etc. which cause the diminishing returns to operate.

Limitations of the Law

Law of variable proportion is criticized on the grounds that-

(i) It does not operate in a dynamic society where technological progress is obvious.

(ii) It does not operate in case of those fields of Production where factor proportions are fixed.

(iii) It does not operate if the units of variable factor are not homogeneous or are heterogeneous, etc.

However, these criticism or limitations are not so significant. Because the law explains the behaviour pattern of production in short-run. But in short-run technology is not expected to change and even if there is change in technology, there is a limit to it. It can't stop the operation of the law. At best it can delay its operation, can't deny its operation. Secondly, the vary name of the law is 'Law of variable Proportion' so the question of applying it to the field of production where factor proportions are fixed does not arise. Of course the limitation regarding the homogeneity of variable factor units bears some significance.

WHAT WE LEARNT

1. Production means creation of utility having exchange value.
2. Four types of utility are created in the production process– form utility, place utility, time utility and service utility.
3. Production in economics is not related to moral value or use value, rather exchange value.
4. Production means creation utility both through material and non-material goods.
5. Those goods and services which are used in the production process are called factors of production or inputs.
6. The outcome of the combined effort of inputs is called output.

7. Factors of production are classified under four broad categories–Land, labour, capital and organization.
8. Land and labour are Primary Factors of Production.
9. Capital is the Secondary Factor or Produced means of production.
10. Land in economics means the surface of the earth and any thing that is permanently attached to it and over whose supply man has no control.
11. Labour means any physical or mental exertion undergone, partly or wholly, for any reward.
12. Capital means those man-made objects which help in further production or in income generation.
13. One who organizes the production process is called organizer or entrepreneur.
14. Organization is a special type of labour.
15. Organizer or the entrepreneur bears all risks in the production process.
16. The functional relationship between factor inputs and output is called production function.
17. In an equation from a normal production function is written as $Q = f(L, K)$
18. On the basis of time period production functions are of two types–(i) Short-run production Function. (ii) Long-run production Function.
19. Short-run refers to that time period in a production venture in which some factors of production can changed to adjust the volume of output to some extent and some others cannot be changed.
20. The factors of production which can be changed during the production process to adjust the volume of output are called variable factors.
21. The factors of production which cannot be changed to adjust the volume of production are called fixed factors.
22. The concept of fixed factor is related to short-run production function only.
23. The concept of variable factor is related to both short-run and long-run production functions.
24. Long-run refers to that time period in the production venture in which all factors of production can be changed, i.e. the scale of production can be changed to fully adjust the volume of output.
25. In long run all factors of production are variable.
26. The law of variable proportion explains the short-run production function.

27. The laws of returns to scale explain the long-run production function.

28. The amount of output produced per unit of the variable factor is called average product (AP = TP/V)

29. The addition made to the total product by employing one more unit of a variable factor is called marginal product ($MP = TP_n - TP_{n-1}$)

30. Marginal product starts decreasing prior to the decrease in the average product.

31. When marginal product decreases, till it is positive, total product increases at a diminishing rate.

32. Total product becomes maximum when marginal product is zero.

33. Total Product decreases when marginal product becomes negative.

34. The law of variable proportion is the new name of the classical law of diminishing return propounded by Alfred Marshall.

35. The law of variable proportion explains the effects of changes in factors proportions on the output.

36. Stage–I of the law of variable proportion is called as the stage of increasing returns or diminishing cots.

37. Stage–II of the law of variable proportion is called as the stage of diminishing return or increasing costs.

38. A rational producer takes production decision in stage–II of the law of variable proportion.

39. Stage–III of the law of variable proportion is called as the staged of negative returns.

40. Production decision in stage-III of the law of variable proportion implies loss.

QUESTIONS FOR REVIEW

A. *Choose the correct answer from the given alternatives in each question. (Each Carrying 1 Mark)*

1. **In economics production means.....**

   (i) Creation of anything material

   (ii) Creation of utility

(iii) Creation of utility having exchange value

(iv) All the above

2. **Which one is created by changing the shape of commodity ?**

(i) Form utility (ii) Time Utility

(iii) Place utility (iv) Service utility

3. **Which one is a primary factor of production ?**

(i) Capital (ii) Land

(iii) Organization (iv) None of these

4. **Which one is a produced mean of production ?**

(i) Land (ii) Labour

(iii)Capital (iv) All the above.

5. **Over the supply of which one man has no control ?**

(i) Capital (ii) Organization

(iii) Organization (iv) Land

6. **Which one is a special type of labour ?**

(i) Organization (ii) Labour

(iii) both (i) and (ii) (iv) None of these

7. **Who bears all risks in the production venture ?**

(i) Labourer (ii) Capitalist

(iii) Entrepreneur (iv) Land owner

8. **A Labour sells his labour for....**

(i) Rent (ii) Wage

(iii) Interest (iv) Profit

9. **Payment made for the use of land is called....**

(i) Interest (ii) Profit

(iii) Wage (iv) Rent

10. **Payment made for the use of capital is called....**

(i) Profit (ii) Interest

(iii) Rent (iv) Wage

11. **For bearing risks in the production venture the entrepreneur is rewarded with....**

(i) Profit (ii) Interest

(iii) Wage (iv) Rent

12. Which factor payment may either be positive or negative ?

(i) Wage (ii) Rent

(iii) Interest (iv) Profit.

13. The functional relationship between factor inputs and output is called...

(i) Production function (ii) Diminishing return

(iii) Increasing return (iv) None of these

14. In short-run which one is not a fixed factor of production ?

(i) Land (ii) Labour

(iii) Machine (iv) Plant.

15. Which one is a fixed factor of production in short-run.

(i) Labour (ii) Raw material

(iii) Permanent employee (iv) All the above

16. In short-run production venture which one falls first ?

(i) Total Product (ii) Marginal Product

(iii) Average Produce (iv) None of these

17. In short-run production function which stage is called the stage of diminishing cost ?

(i) Stage–I (ii) Stage–II

(iii) Stage–III (iv) None of these

18. In short-run production function stage–III is called as....

(i) Stage of increasing returns (ii) Stage of decreasing returns

(iii) Stage of increasing cost (iv) Stage of negative returns.

19. Which stage of production is crucial for taking decision ?

(i) Stage–I (ii) Stage–II

(iii) Stage–III (iv) All the above.

20. Marshall confined the law of variable proportion to ......

(i) Agriculture (ii) Industry

(iii) Fishing (iv) All the above

B. *Correct the statements, if necessary, without changing the underlined portions. (Each Carrying 1 Mark)*

1. <u>In economics production means creation of utility having</u> use value.
2. <u>Production gives rise to</u> exchange value, <u>not necessarily</u> use value.

3. From utility is created by changing the place of a commodity.
4. Labour is a secondary factor of production.
5. Work done for mental pleasure is called labour.
6. Man has no control over the supply of capital.
7. Land is called as the produced mean of production.
8. In short run all factors are variable.
9. In long run at least one factor is variable.
10. Short run production function is written as Q = f(L, K)
11. In short-run production venture raw material is a fixed factor.
12. Plant in long-run production venture is a variable factor.
13. Law of variable proportion explains the short-run production function.
14. In short-run production venture Average product starts falling first.
15. When marginal product becomes zero total product starts decreasing.
16. At the first unit of variable factor Marginal Product > Average Product.
17. The stage of diminishing returns implies loss.
18. Economies of scale is realized in the later stages of production.
19. Division labour in the initial stages of production leads to diminishing returns.
20. Average product become negative in stage–III of the law of variable proportion.

C. *Answer the following questions in 2-3 sentences each (Each Carrying 2 Marks)*

1. What is production in economics ?
2. What are the factors of production ?
3. What is land in economics ?
4. What is labour in economics ?
5. What is capital ?
6. What is organisation ?
7. Who is an entrepreneur ?
8. What is production function ?
9. What is short-run ?
10. What is long-run ?

11. What is variable factor ?
12. What is Fixed factor ?
13. How TP, AP and MP are related ?
14. What is total product ?
15. What is average product ?
16. What is marginal production ?
17. What is short-run production function ?
18. What is long-run production function ?
19. State the law of variable proportion.
20. Point out the assumptions of the law of variable proportion.

D. Distinguish between the concepts in six sentences each. (Carrying 3 Marks)

1. Short-run and Long-run.
2. Fixed factors and variable factors.
3. Short-run production function and Long-run production function.
4. Average product and marginal product.
5. Increasing Returns and Diminishing Returns.

E. Long Answer Type Questions (Carrying 7½ Marks)

1. What do you mean by factors of production ? Briefly discuss different factors of production.
2. Discuss the concepts of TP, AP and MP with the relationship in between them with suitable table and diagram.
3. Explain the law of variable proportion.
4. Discuss the causes of the operation of the law of variable proportion.

Answer to Q. N. A

1.	(iii)	2.	(i)	3.	(ii)	4.	(iii)	5.	(iv)	6.	(i)	7.	(iii)	8.	(ii)
9.	(iv)	10.	(ii)	11.	(i)	12.	(iv)	13.	(i)	14.	(ii)	15.	(iii)	16.	(ii)
17.	(i)	18.	(iv)	19.	(ii)	20.	(i)								

Answer to Q. N. B		
1. Exchange value	2. Correct	3. Shape/Form
4. Primary	5. Reward	6. Land
7. Capital	8. In long run	9. In short run
10. $Q = f(L, \bar{K})$	11. Variable factor	12. Correct
13. Correct	14. Marginal Product	15. Maximizes
16. Equal to (=)	17. Increasing cost	18. Initial stages
19. Increasing returns	20. Marginal product.	

❑ ❑ ❑

UNIT – IV

5. COST, REVENUE AND SUPPLY

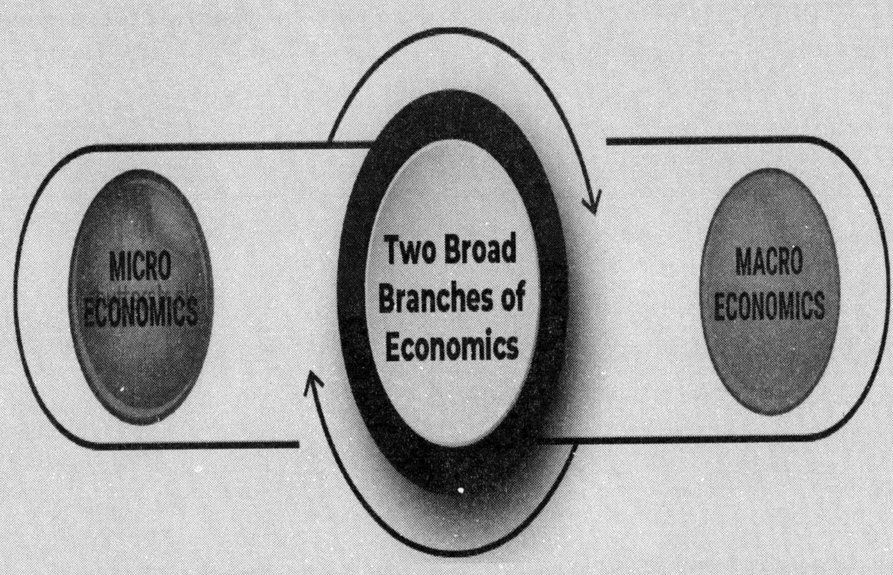

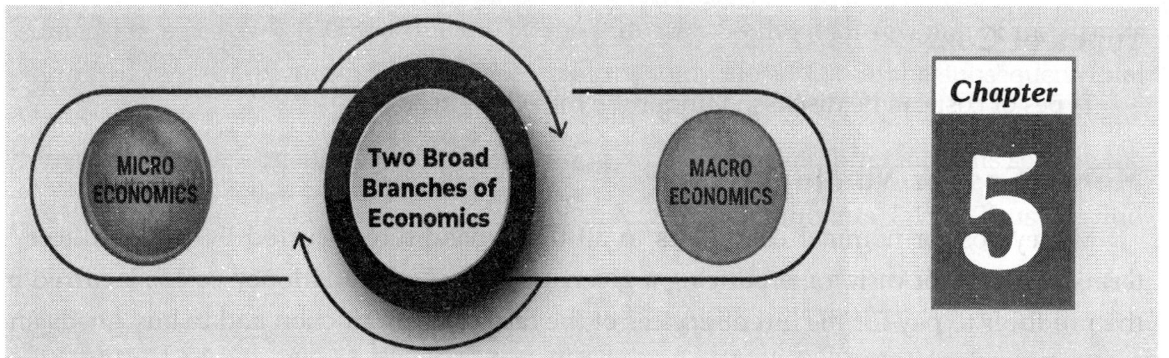

COST, REVENUE AND SUPPLY

The concepts of cost and revenue bear much significance in economics as they influence the decision taking process in the field of production and supply. A producer always aims at maximization of profit which depends upon the difference between the cost of producing a given amount of a commodity and the revenue that he receives from the sale of the amount produced. That's why the concepts of cost and revenue are important in the study of the theory of production and supply of the commodity for sale. Here, let us first discuss on the meaning of cost and its different concepts.

Meaning of Cost

'Cost' in economics is used in the sense of 'cost of production'. So, the cost of production means the sum of all expenditure incurred by the producer to produce the given amount of commodity. In the production process of a commodity a producer incurs different types of expenditure like expenditure incurred on hiring land, labour, capital, for purchasing raw materials, payments for power, fuel, transportation, insurance premiums, tax to the government etc. When all these expenditure incurred by the producer in the production process are summed up, it constitutes the cost of production. It also include the profit of the entrepreneur and the imputed value of the producer's own factors of production for which no formal payment is made. Thus, the cost of production is a very complex concept and includes various types of costs. We must have a clear-cut understanding of the types of cost to understand the equilibrium of the firms or producers in the production venture and the pricing theories.

Types of Cost

Types of cost can be discussed under the following heads.

Money Cost or Nominal Cost

Money cost or nominal cost refers to all the expenditure incurred by the producer in terms of money or cash for producing a given amount of output. Money cost is incurred by the producer to pay for the hired services of the factors of production and to buy goods and services required in the production process. It includes rent for the use of land/building, wages to the labourer, salaries to the employees, interest paid on borrowed funds, expenditure made on the purchase of raw materials, light, fuel, transportation, insurance premiums, depreciation charges, taxes to the government etc. These are those cash payments which the producers made to the outsiders for their services and goods. Since these cash payments are made explicitly, money cost is also called as **explicit cost.** Moreover, since these expenditure are recorded in the accounting register of the producer, are also known as **accounting cost.** As all these payments are made in nominal terms or in cash, these are also called **nominal cost.**

Money costs = Explicit costs = Accounting costs = Nominal costs

Implicit Cost

Often in the production venture the producer also uses some factors of his own for which no formal payment is made. He may have employed his own land/building, his own labour, his own capital etc. in the production venture. For his own factors he makes no formal payment to himself. But all these factors of his own could have fetch him some money or cash in the form of rent, wage/salary and interest, hence constitute a part of cost of production, which is called implicit cost. In this sense implicit costs can be defined as, **"the imputed costs of the producer's own factors of production employed in the production process for which no formal payment is made, but are costs to the producer as they represent an opportunity otherwise."** Since no formal payment is made by the producer for his self-supplied factors, their imputed costs, i.e. the implicit costs are not included in the accounting register of the producer or firm.

Economic Cost

Economic cost is a wider concept which includes both the explicit costs or accounting costs and implicit costs.

Economic costs = Explicit costs + Implicit cost

In the production process a producer hires or buys some factors as production and goods from outsiders for which he makes payments explicitly in terms of money. He also incurs expenditure on paying electric bills, fuel bills, insurance premiums, taxes to the government etc. All these visible expenditure recorded in the accounting register of the producer or firm are called explicit cost. Besides the hired or bought factor services and goods a producer also uses or employs some factor services or goods of his own for which no formal payment is made or recorded in the accounting register of the producer. The imputed costs of his own factor services are called implicit costs. When these two types of costs are added it constitutes the economic costs.

Real Cost

The concept of real cost was propounded by Marshall. It is a broader concept which includes the sum total of pain, sacrifice and toil undertaken by different factors of production in the process of producing a given amount of commodity. The pain, trouble and hardship of the labour, sacrifice involved in saving for capital formation, damages to the environment due to production activities etc. are included in the real cost. In the words of **Marshall, "The exertions of all different kinds of factors that are directly or indirectly used in making a commodity together with the abstinences or rather the waiting for saving the capital used in making it, will be called the real cost of production of the commodity."**

However, real cost is a subjective concept and bears no significance in pricing theory as it cannot be estimated.

Opportunity Cost

Opportunity cost of a factor refers to the income foregone or sacrificed in its next best alternative use. That's why it is also called as alternative cost. In the words of **Benham, "the opportunity cost of anything is the next best alternative forgone, that could be produced instead by the same factor or by an equivalent group of factors, costing same amount of money."**

It can be explained in two senses :

(i) Alternative cost of a factor

(ii) Opportunity cost of producing a commodity instead of an another.

So far as the opportunity cost of a factor is concerned it refers to what it had forgone in its next best alternative use for its present use. For example, suppose a worker is working in a factory and getting ₹ 500/- per day. If he could have been employed anywhere else and earned ₹ 400/- per day, that he has given up, then his opportunity cost or alternative cost is ₹ 400/-. But in terms of opportunity cost of producing a commodity instead of an another, the opportunity cost of producing that commodity is the income that is forgone or sacrificed in producing the present commodity. For example, if a piece of land with a given does of labour and capital can be used for producing wheat of worth ₹ 12,000, is used for producing rice, which worths ₹ 10,500/- then here the opportunity cost of producing rice is equal to the income that is foregone, i.e. ₹ 1500/-

However, in economic analysis opportunity cost is used in the sense of alternative cost which is defined as the value of a resource in its next best use or the amount of income or yield that could have been earned by investing it in the next best alternative use.

Fixed Cost and Variable Cost

In the production process time period plays a significant role in influencing the cost structure of a firm. We know there are two types of production functions on the basis of the time period, i.e. short-run and long-run production. We also know that in short-run production venture some factors of production are fixed and some are variable and in long-run production venture all factors are variable. These fixed and variable factors have their own influence on the cost structure. In this context we come across two concepts of costs :

(i) Fixed costs and (ii) Variable costs.

Fixed Costs :

Fixed costs refers to the expenditure incurred by the producer or firm on the fixed factors of production. Since the concept of fixed factor is related to short-run, fixed cost is exclusively related to the short-run production venture. As fixed factors remain unchanged for any level of output so also the fixed cost. That is fixed cost remains unchanged for all levels of output. So fixed cost is independent of the level of output. Since it equally falls upon all units of output at all level it is also called **over-head cost** or **supplementary cost**. In short-run production venture expenditure incurred on land/building, plant, machinery, salaries of permanent employees, insurance premiums etc. are the examples of fixed costs. Fixed costs have to be borne by the producer or firm even if output is zero.

Variable Costs :

Expenditure incurred by the firm on hiring or buying the variable factors of production to produce a given amount of output. We know in short-run some factors are variable and in long-run all factors are variable. So the concept of variable cost is related to both short-run and long-run production venture. Expenditure incurred in the short-run on hiring labour, purchasing raw-materials, payments on power charges, fuels, transportation, taxes to the government etc. are the examples of variable costs. In long all costs are variable. The firm has to bear variable costs when it starts producing. The variable costs and level of output are directly related, i.e. variable costs increase with the increase in the level of output and the reverse. That's why variable costs are also called **prime costs** or **direct costs.**

Total Cost

From the above discussion on variable costs and fixed costs, we can say that in short-run the total cost of producing a given level of output is the sum of the fixed costs and the variable cost incurred on specific amount of variable factors required to produce that level of output. Thus

$$TC = FC + VC$$

In long-run total cost of producing a given level of output is the sum of the expenditure incurred on hiring or buying all the factors required to produce that level of output.

The behaviour of TC, FC and VC and their graphic trend are presented below in the table and the graph.

Short-run costs.

Units of Output	Total Fixed Cost (₹)	Total Variable Cost (₹)	Total Cost (₹)
0	1000	—	1000
1	1000	130	1130
2	1000	150	1150
3	1000	160	1160
4	1000	165	1165
5	1000	180	1180
6	1000	200	1200
7	1000	230	1280

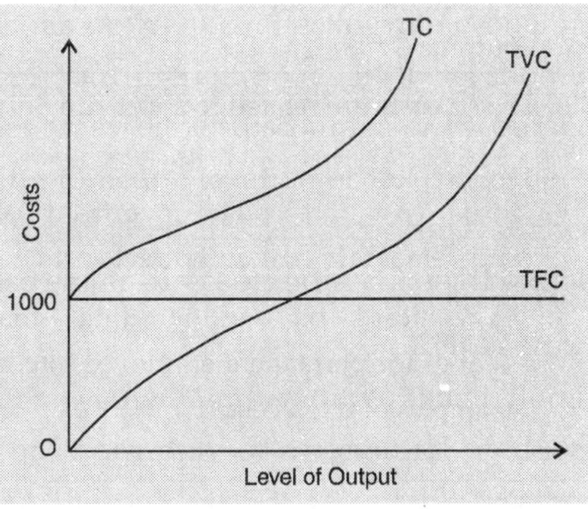

The table shows that when output is zero (0) the variable cost is zero (0), but the firm has to incur the fixed cost of ₹ 1000/- which is independent of level of output and the total cost even at the zero level output is ₹ 1000/- (TC = TFC + TVC). Then to start production the firm has incurred the variable cost worth ₹ 130/-. So the total cost of producing 1 unit has become ₹ 1130/- (₹ 1000/- + ₹ 130/-). Then for producing more and more units, fixed cost has remained unchanged and variable cost is gradually increasing, first at a diminishing rate and in latter stages at an increasing rate and the total cost has increased at the rate of increase in variable costs.

In the figure TFC is the total fixed cost curve which starts from above the origin at the point representing ₹ 1000/- and takes a horizontal shape indicating constant fixed cost at all level of output, presented on the OX-axis. The total variable cost curve TVC starts from the origin indicating zero total variable cost when output is zero. Then the TVC curve moves upward to the right with an increasing slope then after a certain level of output, the rate of its rising trend has declined. Total cost curve TC is obtained by the vertical addiction of the TFC curve and TVC curve.

Distinction between Fixed and Variable Costs

The distinction between the fixed costs and variable costs can be summarized as :

Fixed Costs	Variable Costs
1. Fixed costs are the expenditure incurred for hiring or for the purchase of fixed factors of production.	1. Variable costs are the expenditure incurred for hiring or for the purchase of variable factors of production.
2. Fixed costs are independent of level of output, i.e. donot vary with the level of output.	2. Variable costs are dependent of level of output, i.e. do vary with the level of output.
3. Fixed costs are related to short-run only.	3. Variable costs are related to both short-run and long-run.
4. Fixed costs are called overhead cost or supplementary cost or indirect cost.	4. Variable costs are called prime cost or direct cost.
5. Expenditure on land/building, machine, salaries for permanent employees etc. are the examples of fixed cost.	5. Expenditure on labour, raw-materials, power, fuel etc. are the examples of variable costs in short-run, but all expenditure in long-run are variable costs.

Average Costs

Average cost refers to cost per unit of a commodity. It is obtained dividing the total costs incurred in producing a given amount of output by the amount produced.

Symbolically :

$$AC = \frac{TC}{Q}$$

AC = Average cost

TC = Total cost

Q = Quantity of output produced

Since total cost (TC) has two components in the short-run, i.e. fixed cost and variable costs, we can also give the average cost (AC) by adding the averages of these two types of cost. i.e.

Since STC = TFC + TVC,

where STC = Short-run total cost

TFC = Total fixed cost

TVC = Total variable cost

$$SAC = \frac{TFC}{Q} + \frac{TVC}{Q},$$

$$\therefore \quad SAC = AFC + AVC$$

Thus short-run average cost (SAC) is the sum of Average Fixed Cost (AFC) and Average Variable Cost (AVC).

Average Fixed Cost (AFC)

Average fixed cost refers to fixed cost per unit of output. It is obtained dividing the total fixed cost (TFC) by the units of output produced (Q). Symbolically :

$$AFC = \frac{TFC}{Q}$$

the total fixed cost remains the same for all level of output, as output increases the average fixed cost falls constantly but will never become zero. For example, if a firm incurs ₹ 5000/- on fixed factors then at different level of output, say at 100 units, 200 units ..... 500 units, the AFC will be ₹ 50/-, ₹ 25/- ...... ₹ 10/- respectively, but it will never become zero. So when presented graphically the AFC curve will never touch the OX-axis, rather take the shape of a rectangular hyperbola, as shown in the figure, drawn aside. It is shown in the graph that with increase in the level of output on the X-axis the AFC curve slopes downwards to the right but will never touch the OX-axis.

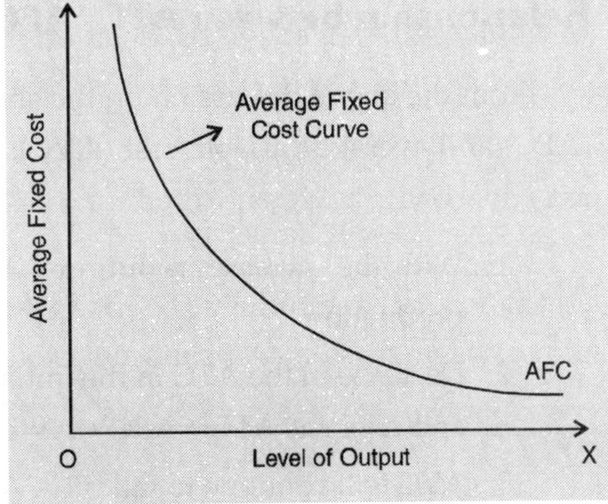

Average Variable Cost (AVC)

Average variable cost refers to the variable cost per unit of output produced. It is obtained dividing the total variable cost (TVC) by the total amount of a commodity produced (Q).

Symbolically :

$$AVC = \frac{TVC}{Q}$$

For example, if a firm is incurring ₹ 5000/- for producing 100 units of a commodity, thus the AVC will be $\frac{5000}{100}$ = ₹ 50.

Average variable cost decreases in the initial stages of production when the firm increases its output, then subsequently reaches a minimum and then increases in the later stages of production. The reason is, in the initial stages when the firm is not producing to its full capacity its fixed factors remain partially absorbed. So when the firm increases its output applying more of variable factors the fuller utilization of the fixed factors and other economies of scale lead to the operation of the increasing returns or diminishing cost, which decreases the average variable cost. But after the fuller utilization of the fixed factors increase in output completely becomes a function of variable factors and subject to the diminishing returns or increasing cost and hence the average variable cost will gradually increase. When this behaviour of the average variable cost is presented graphically the AVC curve will take the shape of English capital letter 'U', as shown in the figure drawn below. (Fig. 1)

Relationship between ATC, AFC and AVC

From the above discussion on the short-run average total cost (ATC), average fixed cost (AFC) and average variable cost (AVC), the relationship between them can be summarised as :

1. With the increase in output ATC, AFC and AVC decrease in the initial stages of production.
2. Decrease in the ATC in the initial stages of production is due to fall in both the AFC and AVC, as ATC = AFC + AVC.
3. ATC will continue to fall till AVC does not rise.

4. Since TFC is constant, AFC will continuously fall throughout all levels of output.
5. ATC reaches the minimum point at that level of output where the fall in AFC just equals the rise in AVC.
6. ATC rises when the rise in AVC outweighs the fall in the AFC.

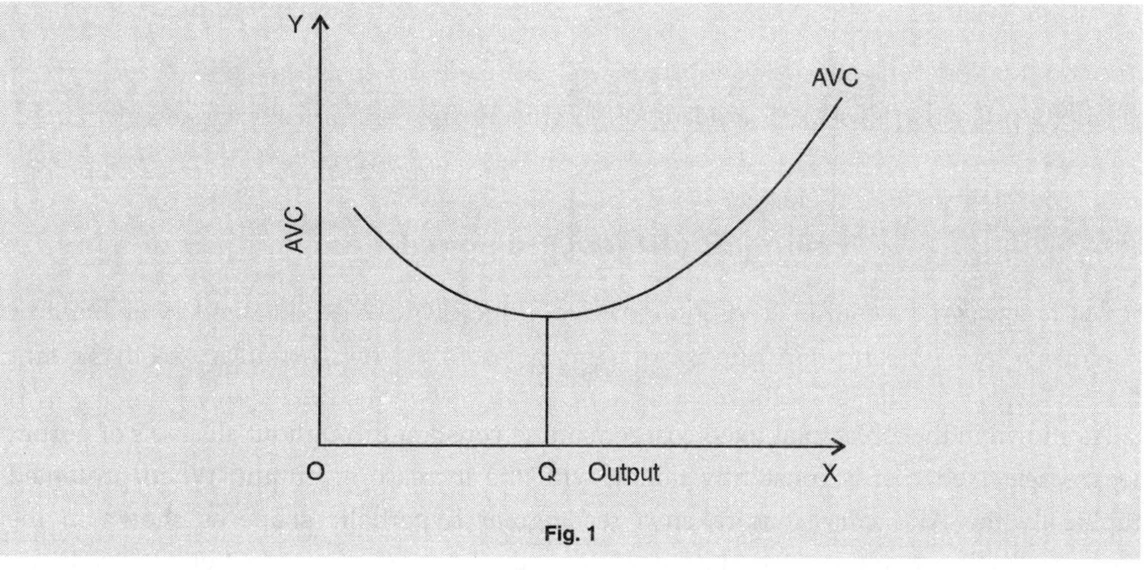

Fig. 1

The relationship between the ATC, AFC and AVC is presented in the table and graph (Fig. 2) drawn below.

Units of Output (Q)	TFC (₹)	AFC = TFC/Q (₹)	TVC (₹)	AVC = TVC/Q ₹	STC = TFC + TVC (₹)	ATC = STC/Q (₹)
0	100	—	—	—	100	—
1	100	100	80	80	180	180
2	100	50	140	70	240	120
3	100	$33.\bar{3}$	190	$63.\bar{3}$	290	$96.\bar{6}$
4	100	25	220	55	320	80
5	100	20	300	60	400	80
6	100	$16.\bar{6}$	410	$68.\bar{3}$	510	85
7	100	14.3	565	80.7	665	95
8	100	12.5	780	97.5	880	110

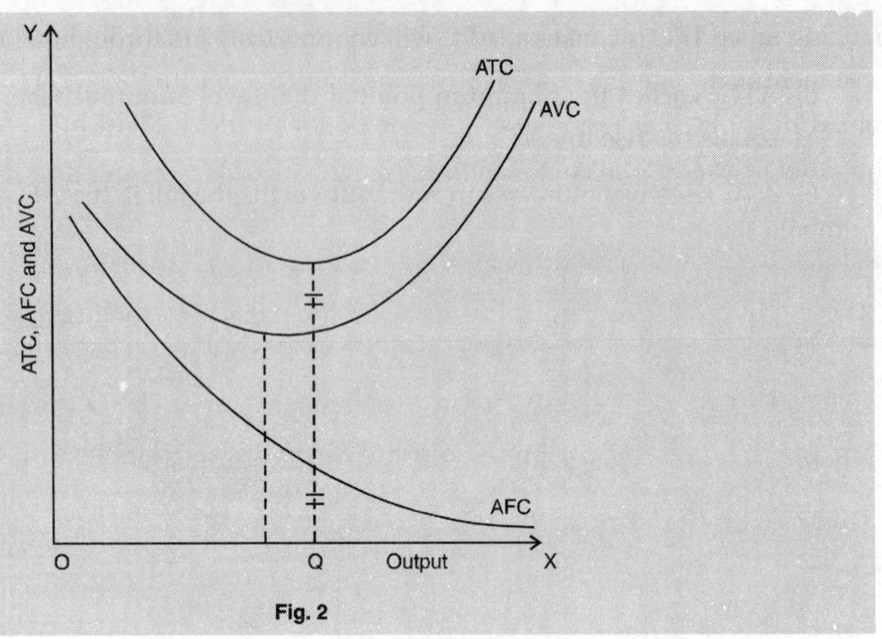

Fig. 2

As shown in the table, total fixed cost remaining constant throughout all levels of output the average fixed cost is constantly falling with the increase in output. When presented graphically the AFC curve has taken a rectangular hyperbolic shape as shown in the diagram. Total variable cost starts incurring with the start of production. It gradually increases with the increase in output but at a diminishing rate till the fuller utilization of fixed factor and hence upto that the AFC decreases. But in the later stages when output completely depends upon variable factor the total variable cost and hence the AVC also starts increasing. When presented graphically the AVC curve slopes downward in the initial stages, then reaching a minimum point starts moving upward with the further increase in the output. It is shown that with the fall in both the AFC and AVC, the ATC also decreases as it is the sum of two decreasing cost. The ATC reaches its minimum when the rising average variable cost just equals the falling average fixed cost. In the figure this situation is reached at OQ level of output. Beyond this level of output the rising average variable cost outweighs the falling average fixed cost. That's why the ATC has increased at an increasing rate. When this tendency of the ATC presented graphically the average total cost (ATC), popularly called as short run average cost (SAC) curve takes the shape of English capital letter 'U'.

Marginal Cost (MC)

The concept of marginal cost bears much significance in determining the equilibrium of a firm and pricing theories. Marginal cost is defined as the addition made to the total cost by producing an additional unit of a commodity. In other words, the increase in the total cost due to increase in one more unit of the commodity concerned is called marginal cost. It is obtained by deducting the total cost incurred for producing last but one units ($n - 1$) of a commodity from the total cost of producing 'n' units.

Symbolically,

$$MC = TC_n - TC_{n-1}$$

or

$$MC = \frac{\partial TC}{\partial Q}$$

where ∂ = change, TC = Total cost, Q = Quantity

Thus marginal cost is the ratio of change in total cost w.r.t. change in quantity produced.

For example : If the total cost of producing 10 units of a commodity is ₹ 120/- and the total cost of producing 11 units of that commodity is ₹ 135/- then the MC = $TC_n - TC_{n-1}$ = 135 – 120 = ₹ 15/-.

Marginal cost reflects the change in the rate of total cost due to change in output. In short run since the fixed cost remains unchanged, in this period marginal cost is governed by the variable cost only, which changes with change in output. But in long-run since also costs are variable, MC reflects the rate of change in the total cost due to change in output. When presented graphically the MC curve, as shown in the figure drawn below first slopes downwards they reaching a minimum point turns upward to take the shape of 'U'.

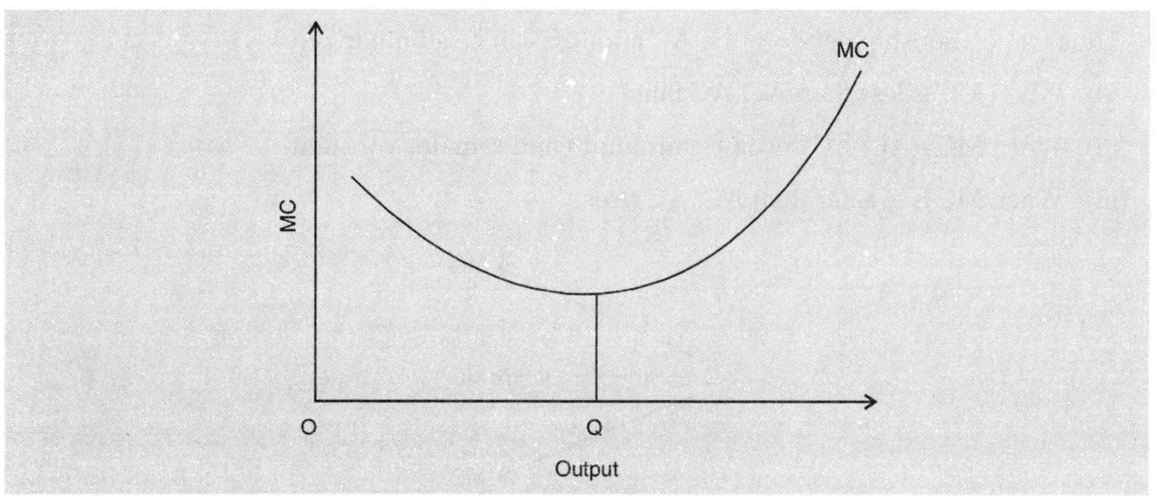

Relationship between Average and Marginal Costs

The relationship between average cost and marginal cost can be explained with the hypothetical table shown below :

Units of Output	Total Cost (₹)	Average Cost (₹)	Marginal Cost (₹)
1	350	350	–
2	450	225	150
3	500	$166.\overline{6}$	50
4	520	130	20
5	550	110	30
6	620	$103.\overline{3}$	70
7	700	100	80
8	800	100	100
9	1080	120	280
10	1400	140	320

The table shows that as production increases, in the initial stages, both average and marginal costs decrease. The average cost is falling upto 7th unit then remaining constant at the 8th unit starts increasing from the subsequent unit. The marginal cost is falling upto the 4th unit and then has started increasing, when the average cost is still falling. Till the fall in the average cost, marginal cost is less than the average cost. At the 8th unit both the average and marginal costs are equal and when average cost starts increasing the marginal cost becomes greater than the average cost.

Thus the relationship between the AC and MC can be summarized as :

(i) When MC is less than AC, AC falls.

(ii) When MC = AC, AC becomes minimum and remains constant.

(iii) When MC is greater than AC, AC rises.

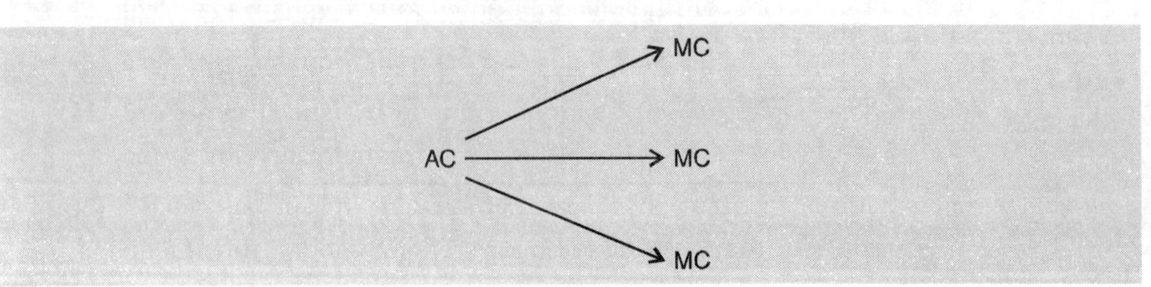

The figure drawn above shows when MC is above AC, it pulls AC to rise, when MC is equal to AC, AC remains the same and when MC is below the AC, it pulls AC down. When we present the average and marginal costs graphically, as shown in the diagram drawn below, we see that in the initial stages of production as output increases, both the average cost curve AC and marginal cost curve MC are sloping downwards indicating the fall in AC and MC. The MC curve is below the AC curve till the AC is falling. The MC curve is intersecting the AC curve at its minimum at output level OQ (8th unit in our example), indicating AC = MC. Beyond this level, as output increases the AC curve turns upward but remains below the MC curve.

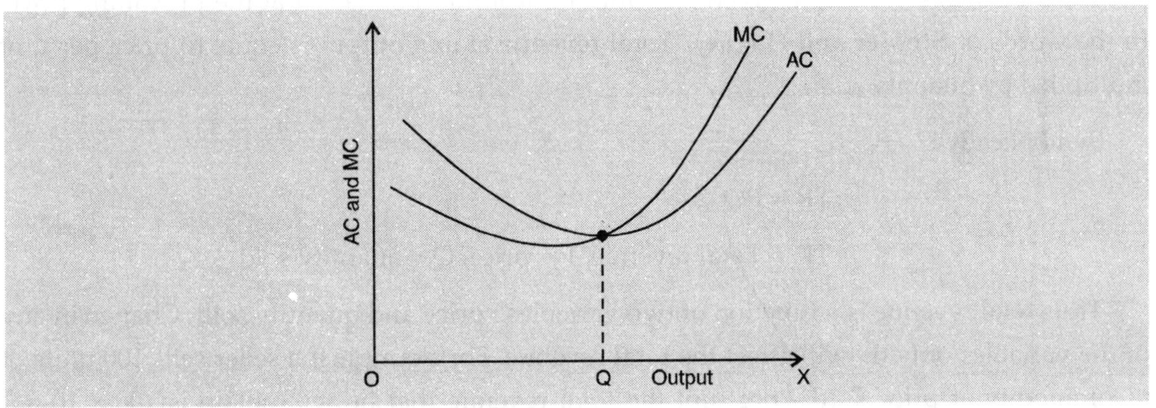

Revenue

The production venture is carried on by a producer or a firm to earn profit by selling the output produced. What a producer or firm earns by selling the produced output in the market at the prevailing prices is called 'revenue'. The profit of the producer or firm is determined by the difference between the income or receipts or the revenue from the sale of the output and the cost incurred for producing that output. That's why the study of revenue is equally important as the study of cost in the price-output analysis.

Revenue of a producer or firm can be defined as 'the money income earned by selling the output produced, in the market at prevailing prices.' In the words of **Prof. Dooley,** "the revenue of a firm is its sales receipts or income." Revenue is also referred to as sale proceeds or turnover. However, revenue is not equal to profit. Profit is the difference between the revenue and cost.

$$\pi = R - C$$

π = Profit, R = Total revenue, C = Total cost

So, in production venture, which is carried on the for the purpose of earning profit, i.e. in the pricing-output theory of firm the study of revenue bears much significance.

Types of Revenue

There are three concepts of revenue. They are : Total revenue, Average revenue and Marginal revenue.

Total Revenue (TR)

Total revenue (TR) refers to the total amount of money income or receipts earned by a producer or firm by selling a given amount of output in the market at the prevailing price. In the words of **Stonier and Hague,** "Total revenue at any output is equal to price per unit multiplied by quantity sold."

Symbolically :

$$TR = PQ$$

TR = Total revenue, P = price, Q = quantity sold

Thus total revenue is a function of two variables : price and quantity sold. Change in any of the variables or both, will affect the total revenue. For example if a seller sells 100 units of a commodity at price ₹ 10/– per unit the total revenue that he will obtain is 100 × 10 = ₹ 1000/-. If number of units remaining of the same the price of the commodity changes, say increases to ₹ 12/- accordingly his total revenue will be 100 × 12 = ₹ 1200/-. Similarly, price remaining the same, ₹ 10/- if the quantity sold changes, say increases, say to 120 units, then his total revenue will increase to 120 × 10 = ₹ 1200/-. Accordingly his total revenue will change with the change in both the variables. However, the behaviour of total revenue depends on the market structure under which a producer works.

Normally total revenue is a direct function of quantity sold, Price remaining constant.

Average Revenue (AR)

Average revenue (AR) can be defined as the revenue earned per unit of output sold. Average revenue is obtained dividing the total revenue (TR) earned from the sale of a given quantity, or units of a commodity by the quantity or units (Q) sold.

Symbolically, $AR = \frac{TR}{Q}$

Since $TR = PQ, AR = \frac{PQ}{Q} = P$, i.e. Average revenue = Price.

But whether average revenue is equal to price or not, that depends upon the market structure. It is to be noted that under perfect competition since each unit of a commodity is sold at uniform price, in such market average revenue equal the price. But under monopoly since the seller has the power to charge discriminatory prices for different units. In such market the average revenue does not equal the price.

Under perfect competition AR = Price

Under monopoly AR ≠ Price

For example, if a seller sells 10 units of a commodity at price ₹ 10/- per unit. His total revenue and average revenue would be

$$TR = PQ = 10 \times 10 = ₹\ 100/-$$

$$AR = \frac{TR}{Q} = \frac{100}{10} = ₹\ 10 = \text{Price } (AR = P)$$

But if he sells the first unit at ₹ 10/- and second unit at price ₹ 12/-, then his TR = 10 + 12 = 22 and AR = $\frac{22}{2}$ = ₹ 11/-, which is neither equal to the price of 1st unit nor equal to that of the 2nd unit.

Marginal Revenue (MR)

Marginal revenue is defined as the addition made to the total revenue (TR) due to the sale of an additional unit of the commodity. Thus it is the change in the total revenue with respect to a change in the quantity of output sold. In the words of **Prof. Ferguson, "Marginal revenue is the change in total revenue which results from the sale of one more or one less unit of output."** Simply speaking, marginal revenue (MR) is the difference between the total revenue earned by selling '*n*' units and the total revenue earned by selling '*n* – 1' units of a commodity.

Symbolically,

$$MR = TR_n - TR_{n-1}$$

Marginal revenue can also be expressed as the ratio of change in total revenue to change in output sold. That is :

$$MR = \frac{\Delta TR}{\Delta Q}$$

As the 1st derivative of the total revenue function

$$MR = \frac{\partial TR}{\partial Q},$$

Marginal revenue indicates the slope of the total revenue curve.

For example, if a seller get ₹ 1250/- from the sale of 10 units of a commodity and ₹ 1400/- from the sale of 11 units of that commodity, then his marginal revenue is :

$$MR = TR_n - TR_{n-1}, \text{ here } n = 11 \text{ and } n - 1 = 10$$

$$= 1400 - 1250 = ₹\ 150/-$$

Relationship between TR, AR and MR

Total revenue, average revenue and marginal revenue are interrelated. However the TR, AR and MR of a firm and their interrelationship depends upon the market structure under which the firm is operating. In this context we can discuss the relationship between TR, AR and MR by dividing the markets broadly under two categories – Perfect competition and imperfect competition.

The relationship between TR, AR and MR of a firm working under perfect competition can be explained with the help of a hypothetical table drawn below.

TR, AR and MR under perfect competition.

Quantity Sold (Q)	Price/Unit (₹)	Total Revenue (P × Q) (₹)	Average Revenue (TR/Q) (₹)	Marginal Revenue ($TR_n - TR_{n-1}$) (₹)
1	15	15	15	15
2	15	30	15	15
3	15	45	15	15
4	15	60	15	15
5	15	75	15	15
6	15	90	15	15
7	15	105	15	15
8	15	120	15	15

Under perfect competition a firm has to accept the price of his commodity prevailing in the market. It cannot influence the price of its commodity determined by the industry. It sells its commodity at the price determined by the market mechanism. In the table we have assumed the price as ₹ 15/- determined by the industry. So the total revenue of the firm is determined by multiplying price with the quantity sold (TR = PQ). So the subsequent total revenue is shown as ₹ 15/-, ₹ 30/-, ₹ 45/- ...... by selling 1, 2, 3. ...... units respectively. Average revenue is obtained in the table dividing total revenue at different units sold by the number of units sold, i.e. $\frac{15}{1}, \frac{30}{2}, \frac{45}{3}$..... respectively, which amounts ₹ 15/-. Thus we find that AR = P. The marginal revenue (MR) is found by deducting the total revenue at each unit from the total revenue earned from the previous units i.e. $TR_n - TR_{n-1}$, which at each unit is ₹ 15/-.

This implies that for a firm working under perfect competition :

$$AR = MR = Price$$

The relationship between TR, AR and MR of a firm working under perfect competition is shown graphically in the diagram drawn below.

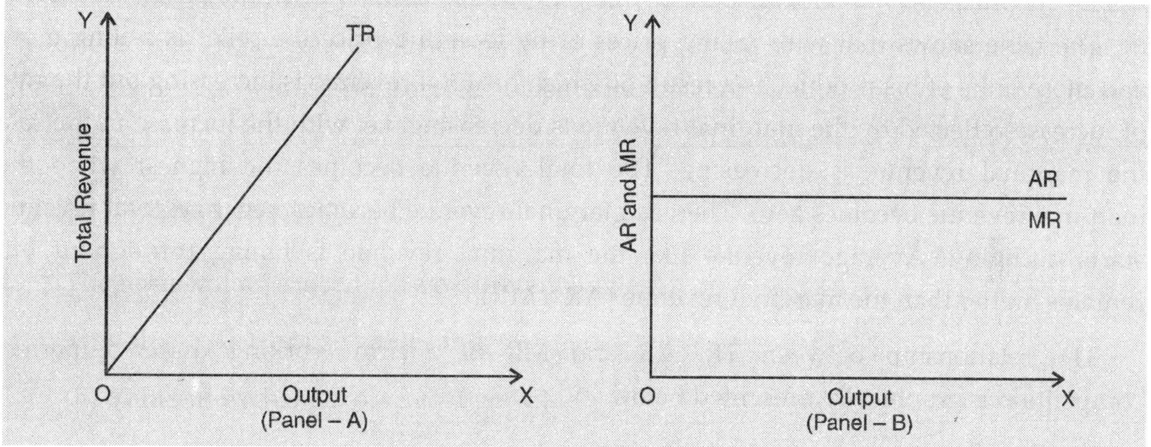

In panel-A of the figure by plotting the total revenue corresponding to different units sold and joining them we have got the total revenue curve TR. It is rising from the origin at a constant rate implying total revenue is rising with the increase in the sale at a constant rate. In panel by plotting the corresponding AR and MR at different units sold and by joining them we get the horizontal AR and MR curve which coincide each other, implying AR = MR at all units sold, which is also equal to price (AR = MR = P).

Under imperfect competition, say monopoly or monopolistic competition a firm has control over the price of its commodity. Under imperfect competition a firm can sell more only when the price of its product falls or by lowering the price. So the average revenue will fall as more and more of the units are sold and so also the marginal revenue.

This is presented in the table drawn below :

TR, AR and MR of a firm under Imperfect Competition

Units Sold (Q)	Price/Unit P (₹)	Total Revenue TR = PQ (₹)	Average Revenue AR = TR/Q (₹)	Marginal Revenue $MR = TR_n - TR_{n-1}$ (₹)
1	100	100	100	100
2	90	180	90	80
3	80	240	80	60
4	70	280	70	40
5	60	300	60	20
6	50	300	50	0
7	40	280	40	– 20

The table shows that with falling prices or by lowering price the seller is selling more and more units of his product as a result of which his total revenue is increasing but the rate of increase reflected by the marginal revenue is decreasing, i.e. with the increase in the sale the marginal revenue is decreasing. The total revenue becomes the highest when the marginal revenue becomes zero. Then as marginal revenue becomes negative, total revenue starts declining. Average revenue like the marginal revenue is falling throughout but remains higher than the marginal revenue (AR > MR).

The relationship between TR, AR and MR of a firm working under imperfect competition is graphically presented below.

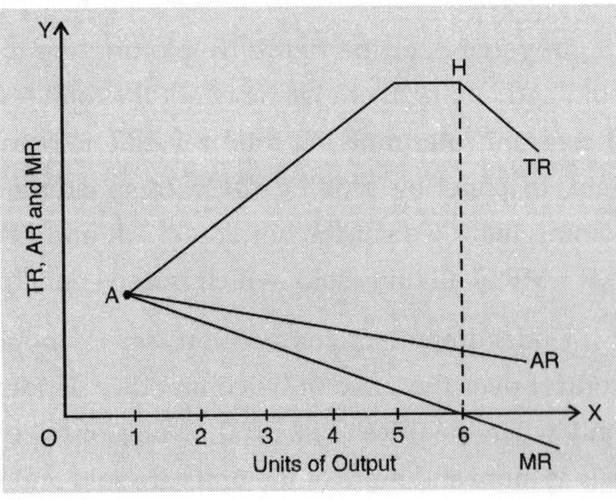

In the figure units of output is presented on the OX-axis and TR, AR and MR are presented on the OY-axis. The total revenue curve TR, average revenue curve AR and marginal revenue curve AR and MR start from the same point 'A' as at the 1st unit of sale TR = AR = MR, i.e. ₹ 100/-. Then with the increase in the sale the TR curve is rising but at a diminishing rate as the MR curve is falling downwards. The TR curve reaches the highest point 'H', right below which the

MR curve intersecting the OX-axis, indicating zero MR (MR = 0), at 6th unit. Then the TR curve turns downwards indicating decrease in total revenue when marginal revenue become negative. Average revenue curve AR is also sloping downwards throughout but is above the MR curve, indicating at all levels of sale AR > MR.

Supply

Meaning

In pricing theory 'supply' along with 'demand' plays a significant role in determining equilibrium prices. It is one of the twin market forces to determine price and output. Supply in economics refer to various quantities of a commodity offered for sale by a producer during a given time at various prices. Thus like demand, supply is always at a price and relates to a period of time. Supply is different from output produced or stock of a commodity in the sense that it is a flow concept and refers to that part of output produced or stock which flows to market for sale at different prices during a given time.

*According to **Prof. J.L. Hansen**, "By supply is meant the amount that will come on to the market over a range of prices."*

Supply Function

Supply of a commodity depends upon a number of factors such the price of the concerned commodity, prices of the factors of production, state of technology, prices of its related commodities, government policy etc. This implies that there is a functional relationship between the quantity supply (S_X) of a commodity and the factors affecting its supply. In this sense supply function refers to the functional relationship between quantity supply of a commodity and the factors influencing its supply.

In the equation from it is written as :

$$S_X = f(P_x, P_r, P_f, T, G_P \ldots.)$$

where, S_X = Quantity supplied of commodity 'X'

P_x = Price of the concerned commodity, i.e. 'X'

P_r = Prices of the related good – substituted or complementaries

P_f = Prices of factors of production

T = State of technology

G_P = Government policies etc.

Factors Affecting Supply

As stated in the supply function, the supply of a commodity depends upon several factors.

Important among them are discussed below.

1. **Price of the Commodity** : The most important factor affecting the supply of a commodity is its price. Generally, there is a positive relationship between price and quantity supply of a commodity. That is they move in the same direction. Normally supply of a commodity increases when its price rises and decreases when its price falls, of course other factors affecting its supply remaining constant. This relationship between the price and quantity supplied is explained in the form of the law of supply, which is discussed later in this chapter. Such relation is guided by the profit motive of the producer.

2. **Prices of Related Commodities** : Prices of related commodities of a good also influence the supply of the good. Related commodities may either be its substitutes or complementaries. For example if the price of wheat increases, price of rice remaining constant, then a farmer may substitute rice for wheat cultivation as it would fetch him more profit and hence the supply of rice will decrease. Thus the price of wheat affects the supply of rice.

3. **Prices of Factors of Production** : Changes in the prices of factors of production affecting the cost of production of a commodity will affect its supply. Fall in the factor prices will encourage the producer to produce more and hence the supply will increase and vice versa. Here it is to be noted that factor prices do not mean the prices of regular factors like land, labour and capital only they also include the prices of raw materials, power, fuel etc. which are taken into account while calculating cost of production.

4. **Means of Transport** : Good and improved means of transport facilitating the mobility of factors of production encourage production and help in mobilizing the products to different regions. This helps in increasing the supply. In the absence of a good and improved transport system supply will not increase even if the price of product increases.

5. **Technology** : State of technology applied in the production process affecting the productivity and production affects the supply of a commodity. Improved technology increases production and decrease the cost of production which encourages a producer to produce more. Hence a change in technology or

technique of production may lead to a change in supply. When production increases by adopting an improved technique of production the producer will be able to supply more even at the same prices.

6. **Objectives of the Producers :** The primary objective of the producer is to maximize profit. Alongwith profit maximization the producers or firms also aim at maximization of output, maximization of sales, minimization of cost, generation of employment etc. These goals of the producers and changes in them also affect the supply of different goods at different times irrespective of prices. For example, a firm may supply more of its product at the same price, which does not maximize its profit. But the firm may do so to maximize its sale or to capture more share in the market.

7. **Price Expectation :** Expectation of the producers on the changes in the prices of their products in near future owing to any reason also affect the supply of different goods. If they expect an increase in the prices of their products in near future they will drop the supply of their products even when the prices are rising and wait for a further rise in the prices. Reverse may happen when they expect a fall in the prices of their products in near future.

8. **Government Policy :** Different government policies such as fiscal and monetary policies, industrial policy, trade policy, labour policy etc. affecting the economic and business activities also affects the supply of different goods in the economy. For example the tax policy of the government may either discourage or encourage the producers to produce less or more owing to heavy taxation or tax concessions respectively. The supply of their products will also be affected accordingly. Other government policies, started above, have also either direct or indirect impact on the production and supply of various goods.

9. **Natural Factors :** Natural factors like climate, weather, temperature, rainfall, flood, cyclone, drought etc. have direct impacts on the supply of agricultural products and indirect impacts on the supply of industrial products. A favourable weather and other natural conditions for agricultural activities increase the production of agricultural products which increases their supply. Increase in the supply of agricultural products will also lead to increase in industrial products and their supply. On the other hand an adverse natural condition will adversely affect agricultural production and their supply which will also affect industrial production and their supply of the industrial products.

Besides the above discussed factors like number of producers of a commodity, availability of the factors of production, changes in the taste and habit, fashion, internal peace and stability of a country, socio-cultural and religious factors etc. also affect the supply of different commodities at different time period.

Law of Supply

From the supply function discussed above we know that supply is a multi-variable function. Though supply of a commodity is influenced by several factors, price a commodity concerned is considered to be the most important factor affecting its supply. The law of supply seeks to explain the functional relationship between the price of a commodity and its quantity supplied assuming the other influencing factors remaining constant.

The Law

The law of supply states that "other factors affecting the supply of a commodity remaining the same, supply of the commodity increases with the rise in its price and decreases with the fall in its price."

This implies that there exists a positive or direct relationship between the price and quantity supplied of a commodity, other factors affecting its supply remaining unchanged.

The functional relationship between the price and quantity supplied of a commodity is explained by the law of supply and is presented as :

$$S_X = f(P_X)$$

where P_X = Price of commodity 'X', S_X = Quantity supplied of 'X',

$\uparrow$ = rise and $\downarrow$ = fall.

If $P_X\uparrow \longrightarrow S_X\uparrow$ and if $P_X\downarrow \longrightarrow S_X\downarrow$

Assumptions

The law of supply is developed on the following assumptions.

1. The supplier is a rational man.
2. There is no change in the factor prices or cost of production.
3. The prices of the related goods are constant.
4. There is no change in the technology or method of production.
5. There is no change in government policy affecting supply.

6. There is no change in the socio-economic and political set up.
7. Natural factors affecting production are constant.

Explanation of the Law

With the above assumptions the law of supply can be explained with the help of a hypothetical supply schedule drawn below.

Supply Schedule

Supply schedule refers to a list or table showing various quantities of a commodity, say 'X', that the producer or supplier is ready to sell at different prices at a given time. The hypothetical supply schedule drawn below shows that other factors affecting supply remaining constant when the price is ₹ 10/- the seller is ready to supply 20 units of his commodity. As the price increases to ₹ 20/-, ₹ 30/-, ₹ 40/- ...... the quantity supplied is increasing to 30, 40, 55 ...... units respectively. Thus the supply schedule presents the direct or positive relationship between the price and quantity supplied of a commodity, other factors affecting its supply remaining constant. It is the tabular presentation of the law of supply.

Supply Schedule

Price (₹)	Q. Supplied (Units)
10	20
20	30
30	40
40	55
50	70

Graphical Presentation (Supply Curve)

The law of supply can be presented graphically to obtain the supply curve as shown below by plotting the pairs of price and quantity supplied on the graph.

In the figure quantity supplied is presented on the OX-axis and price on the OY-axis. By plotting the price and quantity supplied pairs, i.e. OQ quantity at OP price, OQ_1 quantity at OP_1 price and so on we have got the points A, B, C and D respectively. Then by joining these points the curve 'SS' that we have obtained is the supply curve. The normal shape of a supply curve is positive or upward slopping to the right, indicating more is supplied at a higher price and the reverse, other factors affecting supply remaining constant. Thus the supply curve is the graphic presentation of the law of supply.

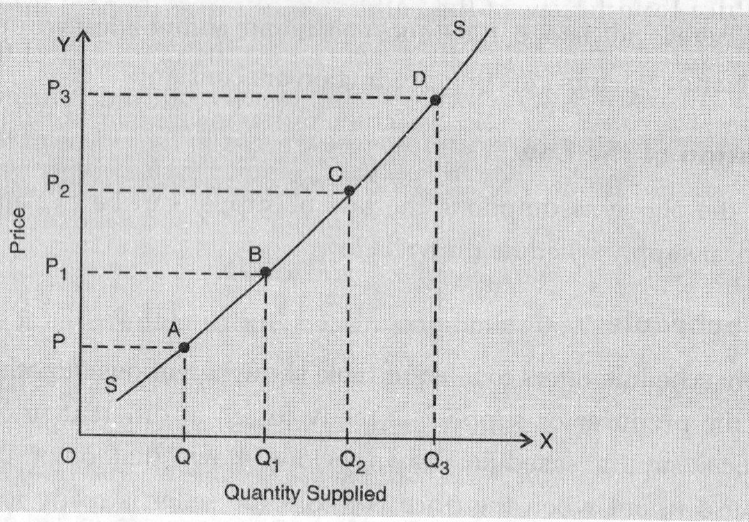

Exceptions or Limitations of the Law

The law of supply does not operate in certain cases which are called as the exceptions or limitations of the law.

Some of these exceptions are discussed below.

1. **Rare Articles :** The law of supply does not operate in case of rare articles such as the paintings of renowned artists, rare art, literature and antiques which cannot be reproduced. The supply of these articles are extremely scarce. So, what ever may be their prices their supply cannot be increased.
2. **Auction Sale :** The law of supply does not operate in case of auction sales. Because in such cases the biders offer higher prices for the same article. The amount of the article does not increase by offering higher prices.
3. **Clearance Sale :** In case of clearance sale the seller is not guided by profit motive. He wants to clear his old stock to store new goods. So he sell large quantity of goods at low or discounted prices, which violates the law of supply.
4. **Distress Sale :** Distress sale takes place when the seller is in financial crisis and needs cash immediately. In such a situation he sells his product in large quantity at very low prices and hence the law of supply does not hold good.
5. **Nature's Dominance :** The law of supply does not work fully in case of the goods in whose production nature plays a dominant role. For example the production of agricultural goods cannot be enhanced at once following increase in prices. Similarly, labour supply cannot be increased at once with the rise in wages.

6. **Price Expectations of the Sellers :** Price expectations of the sellers also often makes the law defunct. When the sellers expect that the prices of their products are going to fall in near future, they will offer to sell more and more even when the prices are falling. Contrarily, when the expect a rise in the prices of their products they stop or reduce supply even when the prices are rising. Both the situation violate the law of supply.

Besides the above discussed cases the law of supply also does not operate in case of goods which are subject to the fear of being out of fashion, in case of perishable goods, the goods whose supply is fixed etc.

Change in Supply and Change in Quantity Supplied

Above we have discussed that supply of a commodity is influenced by several factors. Putting those factors in two broad categories : price and non-price factors, we make a distinction between change in supply and change in quantity supplied.

Change in Supply

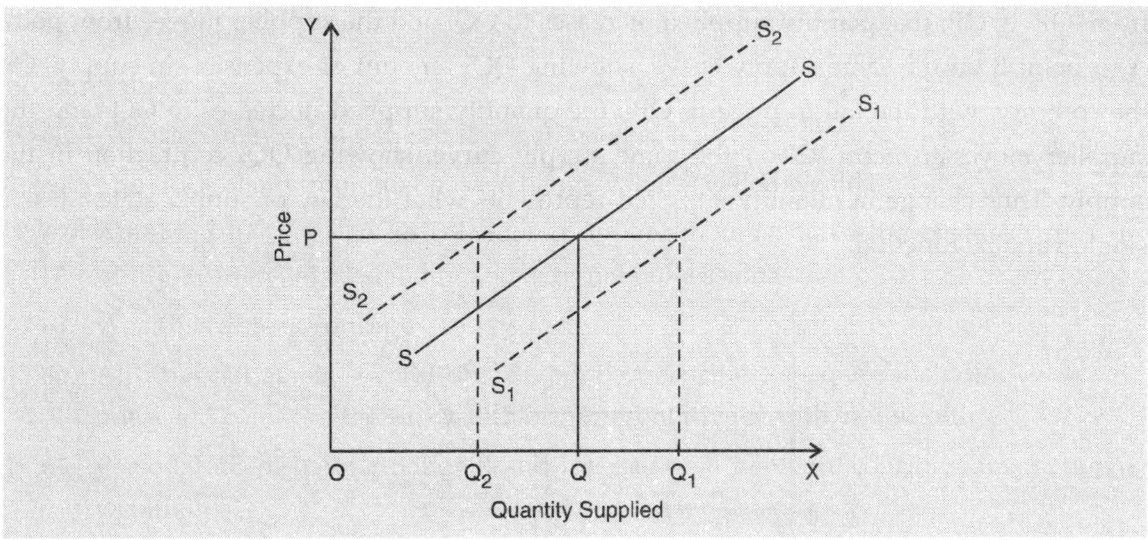

Change in supply refers to the change, i.e. increase or decrease in the supply of a commodity due to changes in the non-price factor(s), price of the commodity remaining unchanged. Simply speaking when the supply of a commodity increases or decreases due to change in the price of related goods or factor prices or change in any other non-price factor (s), price of the commodity remaining constant, it is called change in supply. In such case the supplier shifts from one supply curve to another. Price of the commodity remaining constant, if supply increases due to change in any non-price factor(s) then the seller will shift to a new supply curve, right to the original one, i.e. to S_1S_1 as shown in the figure drawn above. On the other hand of supply decreases to the same reason(s) then the supplier will shift to a new supply curve, left to the original supply curve, i.e. to S_2S_2 as shown in the figure. Thus shift on the supply curve representing change in supply implies increase or decrease in supply, price remaining constant and hence change in supply is a multi-variable function.

Change in Quantity Supplied

Change in quantity supplied occurs when the amount of supply of a commodity changes due to change in its price, other non-price factors remaining constant. Change in quantity supplied implies expansion or contraction in supply with increase or decrease in the price of a commodity respectively. Thus change in quantity supplied is related to the movement along the same supply curve from one point to another, as shown in the diagram drawn below. As shown in the diagram, other factors affecting the supply of the commodity remaining constant when the price is OP, the quantity supplied is OQ. With the rise in price from 'OP' to OP_1 the quantity supplied increases to OQ_1 and the supplier moves from point A to point B on the same supply curve, showing QQ_1 amount of expansion in supply. On the contrary, with the fall in price to OP_2, the quantity supplied decreases to OQ_2 and the supplier moves to point 'C' on the same supply curve, showing QQ_2 contraction in the supply. Thus change in quantity supplied represents what the law of supply states. It is a single-variable function.

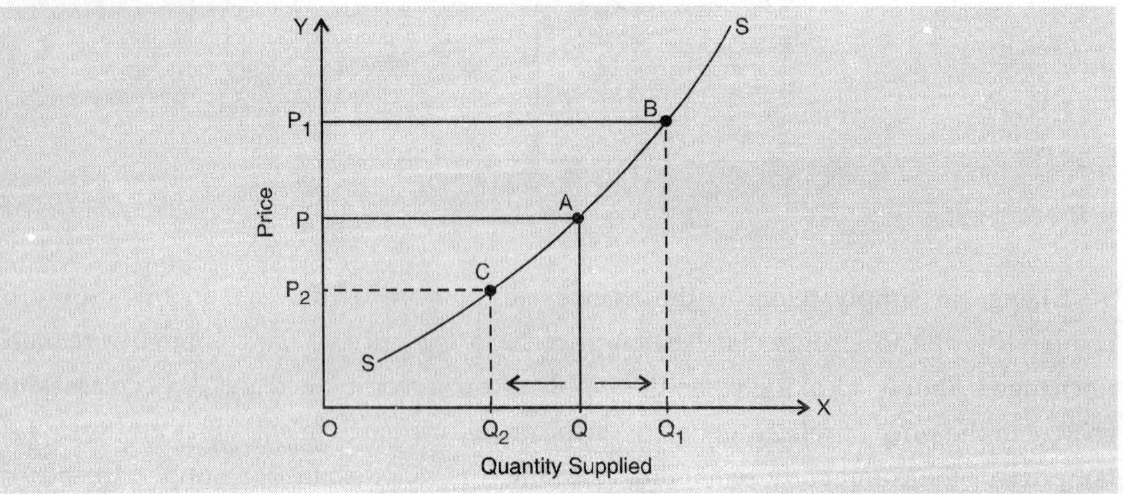

WHAT WE LEARNT

1. Cost of production refers to the sum of all expenditure incurred by the producer to produce a given amount of a commodity.
2. Money cost refers to all expenditure incurred by the producer in terms of money or cash for producing a given amount of a commodity.
3. Money cost is also called nominal cost or explicit cost or accounting cost.
4. Expenditure incurred for hiring or buying factors from outside is called explicit cost.
5. Imputed cost of the producer's own factors or self-employed factors, for which no formal payment is made, is called implicit cost.
6. Economic cost is the sum of explicit costs and implicit costs.
7. The pain, toil, sacrifice etc. of the factors involved in the process of production taking together is called real cost.
8. Real cost is a subjective concept, developed by Alfred Marshall and bears no significance in pricing-output theories.
9. The next best alternative foregone that could have been produced by a factor or combination of factors is called opportunity cost.
10. Expenditure incurred on the Fixed Factors of Production is called Fixed Cost.
11. Fixed cost is output independent and related to short-run production venture.
12. Expenditure incurred on the variable factors of production is called variable cost.
13. Variable cost is output dependent and related to both short-run and long-run production ventures.
14. Fixed cost is also called 'over-head cost' or 'supplementary cost'.
15. Variable cost is also called 'prime cost' or 'direct cost'.
16. Cost of production per unit of a commodity is called average cost.
17. Average cost is the sum of average fixed cost and average variable cost.
18. In long-run production venture all costs are variable costs.
19. The shape of average fixed cost curve is rectangular hyperbolic.
20. The average variable cost curve takes the shape of English capital letter – U.
21. The short-run average cost curve (SAC) curve is U-shaped.

22. The cost of producing an additional unit of a commodity is called marginal cost.
23. When MC is less than AC, AC falls.
24. When MC = AC, AC becomes minimum and remains constant.
25. When MC > AC, AC rises.
26. Income or receipt that a producer gets from the sale of a given quantity of output at the prevailing price is called total revenue. (TR = PQ)
27. Revenue per unit of output sold is called average revenue.
28. Revenue from the sale of an additional unit of a commodity is called marginal revenue.
29. Under perfect competition AR = MR = Price.
30. Under imperfect competition AR > MR.
31. At the sale of the 1st unit of a commodity TR = AR = MR.
32. When MR decreases TR increases at a diminishing rate.
33. When MR becomes zero TR maximizes.
34. When MR becomes negative TR decreases.
35. AR never becomes zero.
36. The part of stock which flows to market for sale at a given price and at a given time is called supply.
37. The functional relationship between quantity supplied and factors affecting supply of a commodity is called supply function.
38. The functional relationship between price of a commodity and its quantity supplied, other factors remaining constant, is explained in the law of supply.
39. The price and quantity supplied of a commodity are related directly.
40. The normal shape of a supply curve is upward sloping to the right. (Positive Slope)
41. Change in supply is a multivariable function.
42. In case of change in supply the supplier shifts to a new supply curve.
43. Change in quantity supplied is a single-variable function.
44. In case of change in quantity supplied the supplier moves on the same supply curve from one point to another.
45. Change in supply implies increase or decrease in supply, whereas change in quantity demanded implies expansion and contraction in supply.

QUESTIONS FOR REVIEW

A. Choose the correct answer from the given alternatives in each question. (Each Carrying 1 Mark)

1. **'Cost' in economics is used in the sense of :**

   (i) Cost of purchasing a good (ii) Cost of production
   (iii) Sacrifice made for a thing (iv) All the above

2. **Expenditure incurred for producing a given amount of commodity in terms of money or cash is called :**

   (i) Nominal cost (ii) Accounting cost
   (iii) Explicit cost (iv) All the above

3. **Expenditure incurred in the production process to hire or purchase factor inputs from outside is called :**

   (i) Total cost (ii) Fixed cost
   (iii) Money cost (iv) Variable cost

4. **Which one of the following is the sum of explicit and implicit costs ?**

   (i) Economic cost (ii) Real cost
   (iii) Accounting cost (iv) Opportunity cost

5. **In economics opportunity cost refers to :**

   (i) Income earned in the next best alternative use
   (ii) Income foregone in the next best alternative use
   (iii) Expected income from an alternative use
   (iv) None of the above.

6. **The concept of which cost was developed by Marshall ?**

   (i) Economic cost (ii) Real cost
   (iii) Nominal cost (iv) None of the above

7. **The sum of toil, pain, sacrifice etc. taken by the factors in the process of production is called:**

   (i) Total cost (ii) Economic cost
   (iii) Real cost (iv) Opportunity cost

8. **Which cost is related to the short-run production venture only ?**
   (i) Fixed cost (ii) Economic cost
   (iii) Money cost (iv) None of the above
9. **Which cost is also called over-head cost ?**
   (i) Total cost (ii) Fixed cost
   (iii) Economic cost (iv) Variable cost
10. **Which cost is related to both short-run and long-run production ?**
   (i) Fixed cost (ii) Opportunity cost
   (iii) Variable cost (iv) All the above
11. **Which one is also called prime cost ?**
   (i) Fixed cost (ii) Explicit cost
   (iii) Implicit cost (iv) Variable cost
12. **Which one is independent of the level of output ?**
   (i) Total cost (ii) Economic cost
   (iii) Fixed cost (iv) Variable cost
13. **In short-run which one is included in fixed cost ?**
   (i) Expenditure on salaries of the permanent employee
   (ii) Expenditure on raw materials
   (iii) Expenditure on power, fuel etc.
   (iv) All the above
14. **Cost of production per unit of a commodity is called -**
   (i) Marginal cost (ii) Average cost
   (iii) Per-head cost (iv) Prime cost
15. **Which one takes the shape of a rectangular hyperbola ?**
   (i) Average cost curve (ii) Average variable cost curve
   (iii) Average fixed cost curve (iv) None of these
16. **Which one takes the shape of English Capital letter – U ?**
   (i) Short-run AC curve (ii) Short-run MC curve
   (iii) Both (i) and (ii) (iv) None of the above
17. **Cost of producing an additional unit of a commodity is called :**
   (i) Marginal cost (ii) Average cost
   (iii) Over-head cost (iv) Nominal cost

18. Income earned from the sale of a given amount of a commodity at prevailing price is called :

(i) Average revenue (ii) Total revenue

(iii) Marginal revenue (iv) None of the above

19. Which one is true under perfect competition ?

(i) AR > MR (ii) MR > AR

(iii) AR = MR (iv) None of the above

20. Which one is true under imperfect competition ?

(i) AR = MR (ii) AR > MR

(iii) MR > AR (iv) None of the above

21. Income earned per unit of a commodity is called :

(i) Average revenue (ii) Marginal revenue

(iii) Total revenue (iv) Over-head revenue

22. Income earned from the sale of an additional unit of a commodity is called :

(i) Total revenue (ii) Average revenue

(iii) Marginal revenue (iv) None of the above

23. What happens to total revenue when marginal revenue becomes zero ?

(i) Increases (ii) Maximizes

(iii) Decreases (iv) Remains constant

24. When marginal revenue becomes negative total revenue :

(i) Starts decreasing (ii) Increases at a diminishing rate

(iii) Remains constant (iv) Becomes maximum

25. When marginal cost is less than average cost, average cost :

(i) Remains constant (ii) Falls

(iii) Increases (iv) Equal marginal cost

26. Average cost becomes minimum and remains constant, when :

(i) MC = AC (ii) AC > MC

(iii) MC > AC (iv) None of the above

27. Average cost rises when :

(i) MC = AC (ii) MC < AC

(iii) MC > AC (iv) All the above

28. **When marginal revenue decreases total revenue :**
(i) Increases at a diminishing rate (ii) Increases at a constant rate
(iii) Remains constant (iv) Becomes maximum

29. **The part of stock of a commodity offered for sale at a prevailing price is called :**
(i) Output (ii) Demand
(iii) Supply (iv) Change in supply

30. **The price and quantity supplied of a commodity are related :**
(i) Inversely (ii) Proportionally
(iii) Absolutely (iv) Directly

31. **The normal shape of a supply curve is :**
(i) Horizontal (ii) Downward sloping to the right
(iii) Vertical (iv) Upward sloping to the right

32. **Shift in the supply curve to the right of the original one implies :**
(i) Increase in supply (ii) Expansion in supply
(iii) Contraction in supply (iv) Decrease in supply

33. **Movement along the supply curve towards the right implies :**
(i) Increase in supply (ii) Expansion in supply
(iii) Decrease in supply (iv) Contraction in supply

34. **Which one of the following is a flow concept :**
(i) Production (ii) Output
(iii) Supply (iv) None of the above

35. **The law of supply does not operate in case of :**
(i) Auction sale (ii) Clearance sale
(iii) Distress sale (iv) All the above

B. *Correct the statement, if necessary, without changing the underlined portions. (Each Carrying 1 Mark)*

1. Expenditure incurred in terms of money to produce a given amount of output is called economic cost.
2. Money cost is the sum of explicit costs and implicit costs.
3. Implicit costs are recorded in the accounting register of a firm.

4. No formal payment is made in case of hired factors of production.
5. The imputed cost of producer's self-employed factor is called implicit cost.
6. The sum of toil, pain, sacrifice etc. involved in the process of production is called total cost.
7. Economic cost bears no significance in pricing theories.
8. Fixed cost is independent of the level of output.
9. Variable cost is also called 'over-head cost'.
10. Fixed cost is also called 'prime cost'.
11. Variable cost is related to short-run production venture only.
12. Average variable cost falls throughout the production process.
13. In short-run production venture all costs are variable.
14. The A.FC curve takes the shape of English chapter letter 'U'.
15. When MC is less than AC, AC rises.
16. When MC is equal to AC, AC becomes maximum.
17. Under perfect competition AR > MR.
18. When MR decreases, TR increases at an increasing rate.
19. TR maximizes when MR becomes negative.
20. MR can never be zero.
21. Under imperfect competition AR > MR.
22. The slope of a normal supply curve is negative.
23. Change in quantity supplied is a multi-variable function.
24. Change in supply implies expansion or contraction in supply.
25. Supply is a flow concept.

C. Answer the following questions in 2-3 sentences each (Each Carrying 2 Marks)

1. What is 'cost' in economics ?
2. What is money cost ? (Also-Nominal cost, Accounting cost, Explicit cost.)
3. What is implicit cost ? (Also-self-employed cost)
4. What is economic cost ?
5. What is real cost ?

6. What is opportunity cost ?
7. What is fixed cost ?
8. What is variable cost ?
9. What is total cost ?
10. What is average fixed cost ?
11. What is average variable cost ?
12. What is average cost
13. What is marginal cost ?
14. How average cost, average fixed cost and average variable costs are related ?
15. How average costs and marginal costs are related ?
16. What is total revenue ?
17. What is average revenue ?
18. What is marginal revenue ?
19. How total revenue, average revenue and marginal revenue are related ?
20. What is supply in economics ?
21. What is supply function ?
22. What is the law of supply ?
23. What is supply schedule ?
24. What is supply curve ?
25. What is change in supply ?
26. What is change in quantity supplied ?

D. *Distinguish between the concepts in six sentences each. (Each Carrying 3 Marks)*

1. Fixed Cost and Variable Cost.
2. Explicit Cost and Implicit Cost.
3. Economic Cost and Real Cost.
4. Average Cost and Marginal Cost.
5. Average Fixed Cost and Average Variable Cost.
6. Total Cost and Marginal Cost.
7. Total Revenue and Average Revenue.

8. Total Revenue and Marginal Revenue.
9. Average Revenue and Marginal Revenue.
10. Change in supply and change in Quantity Supplied.

E. *Long Answer type Questions (Each Carrying 7½ Marks)*

1. Briefly discuss different concepts of cost of production.
2. Discuss various short-run costs and the relationship among them with table and diagram.
3. Discuss different concepts of revenue and the relationship among them in different market conditions.
4. Discuss the factors affecting the supply of a commodity.
5. Explain the law of supply with its limitation.

Answers to Q. N. A

1.	(ii)	2.	(i)	3.	(iii)	4.	(i)	5.	(ii)	6.	(ii)	7.	(iii)	8.	(i)
9.	(ii)	10.	(iii)	11.	(iv)	12.	(iii)	13.	(i)	14.	(ii)	15.	(iii)	16.	(iii)
17.	(i)	18.	(ii)	19.	(iii)	20.	(ii)	21.	(i)	22.	(iii)	23.	(ii)	24.	(i)
25.	(ii)	26.	(i)	27.	(iii)	28.	(i)	29.	(iii)	30.	(iv)	31.	(iv)	32.	(i)
33.	(ii)	34.	(iii)	35.	(iv)										

Answer to Q. N. B

1. Cost of production	2. Economic cost	3. Explicit
4. Self-employed	5. Correct	6. Real cost
7. Real cost	8. Correct	9. Fixed cost
10. Variable cost	11. Fixed cost	12. Average fixed Cost
13. In long-run	14. The SAC curve	15. Falls
16. Minimum	17. AR = MR	18. Diminishing rate
19. Zero	20. AR	21. Correct
22. Positive	23. Single-variable	24. Change in quantity supplied
25. Correct		

❑❑❑

UNIT – V

6. MARKET

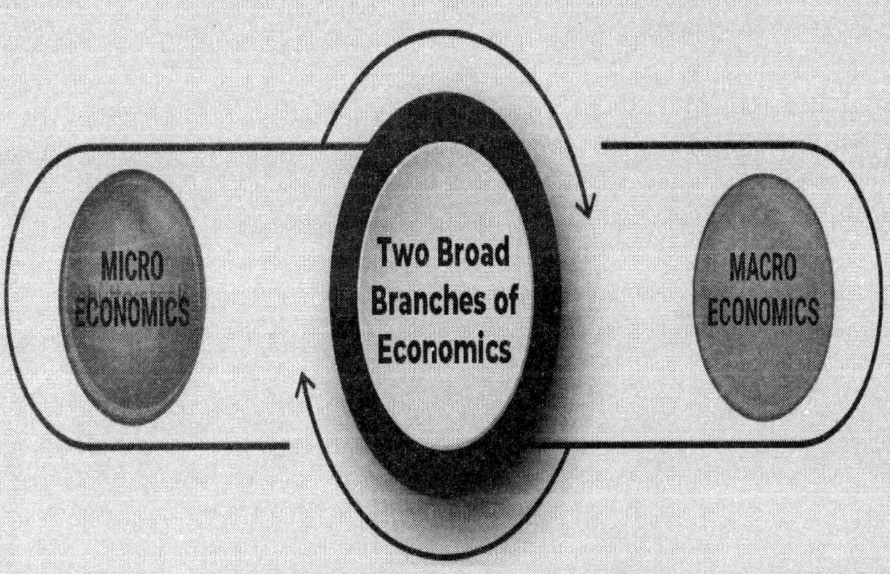

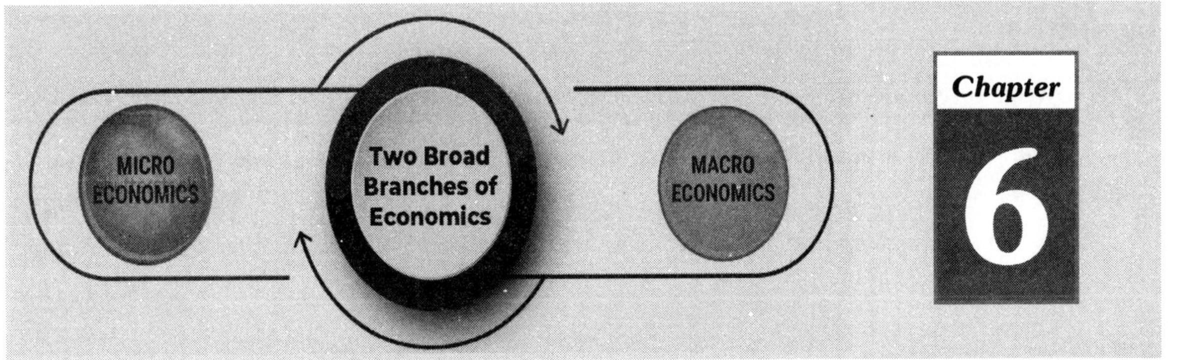

Chapter

6

MARKET

Meaning of Market

For a common man the term 'market' refers to a place where goods and services are bought and sold. In other words, for a common man, market refers to a place where the buyers and sellers of different goods and services meet for the purchase and sale of different goods and services, or a place where transaction of different goods and services takes place. So for a layman a market is known by the name of the place such as Natraj Market, Lokhandwala Market, Janpath Market, China Market (Kolkata). Buxi Bazar, Choudhary Bazar etc. in Cuttack and like. But in economics, 'market' is used in a broader sense and does not refer to any particular place where goods and services are bought and sold. In economics market refers to the relationship established between the buyers and sellers of a commodity or service over its transaction. That's why, in economics a market is known by a commodity and is named after the commodity such as rice market, vegetable market, gold market, share market etc.

In this sense what constitute a market are :

— a commodity or service

— some buyers and sellers of the commodity or service concerned

— direct or indirect contact among those buyers and sellers.

Market can be defined as "an arrangement or a setup in which buyers and sellers of a commodity or service come in contact or communicate with each other, directly or indirectly for the transaction of the concerned good or service at a price."

Definition

Below we have quoted some definitions given by some renowned economists.

"A market is an organization where the buyers and sellers are kept in close touch with each other."

– *Stonier and Hague*

"A group of buyers and sellers in sufficiently close contact with one another so that exchange takes place among them."

— *J.F. Due*

Elements of Market

From the above discussed meaning and definition of market we may draw the following five elements as a market.

1. **Commodity :** A commodity, be it material at or non-material, i.e. service, is the basic element to constitute a market. Because it is the commodity, not the place, that attracts the buyers and sellers to come in to contact with each other. That's why in economics markets are known by the name of the commodity such as rice market, gold market, share market etc.
2. **Buyers and Sellers :** Buyers and sellers are the twin elements of a market who deal with a commodity. Buyers purchase the commodity and sellers sell the commodity. Both are indispensable for each other as without any one transaction cannot take place i.e. the market cannot be constituted.
3. **Communication :** To constitute a market the physical contact between the buyers and sellers does not matter. What matters is the communication between them. It may either be direct or physical or over any other means like letter, fax, telephone, mail or any other electronics device.
4. **Price :** Price is the exchange value of the commodity to be transacted expressed in terms of money. Unless a price is determined exchange or transaction of the commodity cannot take place between the buyers and sellers and hence market cannot be constituted. Price may be determined through competition or negotiation or by arbitration or by legislation.
5. **Area :** Area here does not mean any particular place rather a whole area over which the buyers and sellers of a commodity are spread. It may be a locality, a region, a country or even the whole world.

Types of Market

Markets can be classified on the basis of the area they cover or on the basis of their structure. On the basis of area markets can be classified as local market, regional market, national market, international market. But in microeconomic analysis such classification bears no significance.

In microeconomic analysis we classify markets on the following grounds :

1. The number of buyers and sellers of the commodity.
2. Nature of the commodity.
3. The degree of freedom of the buyers and sellers and the factors of production.
4. Knowledge of the buyers and sellers about market conditions.
5. Degree of competitiveness etc.

On the basis of these factors a broad classification of markets is presented below.

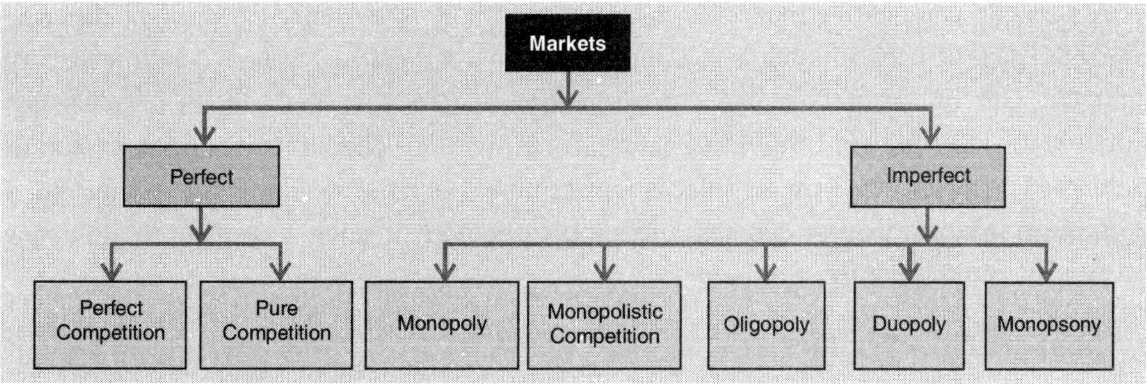

(Here, we will discuss about perfect competition, pure competition, monopoly, monopolistic competition and oligopoly as per the syllabus prescribed for the higher secondary students.)

PERFECT COMPETITION

As an extreme form of market structure perfect competition refers to that market situation where a large number of buyers and large number of sellers deal with a homogeneous products, which are perfect substitutes of each other, having the autonomy of free entry into the market and free exit from the market with perfect knowledge about the market conditions. In such market there is cut-throat competition among the sellers to sell their products but there is no rivalry or no direct competition among any individual sellers of firms.

*According to **Prof. Ferguson,** "Perfect competition describes a market in which there is a complete absence of direct competition among economic group."*

*In the words of **Prof. Cournot,** "A perfect market is one in which the buyers have no preference as between different units of the commodity offered for sale, sellers are quite indifferent to whom they sell and both buyers and sellers have full knowledge of prices in other parts of the market."*

Features of Competitive Market

From the above meaning and definitions we can draw the following features of a perfectly competitive market.

1. Large Number of Buyers and Sellers

A perfectly competitive market is characterised by a large number of buyers and large number of sellers. Their number is so large that each buyer and each seller constitutes a very negligible part of the market, like a drop in the ocean. So no single buyer or seller can influence the market by his individual action. An individual seller or firm sells its product at the prevailing price. The firm or seller is a price taker not price maker. Price is determined by the twin market forces of demand and supply. Similarly a single buyer cannot influence the price by purchasing more or less.

2. Homogeneous Product

The products of all the sellers or firms under perfect competition are homogeneous, i.e. alike in all respects. So no seller can attract the buyers to buy his commodity in the name of differentiation. Likewise no consumer will have any special preference for the commodity of a particular seller or firm. That is, the product of all the sellers are perfect substitutes.

3. Uniform Price

Under perfect competition since the products of all the sellers or firms are homogenous a uniform price is expected to prevail in the market. If any seller charges a higher price he will lose the market. On the other hand if a seller sells his product at a lower price, he may sell his product earlier but cannot influence the market price. Because the supply of the commodity by that seller is a very negligible part of the total market supply.

4. Free Entry and Free Exit

Under perfect competition the buyers and sellers have the autonomy of entering into and exit from the market. It implies, if the existing firms are marking profits, new firms can enter into the market or industry. On the other hand if a firm or seller is facing loss he can quite the market at any time. No other seller can compel him to stay in the market and to face loss. Similarly buyers are also free to enter into market and can quit the market without making any purchase. No seller can compel a buyer to purchase his products. Thus there is a high degree of freedom for both the buyers and sellers under perfect competition.

5. Perfect Knowledge

Under perfect competition the buyers and sellers are expected to have perfect knowledge about the market conditions such as price prevailing in the market, demand and supply positions of the commodity. This implies that no buyer or seller can deceive or be deceived by the other. Moreover the sellers have perfect knowledge about the preferences of the buyers. Thus there cannot be any foul play in the market either by a buyer or by a seller.

6. No Transport Cost

Under perfect competition since a uniform price prevails in the market it obviously implies there is no transport cost, for the movement of goods from one place to another, otherwise if the transport cost will be taken into account then there will be no uniform price. There is also no transport cost for the movement of the factors of production. Otherwise the cost of production will vary and so also the price of the same commodity at different places.

7. Perfect Factor Mobility

Under perfect competition the factors of production are assumed to be perfectly mobile from one place to another, from one use to another so that all firms get equal advantages of the factor services and produce their products at equal cost condition to maintain a uniform price. Otherwise if the factor's movement is restricted the firms will be forced to produce their products at different costs and charge different prices which will be against the nature of perfect competition.

From the above discussion on the features of perfectly competitive market it seems to be an ideal market. But the reality is such type of market is found nowhere in the world. This type of market is purely imaginary and hence is called as an extreme form of market.

PURE COMPETITION

The concept of pure competition as a market form is the brain child of **Prof. E.H. Chamberlin**, a noted American economist. To him pure competition refers to a market situation which is free from monopoly elements of any degree. For example, monopoly elements have a control over price. But pure competition signifies the absence of control over price. Pure competition is characterised by the presence of three important features of perfect competition.

They are :

(i) Large number of buyers and sellers

(ii) Products of all sellers are homogeneous

(iii) There is autonomy of free entry and free exit of the buyers and sellers.

These three features of pure competition seem to make this type of market more close to the real world than the perfect competition. However, the difference between the perfect competition and pure competition is of degree not kind.

Demand Curve of a Firm Under Perfect Competition

Under perfect competition since a uniform price prevails in the market determined by the twin market forces of demand and supply all the firms are bound to follow that price. That is each firm acts as a price-taker. If a firm will charge a slightly higher price than the price prevailing in the market he will lose all customers, i.e. demand for its product will fall infinitely. On the other hand if he will charge a lower price the demand for its product will increase infinitely. This implies that the demand curve faced by an individual firm under perfect competition will be perfectly elastic or horizontal straight line at the prevailing price level as shown in the figure drawn below. Moreover, since a uniform price prevails the revenue from each additional unit of the commodity will be the same, i.e. equal to price which also equals the average revenue of the firm determined by dividing the total revenue by the units or quantity of the commodity sold. Thus the demand curve of the individual firm under perfect competition is also its average revenue (AR) and marginal revenue (MR) curve and the two curves coincide to each other. This is also shown in the figure drawn below. The demand curve of the firm 'PD' is horizontal at prevailing price 'OP' and that is also its average and marginal curves. Thus under perfect competition, for an individual firm Price = AR = MR.

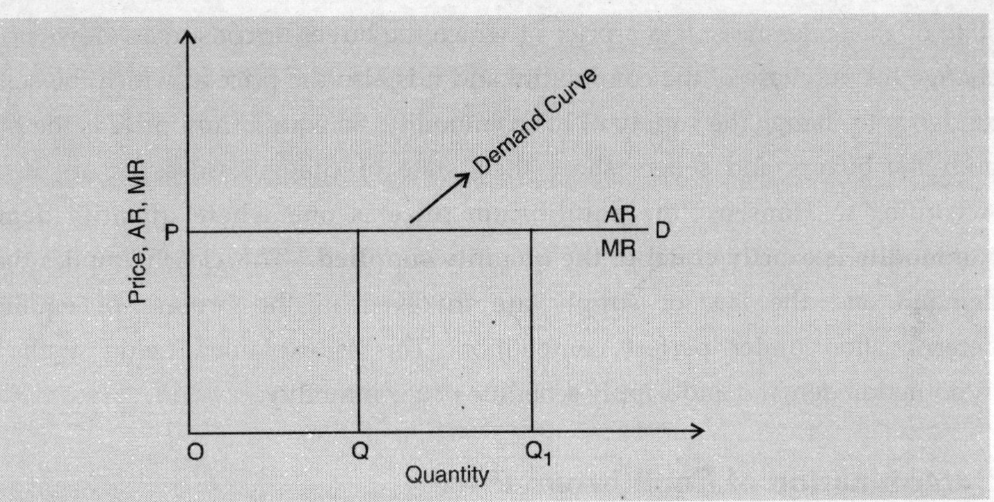

PRICE DETERMINATION UNDER PERFECT COMPETITION

Pricing theories, dealing with how prices are determined in the markets bear much significance in economic analysis as they affect all aspects of economics like consumption, production, distribution etc. The price that prevails in the market is called 'equilibrium price'. Now the question is how this 'equilibrium price' is determined in the market.

Above we have discussed that under perfect competition a uniform price of a commodity prevails in the market and a seller or form as the price-taker, sells its product at that price. But the fact that we are going to study here is : how that equilibrium price is determined. Different economists have given different opinions regarding price determination under perfect competition. Economists like Adam Smith, David Ricardo, J.S. Mill and others considered the 'cost of production' as the sole determinant of price of a commodity. On the other hand utilitarian economists like Jevons consider that the price of a commodity is determined on the basis of the marginal utility derived by a consumer from his consumption. However, both the opinions are one-sided. The first one, considering 'cost of production' as the sole determinant of price, put much emphasis on supply side of a commodity as the determinant of 'equilibrium price'. The second opinion considering the marginal utility of the commodity, put much emphasis on the demand side of a commodity as the determinant of the equilibrium price. However, it was Marshall who made a synthesis of the two complicating opinions and propounded that under perfect competition price is determined by the interaction of the twin market forces of 'demand' and 'supply'.

According to Marshall the price of a commodity determined by the equality between demand for and supply of the commodity is called equilibrium price. Equilibrium means a state of changelessness. It is a price at which the buyer or consumer shows no tendency to change his purchase of the commodity and it is also the price at which the seller shows no tendency to change the supply of his commodity. So equilibrium price is the price at which both the buyers and sellers show their state of changelessness or are in equilibrium. According to **Hansen, "the equilibrium price is one where quantity demanded of a commodity is exactly equal to the quantity supplied."** This clearly implies that the law of demand and the law of supply are involved in the process of equilibrium price determination under perfect competition. This is explained below with the help of hypothetical demand and supply schedule of a commodity.

Determination of Equilibrium Price

Demand Side

From the law of demand we know that the non-price-factors affecting the demand for a commodity remaining constant more will be demanded when its price is less and vice versa. This implies as the price of a commodity will go on decreasing its demand will go on increasing and vice versa. There is an inverse relationship between price and quantity demanded of a commodity. The reason is while purchasing a commodity the consumers always compare the marginal utility of the commodity with its price. As they purchase more and more of a commodity the marginal utility from the successive units will go on diminishing. So they will demand more when the price is low and vice versa. This tendency of the consumers is shown in the hypothetical demand-supply schedule drawn below.

Supply Side

From the law of supply we know that the non-price factors affecting the supply of a commodity remaining constant, there is a direct or positive relationship between the price of a commodity and its quantity supplied. In other words with Ceteris Paribus assumption, more will be supplied when the price is high and less will be the supply when the price is low. The reason is simple, as the seller or supplier wants to maximize his profit and higher profit can be earned at a higher price and lower at a lower price. That's why the sellers or the suppliers will always compare the price with the cost of production. As the cost of production gradually increases with the increase in production, so the seller or supplier charge higher prices for higher level of supply and the reverse. This tendency of the sellers or suppliers is presented below in the hypothetical demand-supply schedule.

Demand and supply schedule taken together.

Price (₹)	Quantity Demanded (Units)	Quantity Supplied (Units)	Explanation
10	100	30	D > S
15	80	40	Price will rise
20	70	50	
25	60	60	D = S Equilibrium Price
30	50	70	D < S
35	40	80	Price will decrease
40	30	90	

The demand-supply schedule drawn above shows that when the price of the commodity is ₹ 10/- the quantity demanded is 100 units where as the supply is only 30 units. Demand being greater than supply (D > S) price of the commodity will rise. With the rise in price quantity demanded has decreased, as per the law of demand, to 80 units. On the other hand due to increase price, as per the law of supply, quantity supplied has increased to 40 units, but still D > S, so there will be further rise in price. Thus the rise in price along with fall in demand and rise in supply will continue till D > S. But at price ₹ 25/- we see that D = S.(60) and hence the equilibrium price is ₹ 25/-. At this price what the buyers or consumers are ready to purchase exactly equals what the seller or firm is ready to sell. This is how the equilibrium price is determined by the interaction of the twin market forces of demand and supply. Neither the demand only guided by the MU of a commodity nor the supply, guided by the cost of production alone can determine the equilibrium price.

Graphical Presentation

In the figure the quantity demanded and supplied are presented on the OX-axis and price on the OY-axis. As shown in the figure when price is OP_1 (higher) the quantity demanded is P_1T. With the fall in price to OP and OP_2 the quantity demanded has increased to PE(OQ) and P_2Q_2. By joining the points T, E and Q_2 we have obtained the downward sloping demand curve DD. On the other hand at those corresponding prices the quantity supplied are shown as P_1Q_1, PE and P_2U respectively. The figure shows at OP_1 price S > D, so the price will fall, at price OP_2, D > S, so price will increase. However, at price 'OP' where the demand curve DD and supply curve SS intersect each other at point E the quantity demand and quantity supplied are exactly equal i.e. PE or OQ. So, OP is the equilibrium price and OQ = PE is the equilibrium output.

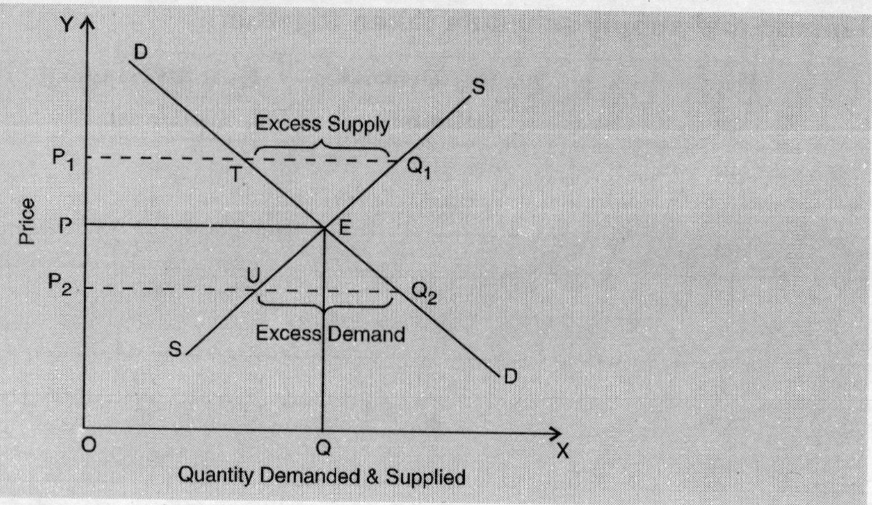

Effects of Change in Demand and Change in Supply

We know change in demand leads to shift in the demand curve. It occurs due to change in non-price factors. Similarly change in supply leads to shift in the supply curve which occurs due to change in non-price factors affecting supply. Shift in the demand curve to the right of the original demand curve implies increase in demand and that to the left of the original demand curve implies decrease in demand. The supply remaining the same, if there is change in demand, it will affect the equilibrium price. Similarly shift in the supply curve implies either increase or decrease in the supply. Demand remaining the same if supply changes it will also affect the equilibrium price. Moreover, change in demand and change in supply simultaneously will also affect the equilibrium price. These are explained diagrammatically in the figures drawn below.

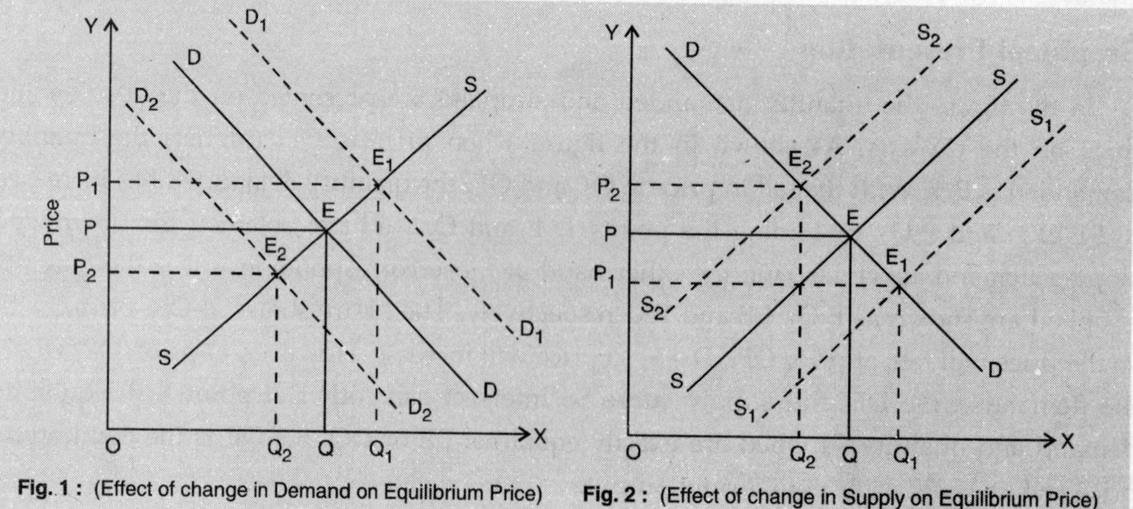

Fig. 1 : (Effect of change in Demand on Equilibrium Price) **Fig. 2 :** (Effect of change in Supply on Equilibrium Price)

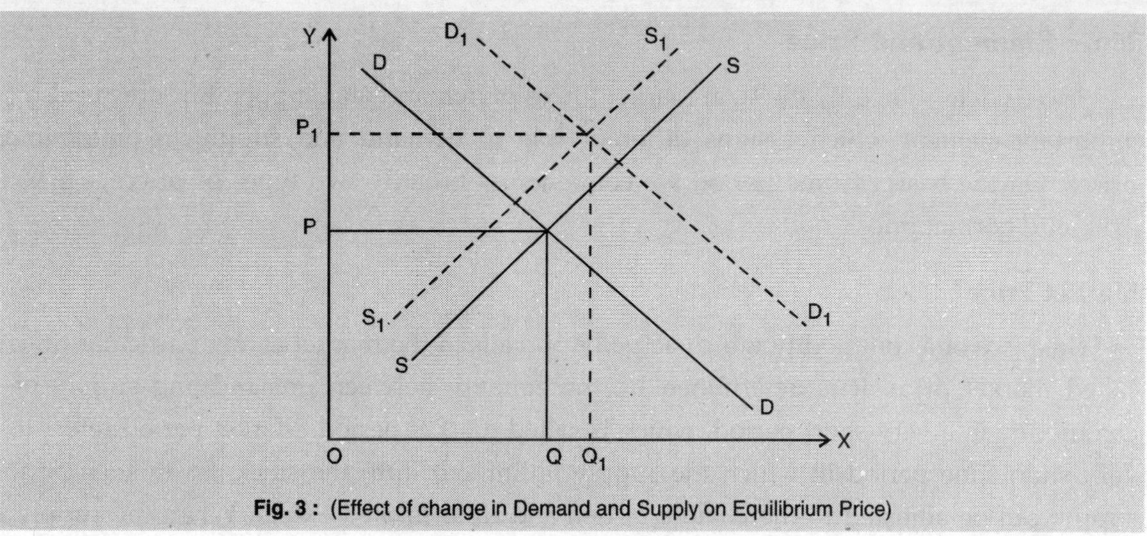

Fig. 3 : (Effect of change in Demand and Supply on Equilibrium Price)

Fig.-1 presents the effects of changes in demand on the equilibrium price. In the figure the original demand curve DD intersects the supply curve SS at point E and thus determines the equilibrium price 'OP'. When the demand curve shifts to right, supply remaining the same, the new demand curve D_1D_1 intersects the supply curve at point E_1, indicating a rise in price to OP_1 with increase in demand. On the other hand, if the demand curve shifts to the left of the original, i.e. to D_2D_2, it intersects the supply curve at point E_2, indicating a fall in price to OP_2 with decrease in demand to OQ_2.

Fig.-2 presents the effects of changes in supply, demand remaining unchanged. As shown in the figure the original supply curve intersects the demand curve at point E and thus determines the equilibrium price OP. When the supply curve shifts to the right of the original one, i.e. to S_1S_1, indicating increase in supply, the new supply curve intersects the demand curve at point E_1 leading to a fall in the equilibrium price to OP_1. On the contrary, when the supply curve shifts to the left of the original one, i.e. to S_2S_2, it intersects the demand curve at point E_2 leading to a rise in the price to OP_2, with decrease in demand to OQ_2.

Fig.-3 presents the effects of change in both the demand and supply on the equilibrium price. The figure shows that the effect on the equilibrium price depends upon the proportionate change in demand and supply. In the figure it is shown that the proportionate change in demand is greater than the proportional change in supply. So at the new point of intersection between the new demand curve D_1D_1 and new supply curve S_1S_1 the price has increased more than proportionately to increase in supply. Contrarily, if the change in supply will be more than proportionate to the change in demand then the new equilibrium price will be lower than the original equilibrium price.

Time Element and Price

Price is determined by the twin market forces of demand and supply. But time is also an important element which assigns different role to demand and supply in determining prices. On the basis of time period we come across broadly two types of prices – market price and normal price.

Market Price :

The price of a commodity which actually prevails in the market at any particular time is called market price. It is determined by the equality between demand and supply of a commodity in a very short period, which is called market period. Market period refers to a very short time period in which the supply is limited, upto the stock. So in such period supply can be adjusted to the change in demand upto limited extent. When the supply is exhausted it ceases to play any role in the price determination. So demand plays all important role in price determination. Market price is temporary and fluctuating as it various frequently with change in demand. However, market price is real.

Normal Price :

Price of a commodity which is expected to prevail in the long run is called normal price. Long run refers to that time period in which supply of a commodity can be fully adjusted according to the changing demand conditions. It implies, in determination of normal price both the demand and supply play equally important role. Normal price is stable. But since the concept 'long run' is ambiguous it makes the concept of normal price imaginary one. In our day to day life we never come across such price. It is hypothetical one.

MONOPOLY

The term 'monopoly' is the congregation of two Greek words : **'Mono'** which means 'Single' and **'Poly'** which means seller. In this sense, as a market structure monopoly refers to that market structure in which there is only seller of a commodity. The existence of a single seller or a single firm obviously implies that there is absence of competition. That single seller constitute the whole market or that single firm constitutes the whole industry. The existence of a single seller also implies that his products have no close substitute. Since the monopolist constitutes the whole market or industry he is the price-maker and price-taker as well. He is the sole determiner of the volume of output and can charge either a uniform price or discriminatory prices from different buyers. Moreover, absence of competition in a monopoly market also implies that entry of new seller into the market or new firm into industry is strictly prohibited.

Features of Monopoly

From the above stated meaning of monopoly as an imperfect market we can draw the following basic features of such market.

1. Single Seller and Large Number of Buyers

Monopoly is a single-seller market or single-firm industry. That single seller or firm is called as the monopolist. The monopolist is the sole decision maker. He is the sole authority to decide his price-output policy, i.e. how much to produce and what price is to be charged etc. The monopolist may be an individual or a group of individuals taking decisions as one. However, the number of buyers in this market is large. But no single buyer can influence the policies of a monopolist, as he has complete control over the entire market.

2. No Close Substitute

The products of the monopolist are unique in the sense that they have no close substitutes. This feature is basic in the sense that if close substitutes are available, there will be competition and monopoly will vanish or it will no more a monopoly market.

3. Barriers to Entry

Entry of new seller or firm into a monopoly market is strictly prohibited. Barriers to entry for a new firm may either by natural or artificial or legal via patent right or so. This entry restriction for the new firm keep the monopolist free from the tension of competition. According to **Prof. J.S. Bains**, "Single firm monopoly occurs when one seller sells a product for which there is no close competitor or rival."

4. Informative Selling Cost

A monopolist may incur a selling cost in the beginning. He may do this to give information to the buyers about his product, but once in the initial stage of his sale. Selling cost is not required to be repeated as the buyers themselves will acquaint the others about his product. No advertisement or propaganda is needed in the subsequent stages of sale.

5. Nature of Demand Curve

Under monopoly since there is only one firm producing a product, the aggregate demand (or market demand) of all the buyers of his product is his demand. We know that the demand curve of an individual buyer as well as the market demand curve slopes downwards to the right, so the demand curve faced by a monopolist also slopes downwards to the right. Since the demand curve is also the average revenue curve, it implies that the AR curve of the monopolist is downward sloping indicating a monopolist will sell more at a lower price and vice-versa. It also implies and another important fact that a monopolist cannot determine both price and quantity of the output at the same time. Since the AR of the monopolist decreases with increase in his sale the MR will Fall Faster than AR and MR curve will lie below the AR curve as shown in the figure drawn below.

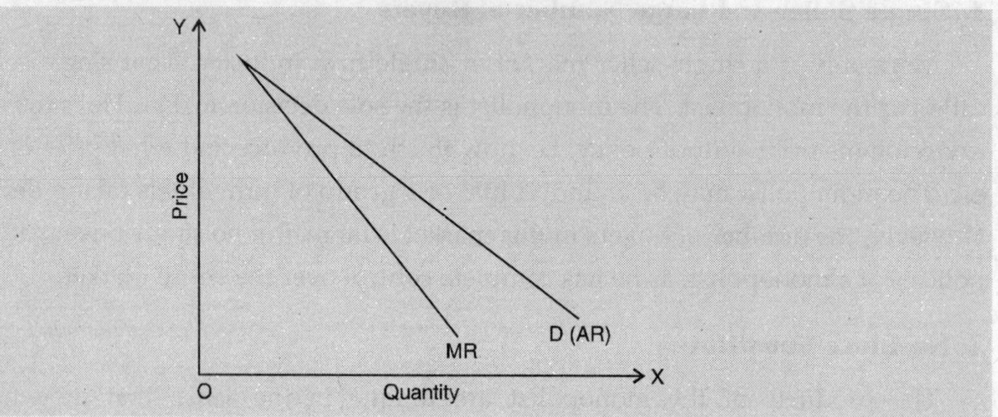

However, monopoly is also an extreme form of market and imaginary only as nowhere in the globe such market is found.

Broad Distinction between Perfect Competition and Monopoly

Perfect Competition	Monopoly
1. Number of buyers and sellers is very large.	1. Only one seller or firm but large number of buyers.
2. The product is homogeneous and hence each seller's product is substitute of that of others.	2. No close substitute of the product, so the buyers have to purchase it from the monopolist or to go without it.
3. The seller or firm has no control over price, it takes the price determined in the market.	3. Monopolist has control over price, he is the price-maker and price taker as well.
4. Entry and exit for a firm is free.	4. There is strong barriers for new firms to enter.
5. Demand curve faced by a firm is horizontal. (AR = MR = Price)	5. Demand curve faced by a monopolist is downward sloping (AR > MR).

MONOPOLISTIC COMPETITION

'Perfect competition' and 'monopoly' are two extreme forms of market. But both these market forms are far from the real world. Because in real world the market forms that we come across are incompatible with the features of perfect competition and monopoly. So there was the need to reformulate the pricing theories to bring them nearer to the actual world. This was accomplished by an English economist **Prof. Mrs. Joan Robinson** and an American economist **Prof. E.H. Chamberlin**, independently and brought out simultaneously "The Economics of Imperfect Competition" and "The Theory of Monopolistic Competition", respectively.

Both the concepts, 'Monopolistic Competition' of Chamberlin and 'Imperfect Competition' of Mrs. Robinson are different is the sense that Mrs. Robinson's 'imperfect competition' includes all forms of markets that we come across in the real world where as Chamberlin's Monopolistic Competition' is just one of those market forms that we come across in case of most of the commodities. Mrs. Robinson's imperfect competition includes – Monopolistic Competition, oligopoly, duopoly, Monopoly and hence is a wider concept.

Meaning and Definition

As the name 'Monopolistic Competition' suggests, it is a market form in which competition takes place among some monopolist sellers or firms of a commodity. In other words in such market there is the presence of some of the features of both perfect competition and monopoly markets. More simply speaking it is a market form where there are large number of firms, like perfect competition, producing and selling similar products each having control over its product and hence face competition. Most of the commodities we require in our day to day life like soap, toothpaste, shoes, cloth etc. constitute such market.

To define, 'Monopolistic Competition' Stonier and Hague pointed out, "There is competition which is keen, though not perfect, among many firms making very similar products."

*According to **Prof. Brain**, "Monopolistic competition is found in the industry where there is a large number of small sellers selling differentiated but close substitute products."*

*According to **Chamberlin**, "It is a market where competition takes place among monopoly firms. It exists between monopoly and perfect competition."*

Features of Monopolistic Competition

From the above discussed meaning and definition we can draw the following features of monopolistic competition.

1. Large Number of Sellers and Buyers

Like perfect competition there are large number of sellers in a monopolistic competitive market. Presence of large number of sellers obviously indicates the presence of competition.

The presence of large number of sellers also indicate that no single seller can influence the market by means of his individual action. But the difference is, the individual firms have nothing to bother about the reaction of the rival firms. A firm can follow an independent price and output policy. Similarly, the presence of large number of buyers indicates that no single buyer can influence the market conditions.

2. Product Differentiation

Product differentiation is a unique feature of monopolistic competition. Under this market each firm produces a differentiated product and the product of each firm are close substitutes of each other, but not perfect substitutes. That is the products of all the firms are alike but not identical. For example we can take the toothpaste market which consists of so many brands like Colgate, Close-up, Pepsodent, Oral-B, Ajanta, Cibaca, Anchor, Promise, Babool, Neem, Miswak etc. These products are close substitutes but not exactly identical or homogeneous. Each of them is different from one another in some way or other. The differentiation may be real in the form of differences in the ingredients or the differentiation may be artificial in the form of differences in packing, shape, size, colour etc. Because of this product differentiation buyers prefer one product to another and because of this product differentiation each seller tries to capture more and more share of the market.

3. Free Entry and Free Exit

Like perfect competition the sellers or firms and the buyers under monopolistic competition have the autonomy to enter into or exit from the market. Since the firms produce close substitutes, each firm is a monopolist, regulating its own products. Each firm has a command over a small part of the whole market. There is open competition with no firms having control over others. So if the existing firms are making profits a new firm can enter into the industry and if a firm is facing loss it can quit the industry. Similarly, under this market the buyers have the autonomy of purchasing a product of any firm or to go away without making any purchase. No firm can compel a buyer to purchase its product.

4. Lack of Perfect Knowledge

There are innumerable products in a monopolistic competitive market. Each product is a close substitute of the others. So the buyers do not have perfect knowledge about the products, i.e. about their quality, prices etc. It is also not possible on their part. Similarly, the sellers or firms do not have perfect knowledge about the choice and preferences of the buyers, which is also not possible on their part.

5. Selling Cost

Though this feature is also found in some other form of markets but it is unique to monopolistic competition. Under monopolistic competition there are many firms and their products are close substitutes of each other. So each firm wants to capture a larger part of the market or to maximize its sale. For this the firms resort to different types of salesmanship like advertisement, propaganda, offer sale, discount etc. and the expenditure incurred on these salesmanship is called selling cost. Because all these expenditure are included in the cost of production and are included in the price of their product. Selling cost bears much significance under monopolistic competition as it influences price significantly.

6. Downward Sloping Demand Curve

Like a monopolist a firm under monopolist competition faces a downward sloping demand curve. Because in such market when a firm of certain brand increases its price, some buyers will give up their purchase and buy its substitute. But some buyers continue to buy the same brand even if its price rises. This implies that the firm will be able to sell less at higher price. Similarly, when a firm reduces the price of its product it will attract some of the buyers of his competitors, but not all.

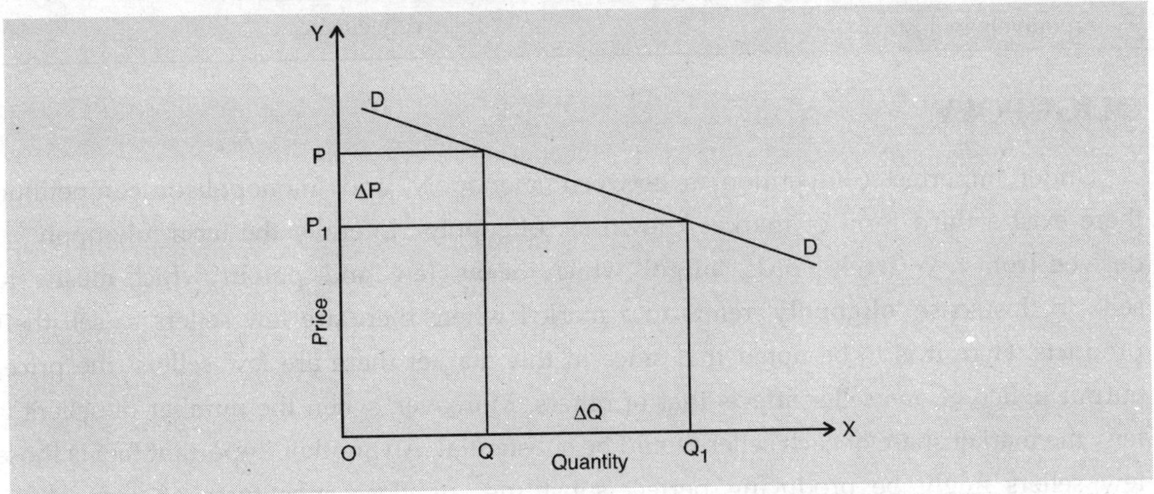

This implies that the firm's sale will increase at a lower price but not infinitely. Therefore, the demand curve faced by a monopolistic competitive firm slopes downwards. Moreover, since the substitutes of the product of a firm are available in the market, the demand for the product is more elastic and the demand curve becomes flatter as shown in the figure drawn above. In the figure the change in quantity demanded is OQ_1 (ΔQ) due to the change in price by PP_1 (ΔP). Geometrically OQ_1 is greater than $PP_1(\Delta Q > \Delta P)$. So the price elasticity of demand for the product is greater the 1 $\left(E_P = \frac{\Delta Q}{\Delta P} > 1\right)$.

Distinction between Monopoly and Monopolistic Competition

On the basis of the above discussion on both the forms of market – Monopoly and Monopolistic competition we can summarize the distinction between them as follow.

Monopoly	Monopolistic Competition
1. Single seller or firm.	1. Large number of firms.
2. Product has no close substitute.	2. Products of each firm are close substitutes.
3. Monopolistic has full control over the market and constitute the whole market or industry.	3. A firm has partial control over the market and constitutes a part of the market or industry.
4. No rival to compete.	4. Competition among the firms is cut throat.
5. Barriers for new firm to enter.	5. Entry for new firms is free.
6. Demand curve faced by a monopolist is relatively inelastic.	6. Demand curve faced by a firm is relatively elastic.

OLIGOPOLY

Under imperfect competition in between 'monopoly' and 'monopolistic competition there exist a third form of market known as 'oligopoly'. Literally the term 'oligopoly' is derived from two Greek words, **'oligoi'** which means 'few' and **'polein'** which means 'to sell'. In this sense **'oligopoly'** refers to a market where there are few sellers to sell their products. Here it is to be noted that since in this market there are few sellers, the price-output policy of one seller affects that of others. Moreover, when the number of sellers is few, the market share of each seller would be substantial. An another important fact is those few sellers might be producing perfect substitutes or close substitutes of each others product.

With the above meaning of this market from we can define oligopoly as *"a market structure where a few sellers producing either homogeneous or differentiated products, each having control over a significant portion of the whole market, compete with each other affecting each others price-output policy."* Thus in this market there is competition among the few.

Types of Oligopoly

On the basis of the nature of products produced by the oligopolistic firms as stated above oligopoly markets can be put under two categories :

(i) Pure or perfect oligopoly

(ii) Differentiated or imperfect oligopoly

Pure Oligopoly : When a few sellers or firms comprising an oligopoly market are producing a homogeneous product then it is called a pure or perfect oligopoly. Since the number of sellers is few and their products are homogeneous and hence perfect substitutes of each others, each firm's decision on price and output is sharply reacted and reflected in others. Pure oligopoly is found primarily among the producers of iron and steel, aluminium, copper, zinc, cement and like industrial products.

Differentiated Oligopoly : When a few sellers or firms comprising an oligopoly market are producing differentiated products, i.e. similar products which are close substitutes of each others, not perfect substitutes, then it is called differentiated or imperfect oligopoly. In such market the reaction of each firm on others price output policy is notable but not so sharp as under pure oligopoly. Producers of automobiles, cigarettes, TVs, cell phone, refrigerators, computers, laptops etc. constitute differentiated oligopoly markets.

Features of Oligopoly Market

Besides the nature of the products most of the oligopolistic markets have several common features which are discussed below.

1. **Few Sellers :** In monopoly markets the number of sellers is few. Though there is no unanimity among the economists regarding the number of sellers in this type of markets, yet their number is supposed to be more than two and generally around ten to twenty who compete among themselves. Each firm controls a significant portion of the market demand, so the price-output policy of one affects that of others. However, the number of buyers like any other market is large.

2. **Interdependence :** In oligopoly markets since there are few sellers of the products, whether homogeneous or differentiated, each seller or firm knows that changes in its price-output policy may lead to countermoves by the rivals. This implies that each firm can influence and be influenced by others price-output policy. Therefore, while taking any decision a firm has to consider the possible reaction of its rival firms. In this sense there is a recognised interdependence among the sellers in the oligopolistic markets.

3. **Competition :** Oligopoly refers to competition among the few. Here each firm competes with its rivals 'tooth and nail' to get a greater share of the market. The competition among the oligopolistic firms is different from the competition under perfect competition or monopolistic competition. Because under those markets there are large number of firms, so the influence of a single firm is negligible. But under oligopoly since the market consists of few sellers, the action taken by one immediately affects the others. So the competition is more acute and retaliastic.

4. **Group Behavior :** The pricing-output theory under oligopoly is a theory of group behaviour. It is not a theory of mass behaviour as under perfect competition or monopolistic competition where the number of sellers is large. It is also not a theory of individual behaviour as in case of monopoly, where there is only one firm. In oligopoly markets the firms are inter-dependent in their decisions on price-output policy and may join hands together for their common interest of profit maximization, what is called as 'cartel', which may either be open or tacit.

5. **Selling Cost :** Selling cost is also an important feature of oligopoly markets. In order to capture more share of the market an individual firm resorts to various salesmanship methods like advertisement, propaganda, offers etc. The expenditure incurred on these heads is called selling cost. When one firm adopts these methods others are also influenced to do so.

6. **Price Rigidity :** In oligopoly markets in order to increase the sale of its product no individual firm depends on price reduction. Because it may result in 'price-war'. In this market each firms knows if it will reduce price the others will follow it but if will increase the price others may not follow it. Thus price reduction will not benefit the individual firm on the other hand raising price an individual firm may face loss. That's why the individual firms try to stick to their price, which is called price rigidity.

7. **Indeterminateness of Demand Curve :** In this type of market it is not easy to trace out the demand curve for the product of an oligopolist. Because under oligopoly the exact behaviour pattern of a firm cannot be ascertained as one firm's price-output moves lead to unpredictable reaction on price-output policies of his rivals, which may have further repercussions on his price and output. The chain of action and reaction as a result of an initial change in price and output can only be guessed not ascertained which make the demand curve faced by an oligopolistic inderminate.

For the easy understanding of the students about the types of market discussed above a comparative picture of these markets is presented in a chart drawn below.

Differences among Different Forms of Market

Features	MARKET FORMS			
	Perfect Competition	Monopoly	Monopolistic Competition	Oligopoly
Number of Sellers or Firms	Large	One/Single	Large	Few
Nature of Product	Homogeneous or Perfect Substitutes	One Type	Differentiated or Close Substitutes	Homogeneous and Differentiated
Degree of Monopoly or Influence	Zero	Complete or Full	Limited (As close substitutes available)	Limited (As close substitutes available)
Price Policy	Price-taker	Price-maker and taker as well	Price-maker	Price-maker
Barriers to Entry and Exit	Autonomy	No Entry	Autonomy	Restricted
Market Knowledge	Complete or Perfect	Incomplete	Incomplete	Incomplete
Elasticity of Demand	Perfectly elastic	Relatively inelastic	Relatively elastic	Relatively elastic
AR and MR	Equal	Different (AR > MR)	Different (AR > MR)	Different (AR > MR)
Control over price	Zero (No control)	Larger Control	To some extent	To some extent
Selling cost	Nil	Negligible	Large	Some

WHAT WE LEARNT

1. In economics market refers to the relationship established between the buyers and sellers of a commodity over its transaction.
2. The basic elements of a market are : a commodity, some buyers and some sellers.
3. In economics markets are named after commodity not place.
4. Perfect competition and monopoly are two extreme forms of markets.

5. Under perfect competition there are large number of buyers and sellers.
6. Under perfect competition the products of all the sellers or firms are homogeneous i.e. perfect substitutes.
7. A uniform price prevails in the market under perfect competition.
8. Under perfect competition firm is the price-taker, industry or market is the price determiner.
9. Under perfect competition there is free entry and free exit for the buyers and sellers.
10. Under perfect competition the buyers and sellers have perfect knowledge about the market conditions.
11. Under perfect competition there is no transport cost for the movements of the products and factors of production.
12. Factors of production are perfectly mobile.
13. The concept of pure competition was developed by E.H. Chamberlin.
14. The demand curve faced by a firm under perfect competition is horizontal.
15. Under perfect competition equilibrium price is determined by the equality between the market demand and market supply.
16. Equilibrium price is one where quantity demanded of a commodity is exactly equal to the quality supplied.
17. The price of a commodity which actually prevails in the market at any particular time is called market price.
18. Price prevailing in very short period is called market price.
19. Market price is real and fluctuates frequently (unstable).
20. The price of a commodity which is expected to prevail in the long run is called normal price.
21. Normal price is imaginary and stable.
22. Monopoly is derived from two Greek words, 'Mono' which means single and 'poly' which means seller.
23. There is only one seller in a monopoly market.
24. The product of a monopoly market has no close substitute.
25. A monopolist seller or firm is the price-maker and price-taker as well.
26. Under monopoly the single seller or firm constitutes the whole market or industry.
27. There is strong entry barriers, for new firms, under monopoly.
28. The demand curve faced by a monopolist is downward sloping.

29. The MR curve of monopolist remains below his AR curve.
30. The concept of imperfect competition was developed by Mrs. Joan Robinson.
31. The concept of monopolistic competition was developed by an American economist E.H. Chamberlin in 1933.
32. Under monopolistic competition large number of sellers deal with differentiated but close substitute products.
33. Under monopolistic competition, competition takes place among some monopolist firms producing close substitute products.
34. Selling cost is a unique feature of monopolistic competition.
35. Under monopolistic competition the buyers and sellers lack perfect knowledge about the market conditions.
36. Degree of price elasticity of demand for the products of monopolistic competitive market is high (relatively elastic).
37. Oligopoly is derived from two Greek words : 'Oligoi' which means 'Few' and 'Poleein' which means 'to sell'.
38. Under oligopoly few sellers producing either homogeneous or differentiated products compete with each other.
39. Under oligopoly markets the sellers behave in group.
40. Demand curve of a oligopolist firm is inderminate.
41. In oligopoly markets the individual firms believe in price rigidity.
42. Interdependence of firms is a unique feature of oligopoly market.

QUESTIONS FOR REVIEW

A. *Choose the correct answer from the given alternatives in each question. (Each Carrying 1 Mark)*

1. **In economics market refers to :**
   (i) A place where goods are sold
   (ii) The relationship between the buyers and sellers
   (iii) An organization of sellers
   (iv) None of the above
2. **Which one is not a basic element of a market ?**
   (i) A place (ii) A commodity
   (iii) Some buyers (iv) Some sellers

3. **In economics markets are named after :**
   (i) Place (ii) Locality
   (iii) Commodity (iv) None of the above
4. **Which one of the following is an extreme form of market ?**
   (i) Oligopoly (ii) Monopolistic competition
   (iii) Perfect competition (iv) Pure competition
5. **Under which market a uniform price is expected to prevail ?**
   (i) Perfect competition (ii) Pure competition
   (iii) Monopolistic competition (iv) Monopoly
6. **In which market the factors of production are perfectly mobile ?**
   (i) Pure competition (ii) Perfect competition
   (iii) Monopolistic competition (iv) Pure oligopoly
7. **Who developed the concept of pure competition ?**
   (i) Alfred Marshall (ii) Mrs. Joan Robinson
   (iii) E.H. Chamberlin (iv) Prof. Hansen
8. **The demand curve (AR curve) faced by a firm under perfect competition is :**
   (i) Horizontal (ii) Vertical
   (iii) Downward sloping (iv) Upward sloping
9. **The price at which the quantity demanded is equal to quantity, supplied is called:**
   (i) Market price (ii) Normal price
   (iii) Equilibrium price (iv) None of the above
10. **Price prevailing in very short period or at a particular point of time is called :**
    (i) Normal price (ii) Market price
    (iii) Equilibrium price (iv) All the above
11. **Price which is expected to prevail in the long run is called :**
    (i) Normal price (ii) Equilibrium price
    (iii) Market price (iv) None of the above
12. **In which market there is only one seller ?**
    (i) Oligopoly (ii) Monopoly
    (iii) Pure competition (iv) Pure oligopoly
13. **Which one of the following is a feature of monopoly ?**
    (i) Single seller (ii) Absence of a close substitute
    (iii) Barriers to entry (iv) All the above

14. **The AR curve of a monopolist is :**
   (i) Downward sloping (ii) Horizontal
   (iii) Upward sloping (iv) Vertical

15. **Which one is not a characteristic of monopolistic competition ?**
   (i) Large number of sellers (ii) Product differentiation
   (iii) Absence of selling cost (iv) Free entry and free exit

16. **In which market the AR and MR curves coincide ?**
   (i) Perfect competition (ii) Monopolistic competition
   (iii) Monopoly (iv) Oligopoly

17. **The demand curve faced by a monopolist is :**
   (i) Horizontal (ii) Downward sloping
   (iii) Upward sloping (iv) Vertical

18. **Which one of the following is a unique feature of monopolistic competition ?**
   (i) Selling cost (ii) Barriers to entry
   (iii) Single seller (iv) Group behaviour

19. **In which market the sellers and buyers have perfect knowledge about the market conditions ?**
   (i) Monopolistic competition (ii) Perfect competition
   (iii) Differentiated oligopoly (iv) Monopoly

20. **In which market the sellers behave in group ?**
   (i) Monopoly (ii) Oligopoly
   (iii) Perfect competition (iv) Monopolistic competition

21. **Interdependence of sellers is a feature of which market ?**
   (i) Oligopoly (ii) Perfect competition
   (iii) Monopolistic competition (iv) None of the above

22. **In which market an individual firm believes in price rigidity ?**
   (i) Monopoly (ii) Monopolistic competition
   (iii) Oligopoly (iv) Perfect competition

23. **Demand for the products in which market is perfectly elastic ?**
   (i) Monopoly (ii) Monopolistic competition
   (iii) Oligopoly (iv) Perfect competition

24. Under oligopoly market the number of sellers is :

(i) Large (ii) Few

(iii) One (iv) None of the above

25. In which market the demand curve faced by a firm is indeterminate ?

(i) Monopoly (ii) Perfect competition

(iii) Oligopoly (iv) Monopolistic competition

B. *Correct the statement, if necessary, without changing the underlined portions. (Each Carrying 1 Mark)*

1. In economics markets are named after the place.
2. Perfect competition and oligopoly are two extreme forms of markets.
3. Under perfect competition the number of sellers is few.
4. Under monopolistic competition the products of all the sellers are perfect substitutes.
5. A uniform price prevails in the market under perfect competition.
6. Under perfect competition a firm is the price-maker.
7. Under monopoly there is free entry and free exit.
8. Factors of production are perfectly mobile under oligopoly.
9. The concept of imperfect competition was developed by Chamberlin.
10. The demand curve faced by a competitive firm is downward sloping.
11. Price prevailing in very short period is called normal price.
12. Normal price is stable.
13. Market price is imaginary.
14. The products of a competitive market has no close substitutes.
15. There is strong entry barriers for new firms in oligopoly markets.
16. The MR curve of a monopolist remains above its AR curve.
17. Under monopolistic competition there is competition among few.
18. Product differentiation is a unique feature of monopoly market.
19. The price elasticity of demand for the products of the monopolistic competitive firm is relatively low.
20. The demand curve faced by a monopoly firm is inderminate.

C. Answer the following questions in 2-3 sentences each (Each Carrying 2 Marks)

1. What is market in economics ?
2. What are the features of market ?
3. What is perfect competition ?
4. What is pure competition ?
5. What is monopoly ?
6. What is monopolistic competition ?
7. What is product differentiation ?
8. What is selling cost ?
9. What is oligopoly ?
10. What is pure oligopoly ?
11. What is differentiated oligopoly ?
12. What is equilibrium price ?
13. What is market price ?'
14. What is normal price ?

D. Distinguish between the concepts in six sentences each. (Each Carrying 3 Marks)

1. Perfect Competition and Pure Competition.
2. Perfect Competition and Monopoly.
3. Monopoly and Monopolistic Competition.
4. Perfect Competition and Monopolistic Competition.
5. Monopoly and Oligopoly.
6. Pure Oligopoly and Differentiated Oligopoly.
7. Market Price and Normal Price.

E. Long Answer Type Questions (Each Carrying 7½ Marks)

1. Define market. Discuss the features of market in economics.
2. What is Perfect Competition ? Discuss the features of Perfectly Competitive Market.

3. Explain how equilibrium price is determined under perfect competition.
4. What is Monopoly ? Discuss the features of monopoly market.
5. What is monopolistic competition ? Discuss the features of monopolistic competitive market.
6. What is oligopoly ? Discuss the features of oligopoly market.

Answers to Q. N. A

1.	(ii)	2.	(i)	3.	(iii)	4.	(iii)	5.	(i)	6.	(ii)	7.	(iii)	8.	(i)
9.	(iii)	10.	(ii)	11.	(i)	12.	(ii)	13.	(iv)	14.	(i)	15.	(iii)	16.	(i)
17.	(ii)	18.	(i)	19.	(ii)	20.	(ii)	21.	(i)	22.	(iii)	23.	(iv)	24.	(ii)
25.	(iii)														

Answer to Q. N. B

1. the commodity	2. Monopoly	3. large
4. Perfect competition	5. Correct	6. Price-taker
7. Under perfect competition	8. Perfect competition	9. Mrs. Joan Robinson
10. horizontal	11. Market price	12. Correct
13. Normal price	14. Monopoly market	15. Monopoly
16. below	17. Under oligopoly	18. Monopolistic competition
19. relatively high	20. Oligopoly firm	

❑ ❑ ❑

UNIT – VI

7. INTRODUCTORY MACROECONOMICS

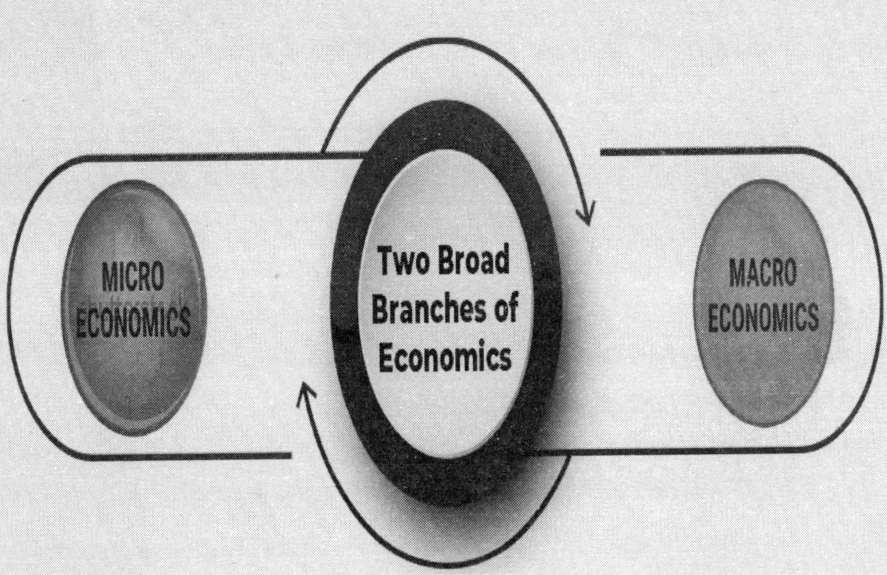

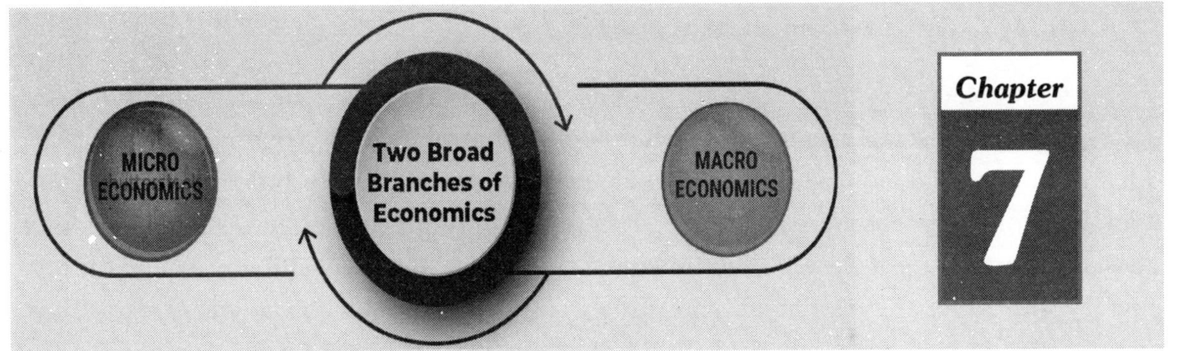

Chapter 7

INTRODUCTORY MACROECONOMICS

Introduction

Modern economic analysis has been divided into two broad branches—Microeconomics and Macroeconomics. The terms **'micro'** and **'macro'** were first introduced in economics by **Prof. Ragner Frisch** of Oslo University in 1933. But it was the Great Depression of 1930s after which the distinction between the two approaches has become necessary and widely accepted. In fact, the concept of 'macroeconomics' is not a new concept. Only the term 'macro' added to 'economics' made 'macroeconomics' a separate, rather an important branch of economic analysis. Because, 'macroeconomics' which is now studied as an aggregative economics concerning the economic system as a whole, is also found in the writings of even the predecessors of the classical economists. It was in the writings of the mercantilists, physiocrats and in the writings of classical economists like Adam Smith, David Ricardo and others and in the writings of neo-classical economists like Marshall, Pigou, Fisher, Robertson and others. But it was **J.M. Keynes** who brought about a revolutionary change in the economic thinking by pointing out the causes of economic debackles of 1930s and failure of the classical or traditional economic theories in reviving the European and American economies from the grip of depression in his monumental work **'The General Theory of Employment, Interest and Money'** published in 1936. In his book he put emphasis on the study of economic problems in aggregate level separately which divided economics into two separate branches-Microeconomics and Macroeconomics.

Meaning and Definitions of Macroeconomics

The term 'Macro' is derived from the Greek word **'Makros'** which means 'large' or 'aggregate'. In this sense macroeconomics refers to that branch of economics which deals with the nature, behaviour and problems of not one particular unit, rather all units taken together or of the economy as a whole. It deals with aggregate economic variables like national income, output, level of employment, aggregate demand and aggregate supply, general price level, development and growth of an economic as a whole etc. Thus macroeconomics is an aggregate study and hence is called aggregative economics.

Definitions

Macroeconomics has been defined by economists in different ways. Some of them are quoted below.

*According to **Gardner Ackley**, "Macroeconomics deals with economic affairs 'in the large', it concerns the overall dimensions of economic life. It looks at the total size and shape and functioning of the 'elephant' of economic experience, rather than working of articulation of dimensions of the individual parts. It studies the character of the forest, independently of the trees which compose it."*

*According to **Boulding**, "Macroeconomics deals not with individual quantities as such, but with aggregates of these quantities, not with individual income but with national income, not with individual prices but with general price levels, not with individual output but with national output."*

***Prof. Edward Shapiro** simply defined our subject as "Macroeconomics deals with the functioning of the economy as a whole."*

*According to **P.A. Samuelson**, "Macroeconomics is the study of the behaviour of the economy as a whole. It examines the overall level of a nation's output, employment, prices and foreign trade."*

However, for proper understanding of macroeconomics as a branch of economic analysis a distinction between microeconomics and macroeconomics is essential. Before doing that let's know first what is microeconomics ?

Microeconomics

The term 'micro' is derived from the Greek and **'Mikros'** which means 'small' or 'individual'. In this sense 'microeconomics' refers to that branch of economics which deals with the problems of the small or individual economic units of an economy. Such individual economic units include an individual or household, a firm or an industry. In the words of **Prof. Boulding, "Microeconomics is the study of particular firm, particular households, individual prices, wages, income, individual industries, particular commodity and so on."**

Distinction between Microeconomic and Macroeconomics

From the above discussed meaning and definitions of micro and macroeconomics we can draw the following distinctions between them.

1. Microeconomics is the study of individuals or small group of individuals' economic actions and problems whereas macroeconomics deals with aggregate economic actions and problems of an economy as a whole.
2. The objectives of microeconomics is to maximize utility, maximize profit and minimize cost of individual consumers or producers, where as the macroeconomics deals with the objectives like full employment, price stability, economic growth, balance of payments etc.
3. The basis of microeconomics is the price mechanism which operates with the help of twin market forces of demand and supply, where as the basis of macroeconomics is national income, output and employment which is determined by the aggregate demand and aggregate supply.
4. Microeconomic is based on different assumptions with rational behaviour of individuals where as macroeconomics bases its assumptions on the variables such as aggregate volume of output of an economy with the extent to which its resources are employed, with the size of national income and with the general price level.
5. Microeconomics theories are based on the assumption of full employment and its theories are developed on partial equilibrium technique, where as macroeconomic theories are based on under-employment assumption and are developed on general equilibrium technique.
6. In microeconomics the study of equilibrium conditions are analysed at a particular period where as in macroeconomics the study of equilibrium is based on time lags, rates of change, past and expected values of different values of the macro variables.

However, the distinction between micro and macroeconomics is not very much clear cut. Because what is macroeconomics in one situation or from one view point may become microeconomics from an another view point. For example, in case of a closed economy, the study of income, expenditure, saving, investment, employment etc. For the whole economy is the matter of macroeconomics. However if the country has trade relations with other countries, then a single country becomes just one unit of the international set up and becomes the subject matter of microeconomics. Moreover the study of microeconomics is not necessarily confined to individual units. It also studies aggregates. For example, the study of an industry which consists of several firms. So, we can say that the distinction between micro and macroeconomics is largely one of convenience. Certainly the two branches of economics study different types of problems and use different analytical tools and knowledge of each branch is necessary to understand the functioning of the economic system, unit-wise and as a whole.

Subject Matter of Macroeconomics

From the meaning and definitions of the 'Macroeconomics' discussed above we can say that the study of macroeconomics covers a broad area. It includes the issues, problems and parameters related to the working of the economy as a whole. They may be with regard to national income, employment and unemployment, aggregate demand and supply, economic stability and growth, macroeconomic policies of the government etc. Which constitute the subject matter of macroeconomics. Moreover, it is to be noted that the economic systems are dynamic and hence the scope of our subject is also dynamic. Because with changing economic scenarios, with new issues and problems the scope of macroeconomics also expands. Yet the broad subject matter of macroeconomics can be discussed under the following heads.

1. National Income

Macroeconomic studies different concepts related to the study of national income. Such concepts are GDP, NDP,. GNP, NNP (both at market price and factor costs), Real GDP, nominal GDP. It also studies other concepts related to nation income accounting such as personal income, personal disposable income, private income. Macroeconomics also studies the methods of measuring national income.

2. Level of Employment and Unemployment

The study of factors affecting the problems relating to aggregate employment and unemployment in the economy as a whole also constitute the subject matter of macroeconomics. In this context, the macroeconomic variables which determine the level of employment in the economy such as aggregate demand, aggregate supply, effective demand, aggregate saving and investment, factors affecting these variables are studied in macroeconomics.

3. General Price Level

The study of general price level is related to the study of inflation and deflation, which are the main issues of macroeconomic studies. These are responsible for instabilities in the working of the economy as a whole. Inflation refers to a situation in which the general price level is rising leading to the fall in the value of money. Deflation on the other hand refers to a situation of falling prices. Both the situations have adverse effects and not good for the economic health of a country. So the study of the nature and causes of inflation and deflation, their effects on the economy, measures to control these economic diseases also constitute a part of the subject matter of macroeconomics.

4. Theories of Money

Money is a macroeconomic variable. Variations in the demand for and supply of money have significant effects on the level of investment, employment, output, price level and economic stability etc. That's why money and the institutions related to money i.e. the financial system and theories related to the determination of demand and supply of money, value of money, all constitute a part of the subject matter of macroeconomics.

5. Business Cycles

Business cycles or trade cycles refer to the ups and downs in the economic activities of an economy. The study of economic growth of different countries shows that the economic growth does not follow a steady and smooth upward trend. No doubt, there has been a secular upward trend in the growth process of the economies, but characterized by a number of short-run fluctuations in the economic activities around the secular trend. The short-run fluctuations in the economic activities are due to the fluctuations in the macroeconomic variables like output, income, employment, prices etc. That's why, why these fluctuations take place ? What measures should be taken to achieve steady and smooth growth rate etc. also come under the subject matter of macroeconomics.

6. Economic Development and Growth

Economic development and economic growth are macroeconomic concepts as both are related to the economy as a whole. Economic development is a multidimensional concept, as it is related to increase in output along with the transition in the economic arrangements involved in the process of production, consumption and distribution. Economic growth on the other hand refers to increase in output over a long period of time or to maintain the already achieved development. Economic development is related to underdeveloped or developing countries where as economic growth is related to developed countries. However, both the concepts are dependent on various macroeconomic variables and hence come under the subject matter of macroeconomics.

7. International Trade

Present days economics are open economics having trade relations with each other. International trade and financial relations of a country with the other countries have far reaching effects on the working of its economy as a whole. That's why the theories of international trade, factors affecting international trade, balance of payments, tariff, protection, trade barriers etc. bear much significance in the study of macroeconomic analysis and come under the subject matter of macroeconomics.

8. Public Finance

Public finance is the study of income and expenditure of the public authorities. It includes the study of government revenue, government expenditure, public debt, financial management of the government etc. The classical economists believed in the concept of laissez-faire economy. But the lessons from the Great Depression made Keynes to suggest for the government intervention into the economic activities. Now the governments of different countries, with the concept of welfare state, are interfering more and more in to the economic activities with their budgeting instruments to streamline the economic activities of the country as a whole. That's why Public Finance has become a significant part of the subject matter of macroeconomics.

Importance of the Study of Macroeconomics

The theoretical and practical importance of macroeconomics can be discussed under the following heads.

1. Formulation of Economic Policies

Macroeconomic is of great help in formulation of economic policies. Modern governments, specially of the underdeveloped countries are confronted with innumerable national problems like problems of inflation, unemployment, underproduction, balance of payments crisis etc. The main responsibility of these governments rests in the regulation and control of these problems. As **Prof. Timbergen** says, **"Working with macroeconomic concepts is a bare necessity in order to contribute to the solutions of the great problems of**

our times." Because no government can solve these problems in terms of individual behaviour.

2. Understanding Microeconomics

The study of macroeconomics is essential for the proper understanding of microeconomics. Because no microeconomics law could be framed without a prior study of the aggregate.

3. Functioning of an Economy

For the understanding of the functioning of an economy macroeconomic analysis is of paramount importance. Because without knowing the behaviour pattern of the aggregative variables, which are the subject matter of macroeconomics we can't understand the working of the complex economic system.

4. Understanding and Controlling Economic Fluctuations

Economic fluctuations are a characteristic feature of almost all types of economy. Economic fluctuations creating instabilities in the economic activities are not good for the economic health of a country. Fluctuations, their causes and measures to control them are related to aggregate variables. For this the study of macroeconomics is essential.

5. Economic Development

Study of macroeconomics reveals the presence of inequalities in the distribution of income and wealth, differences in the standard of living of the people. By this the government can adopt various measures to eradicate the inequalities and ensure economic welfare, which is termed as economic development. So the study of macroeconomics bears much importance.

6. Inflation and Deflation

Macroeconomics analysis is of utmost importance to understand the causes and effects of inflation and deflation and to take the steps to counteract the adverse effects of these economic diseases.

7. Study of National Income

Without studying the national income we can't understand the economic status of the country and formulate correct economic policies. We know national income is a subject matter of macroeconomics. Hence, the study of macroeconomics bears much significance.

8. Performance of the Economy

The study of macroeconomics helps us to understand and analyse the performance of an economy. The study of GDP gives information about the contribution of each sector of the economy to the national income, their performance over time and so on. This helps in formulating policies in required sectors.

To conclude on the importance of studying macroeconomics we can say that it enriches our knowledge of the functioning of an economy by studying the behaviour of national income, output, saving and investment, consumption etc. Moreover, it throws light on solving the problems of unemployment, economic instability, balance of payments crisis, economic development and growth etc.

Limitations of Macroeconomics

No doubt macroeconomics and its analysis have been gaining strength ever since the publication of J.M. Keynes's 'General Theory of Employment, Interest and Money' in 1936. But it is to be noted that out of the two methods of studying and analysing-Inductive method and Deductive Method, the macroeconomic problems, inductive method has, however, possed the danger at excessive generalization of individual experiences to the system as a whole. Such pitfalls seem to be avoided to make macroeconomics serve as a handmaid of public policy.

Let us outline such pitfalls as the limitations of macroeconomics.

1. Excessive Generalization

Generalization of individual observation to the system as a whole may lead to erratic inferences about the system as a whole. For example, a loss incurred by one firm in an industry does not necessarily imply losses to all other firms in the industry.

2. Obsession of Aggregative Approaches

Excessive thinking in terms of lumping the individual units together may lead to erratic inferences. Individual units possess individualistic traits. They are non-homogeneous in character. One cannot add up two apples and three oranges to make any meaningful aggregate.

3. Fallacy of Deductive Inferences

Inferences deduced about individual units from the aggregative tendency may not always be true in respect of individual units as well. For example, a general rise in prices may not affect all sections of the community in the same manner. A consumer suffers from rising prices but rising prices benefit the producers.

4. Inconsistency between Overall and Individual Changes

A hike on prices of industrial output and a fall on prices of agricultural products may offset each other leading to no rise in the general price level. On the basis of stability of the general price level, if one will believe that no policy changes are required then it would certainly jeopardize the interest of the cultivators.

5. Problems of Measuring the Aggregates

Measurement of aggregative variables for the macroeconomic analysis involves a number of conceptual, statistical and practical problems due to their complexities.

To conclude, macroeconomic analysis by itself may not provide a true picture of an economy. It may appear like the top surface of an oceans appearing calm and unruffled from above, yet harbouring quite a few storms underneath. To look into the trouble spots, it is microeconomics analysis that is called for.

Distinction between Micro and Macroeconomics can be summarized as

Microeconomics	Macroeconomics
1. Microeconomics is the study of the economic actions and problems of the small or individual economic units.	1. Macroeconomics is the study of the economic actions and the problems of the economy as a whole.
2. The objectives of microeconomics are to maximize utility or profit or minimize cost, i.e. optimum utilization of resources at the disposal of individual economic units.	2. Macroeconomics deals with the objectives of aggregate economic welfare via full employment, increase in national income, stability, economic development and growth.
3. Microeconomic theories are based on full employment assumption.	3. Macroeconomic theories are based on under-employment assumption.
4. Microeconomic laws are developed on the basis of partial equilibrium.	4. Macroeconomic laws are developed on the basis of general equilibrium.
5. In microeconomics the study of equilibrium conditions are analysed at a particular period.	5. In macroeconomics the study of equilibrium is based on time lags, rates of change, past and expected values of the macro variables.

WHAT WE LEARNT

1. The term 'Micro' and 'Macro' was introduced in economics by Prof. Ragner Frisch in 1933.
2. The distinction between microeconomics and macroeconomics became a necessity because of the Great Depression of 1930s.
3. J.M. Keynes brought a revolution in economic thinking with the publication of his book "The General Theory of Employment, Interest and Money' in 1936.
4. J.M. Keynes is called as the father of macroeconomics.
5. The term 'Macro' is derived from the Greek word 'Makros' which means 'large' or 'aggregate'.
6. Macroeconomics is also called as 'aggregative economics'.
7. The term 'Micro' is derived from the Greek word 'Mikros', which means 'small' or 'individual'.
8. Microeconomics deals with the actions and problems of small or individual economic units like a household, firm etc.
9. Macroeconomics deals with the actions and problems of an economy as a whole.
10. The objectives of microeconomics are to study maximization of utility, maximization of profit, minimization of cost etc. of consumers or producers.
11. The objectives of macroeconomics are maximization of welfare national income and output, full employment, price stability, economic development and growth, balance of payments etc.
12. The basis of microeconomics is the price mechanism which operates with the help of twin market forces of demand and supply.
13. The basis of macroeconomics are national income, output, employment etc. which are determined by aggregate demand and aggregate supply.
14. Microeconomic theories are based on full employment assumption.
15. Macroeconomic theories are based on underemployment assumption.
16. Microeconomic laws are developed on partial equilibrium technique.
17. Macroeconomic laws are developed on general-equilibrium technique.
18. In microeconomics the study of equilibrium conditions are analysed at a particular period.

19. In macroeconomics the study of equilibrium is based on time lags, rates of change, part and expected values of the macro variables.

20. The distinction between microeconomics and macroeconomics is not very much clear cut.

21. National income, general employment, general price level, money and financial system, business cycles, international trade, economic development and growth, public finance etc. which are related to the economy as a whole are the subject matter of macroeconomics.

22. Consumption, production, distribution, welfare etc. related to individual economic units are the subject matter of microeconomics.

23. Study of macroeconomics is essential to understand the functioning of the economy as a whole.

QUESTIONS FOR REVIEW

A. Choose the correct answer from the given alternatives in each question. (Each Carrying 1 Mark)

1. **Who introduced the terms 'Micro' and 'Macro' in economics ?**
   (i) Adam Smith (ii) J.M. Keynes
   (iii) Ragner Frisch (iv) Alfred Marshall

2. **Who wrote 'The General Theory of Employment, Interest and Money' ?**
   (i) J.M. Keynes (ii) Ragner Frisch
   (iii) David Ricardo (iv) Robertson

3. **Who is called as the father of macroeconomics ?**
   (i) Ragner Frisch (ii) J.M. Keynes
   (iii) A.C. Pigou (iv) Fisher

4. **The term 'Macro' means -**
   (i) Small (ii) Individual
   (iii) Large (iv) None of the above

5. **Which one is an objective of microeconomics ?**
   (i) Maximization of utility (ii) Price stability
   (iii) Increase in national income (iv) All the above

6. **Which one is not related to macroeconomics ?**
   (i) Determination of national income
   (ii) Economic growth
   (iii) Price Stability
   (iv) Price determination by a firm

7. **Which one is not a subject matter of microeconomics ?**
   (i) Consumption (ii) Production
   (iii) National Income (iv) Distribution

8. **Which one is a subject matter of macroeconomics ?**
   (i) National Income (ii) Price Stability
   (iii) International Trade (iv) All the above

9. **Which one of the following is the basis of microeconomics ?**
   (i) Aggregate demand and supply (ii) Price mechanism
   (iii) Business cycle (iv) All the above

10. **In microeconomics the study of equilibrium conditions are based on-**
    (i) A particular period
    (ii) Over a period of time
    (iii) Rates of change in micro variables
    (iv) All the above

11. **Which one is not related to macroeconomic analysis ?**
    (i) Price stability (ii) Price mechanism
    (iii) Balance of payments (iv) Economic growth

12. **Microeconomic theories are based on which assumption ?**
    (i) Full employment (ii) Under employment
    (iii) Unemployment (iv) Over employment

13. **'The General Theory of Employment, Interest and Money' was published in which year?**
    (i) 1933 (ii) 1936
    (iii) 1939 (iv) 1956

14. **The terms 'Micro' and 'Macro' were coined in economics in which year ?**
   (i) 1969 (ii) 1948
   (iii) 1933 (iv) 1914
15. **For the development of the studies in macroeconomics all credit goes to –**
   (i) Adam Smith (ii) Ragner Frisch
   (iii) Alfred Marshall (iv) J. M. Keynes

B. *Correct the statement, if necessary, without changing the underlined portions. (Each Carrying 1 Mark)*

1. The term 'Macro' is derived from the Greek word Mikros.
2. Microeconomics is called as aggregative economics.
3. Macroeconomics studies the actions and problems of individual economic units.
4. J.M. Keynes introduced the terms 'micro' and 'macro' in economics.
5. Great Depression of 1930s divided economics into two branches.
6. Maximization of profit is an objective of macroeconomics.
7. Microeconomics studies the determination of national income.
8. Microeconomic theories are developed on underemployment assumption.
9. Macroeconomic laws are developed on partial equilibrium technique.
10. Distinction between microeconomics and macroeconomics is not clear cut.
11. Public finance is a subject matter of microeconomics.
12. The classical economists believed in welfare economy.

C. *Answer the following questions in 2-3 sentences each. (Each question carrying 2 Marks)*

1. What is macroeconomics ?
2. What is microeconomics ?
3. What are the broad objectives of microeconomics ?
4. What are the broad objectives of macroeconomics ?
5. What are the subject matters of microeconomics ?
6. What are the subject matters of macroeconomics ?
7. Point out two importances of studying macroeconomics.

8. Point out two limitations of macroeconomics.
9. Point out the differences in the micro and macroeconomic laws.
10. Why the distinction between microeconomics and macroeconomics in not clear cut?

D. Distinguish between in Six Sentences (Carrying 3 Marks)

1. Microeconomics and Macroeconomics.
2. Pricing theory and Income theory.
3. Microeconomic equilibrium and Macroeconomic equilibrium.

E. Long Answer Type Questions (Carrying 7½ Marks)

1. What is Macroeconomics ? Make a distinction between microeconomics and macroeconomics.
2. What is macroeconomics ? Briefly discuss the subject matters of macroeconomics.
3. Discuss the importance of the study of macroeconomics.
4. What is macroeconomics ? Discuss the limitations of macroeconomics.

Answer to Q. N. A

1.	(iii)	2.	(i)	3.	(ii)	4.	(iii)	5.	(i)	6.	(iv)	7.	(iii)	8.	(iv)
9.	(ii)	10.	(i)	11.	(ii)	12.	(i)	13.	(ii)	14.	(iii)	15.	(iv)		

Answer to Q. N. B

1. Makros	2. Macroeconomics	3. Microeconomics
4. Ragner Frisch	5. Correct	6. Microeconomics
7. Macroeconomics	8. Full employment	9. General equilibrium
10. Correct	11. Macroeconomics	12. Laissez-Faire

❑❑❑

UNIT – VII

8. NATIONAL INCOME AND RELATED AGGREGATES

9. INCOME DETERMINATION

(AGGREGATE DEMAND AND AGGREGATE SUPPLY AND THEIR COMPONENTS, SIMPLE KEYNESIAN THEORY OF INCOME DETERMINATION)

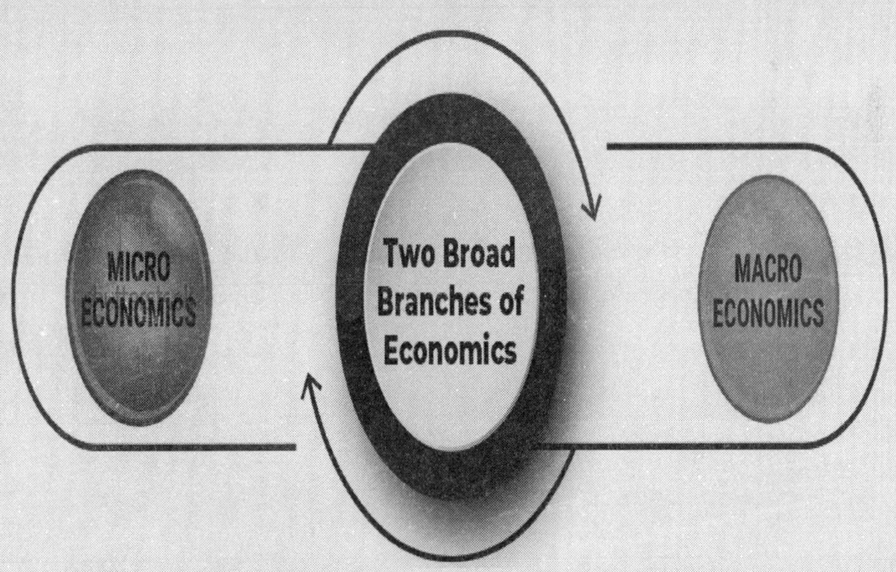

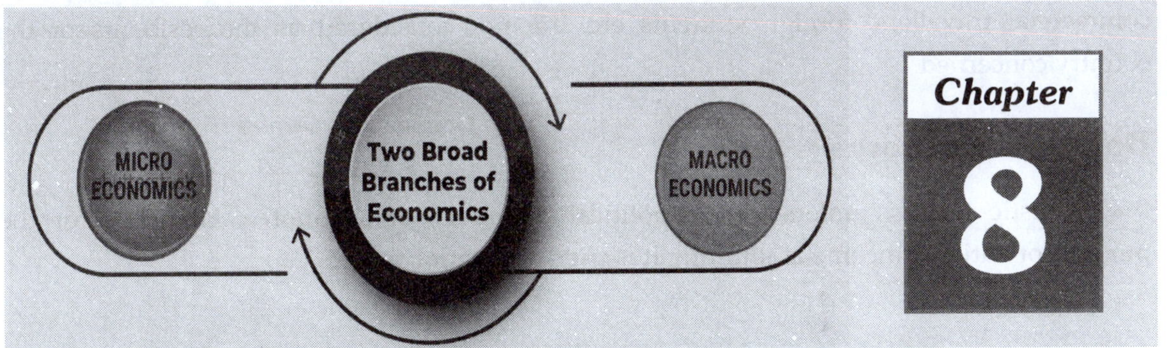

NATIONAL INCOME AND RELATED AGGREGATES

National income is a significant part of macroeconomic studies. As an important indicator of the overall economic performance of a country. National Income or the Net National Product can be defined as "the money value of all final goods and services produced in an economy by all the normal residents during an accounting year, including the net factor income received from abroad." The concept of 'national income' is very complex one and its understanding needs to understand some terms associated with it and some other aggregates related to national income studies.

Let us first understand the terminologies associated with the concept of national income.

Normal Residents

As stated above, national income is the money value of all final goods and services produced by the normal residents.

Here normal residents refer to –

(i) A citizen or may be an institution living or working in a country.

(ii) One who is residing in a country for a period of more than one year.

(iii) One whose centre of interest lies in the country where he/she is residing.

(iv) Nationals of a country residing in a foreign country temporarily.

However international organizations or institutions and the foreign employees working in those are not considered as the residents of that country. Similarly foreign tourists, staffs of the embassies, diplomats, members of foreign armed forces living in a country, commercial travellers, foreign students etc. are not considered as the residents of the country concerned.

Domestic Territory

Domestic territory refers to the political boundary of a country. However for the purpose of national income accounting it is used in a wider sense.

It includes –

1. The geographical area or political boundary of a country.
2. Territorial waters of the country.
3. Embassies, consulates and military establishments of a country established abroad.
4. Ships and aircrafts owned and operated by normal residents between two or more countries.
5. Fishing vessels, oil and natural gas rigs operated by the residents of a country on international water.

However the embassies, consulates and military establishment of foreign countries in a domestic country are not considered as its domestic territory. The branches of international organization and institution like that of the UNO, WHO etc. are not included in the domestic territory of the concerned country.

Accounting Year

Accounting year refers to a current year of which the national income is to be estimated. In India, 1st April to 31st March is considered as a financial accounting year.

Some Concepts related to National Income Accounting

While estimating national income and other related aggregates we come across certain concepts.

Let us first understand them.

1. Factor Income

Factor income refers to the income received by the factors of production (or their owners) for providing factor services in the process of production. Factor incomes include rent (paid for the use of land), wages (paid to the labourers), interest (paid for the use of capital) and profit (paid to the entrepreneur)

While estimating national income or domestic income the factor incomes of all the normal residents of a country are taken into account. Thus it is an earning concept. When the national income is estimated on the basis of these factor payments in producing the domestically produced output it is called as the national income at factor cost.

2. Transfer Income

Transfer income refers to the income received by individuals or institutions from the government or from any foreign source without providing any productive service. While estimating national income of a country transfer incomes received by its normal residents or institutions are not taken into account. These incomes are mostly received on social security grounds. Old age pension, widow pension, disabled pension, unemployment allowance, scholarship etc. are examples of transfer income.

Depreciation Cost

The cost incurred in the production process on the capital goods to keep them in working condition is called depreciation cost. The expenditure incurred on repairing a machine, replacing any part of it etc. are included in depreciation cost. It is also called cost of capital consumption. Depreciation cost is deducted from the gross value of output to get the net value.

Gross Value = Net Value + Depreciation

Net Value = Gross Value – Depreciation

Factor Cost

The cost incurred in the production process for making payments to various factors of production for rending their services is called factor cost. In national income estimation it is calculated by deducting Net Indirect Taxes imposed by the government on goods and services from the value of the products at market prices.

Value at Factor Cost = Value at Market Price – NIT

or, Value at Market Price = Value at Factor Cost + NIT

Value at market price refers to the money value of goods and services estimated on the basis of their prices prevailing in the market.

Net Indirect Tax (NIT)

Net Indirect Tax (NIT) is the difference between the indirect taxes imposed by the government on different goods and services and the subsidies or financial assistance given by the government to the enterprises for producing certain commodities.

NIT = IT – S   IT = Indirect tax
S = Subsidy

The concept of NIT is important in the sense that when the value of output produced in the country is estimated at factor cost at that time the value of NIT is deducted from the value of output at market price which helps in knowing the contribution of different factors of production towards the national income. NIT is always supposed to be positive.

Net Factor Income from Abroad (NFIa)

Net factor income from abroad is the difference between the factor income received from abroad, i.e. from the rest of the world and the factor income paid to the rest of the world.

NFIa = Factor income received from abroad – Factor income paid to abroad

NFIa may be either positive or zero or negative. That is –

(i) If factor income from abroad > Factor income paid to abroad then NFIa is positive.

(ii) If factor income from abroad = Factor income paid to abroad then NFIa is zero.

(iii) If factor income from abroad < Factor income paid to abroad then NFIa is negative.

NFIa has three components –

(i) Net compensation of employees.

(ii) Net income from property and entrepreneurship.

(iii) Net retained earnings.

While estimating national income NFIa is added to the domestic income. In this sense

National Income = Domestic Income + NFIa

Or, NFIa = National Income – Domestic Income

National Income and Related Aggregates

As stated earlier, national income refers to the money value of all final goods and services produced by the normal residents of the concerned country during an accounting year including the net factor income from abroad. However there are various concepts of national income which are called as aggregates related to national income. Each of these aggregates has a specific meaning in national income estimation.

On the basis of their gross and net value the aggregates related to national income are of four types :

(i) Gross Domestic Product (GDP)

(ii) Gross National Product (GNP)

(iii) Net Domestic Product (NDP)

(iv) Net National Product (NNP)

When these four aggregates are estimated at market prices and factor costs they give rise to 8 types of aggregates such as –

1. Gross Domestic Product at Market Price (GDP_{MP})
2. Gross Domestic Product at Factor Cost (GDP_{FC})
3. Net Domestic Product at Market Price (NDP_{MP})
4. Net Domestic Product at Factor Cost (NDP_{FC})
5. Gross National Product at Market Price (GNP_{MP})
6. Gross National Product at Factor Cost (GNP_{FC})
7. Net National Product at Market Price (NNP_{MP})
8. Net National Product at Factor Cost (NNP_{FC})

Let us discuss these aggregate concepts.

1. Gross Domestic Product at Market Price (GDP_{MP})

Gross Domestic Product at Market Price (GDP_{MP}) can be defined as the gross market value of all final goods and services produced with in the domestic territory of a country by all the producers, both residents and non-residents, during an accounting year. It is estimated by multiplying the volume of final goods and services with their prices prevailing in the market in the accounting year.

It is to be noted that GDP_{MP} is a gross value which includes the value of newly produced final goods and services, not the value of second hand goods. Moreover, since it is a gross value the cost of depreciation or capital consumption is included in it. The concept of GDP_{MP}

is the most basic concept. After calculating GDP_{MP} we can compute the other aggregates related to national income.

$$GDP_{MP} = \text{Domestic Output} \times \text{Market Price}$$

2. Gross Domestic Product at Factor Cost (GDP_{FC})

Gross domestic product at factor cost (GDP_{FC}) can be defined as the value of all final goods and services produced with in the domestic territory of a country by all producers during an accounting year estimated on the basis of payments made to the factors of production involved in producing those goods and services. GDP_{FC} is calculated by deducting the Net Indirect Taxes from the value of GDP_{MP}.

So symbolically,

$$GDP_{FC} = GDP_{MP} - NIT$$

It is to be noted that GDP_{FC} is always less than the GDP_{MP}.

$$GDP_{FC} < GDP_{MP}$$

3. Net Domestic Product at Market Price (NDP_{MP})

As an aggregate related to national income Net Domestic Product at market price (NDP_{MP}) can be defined as the value of all final goods and services produced with in the domestic territory of a country by all the producers, residents and non-residents, during an accounting year estimated on the basis of their market prices minus the depreciation cost or value of capital consumption. In other words it is estimated by deducting the depreciation cost (D) from the value of Gross Domestic Product at Market Price (GDP_{MP}).

Symbolically,

$$NDP_{MP} = GDP_{MP} - D$$

Thus, NDP_{MP} is always less than GDP_{MP} ($NDP_{MP} < GDP_{MP}$)

4. Net Domestic Product at Factor Cost (NDP_{FC})

As an aggregate related to national income Net Domestic Product at Factor Cost (NDP_{FC}) can be defined as the value of all final goods and services produced with in the domestic territory of a country by all the producers, residents or non-residents, during an accounting year estimated on the basis of the payments made to the factors of production involved in their production minus the depreciation cost or value of capital consumption. It is estimated either by deducting Net Indirect Taxes (NIT) from Net Domestic Product at Market Price (NDP_{MP}) or by deducting Depreciation Cost (D) and Net Indirect Taxes (NIT) from the Gross Domestic Product at Market Price (GDP_{MP}).

Symbolically,

$$NDP_{FC} = GDP_{MP} - D - NIT$$

$$\text{or, } NDP_{FC} = NDP_{MP} - NIT$$

NDP_{FC} is always less than NDP_{MP}

Thus $NDP_{FC} < NDP_{MP} < GDP_{MP}$

5. Gross National Product at Market Price (GNP_{MP})

Gross National Product at Market Price (GNP_{MP}) can be defined as the value of all final goods and services produced by the normal residents of a country during an accounting year estimated on the basis of their prices prevailing in the market in that accounting year. It is estimated by adding the Net Factor Income from abroad (NFIa) to the Gross Domestic Product at Market Price (GDP_{MP}).

Symbolically,

$$GNP_{MP} = GDP_{MP} + NFIa$$

Since NFIa may be either positive or zero or negative, so –

(i) If NFIa is positive then $GNP_{MP} > GDP_{MP}$

(ii) If NFIa is zero then $GNP_{MP} = GDP_{MP}$

(iii) If NFIa is negative then $GNP_{MP} < GDP_{MP}$

6. Gross National Product at Factor Cost (GNP_{FC})

Gross National Product at Factor Cost (GNP_{FC}) can be defined as the value of all final goods and services produced by the normal residents of a country during an accounting year estimated on the basis of the payments made to the factors of production involved in producing those goods and services. Thus it is estimated by deducting the Net Indirect Taxes (NIT) from the Gross National Product at Market Price (GNP_{MP}).

Symbolically,

$$GNP_{FC} = GNP_{MP} - NIT$$

or, $GNP_{FC} = GDP_{MP} + NFIa - NIT$ (Since $GNP_{MP} = GDP_{MP} + NFIa$)

GNP_{FC} can also be estimated by adding NFIa to the GDP_{FC}, that is –

$$GNP_{FC} = GDP_{FC} + NFIa$$

So, GNP_{FC} is less than GNP_{MP} and more than GDP_{FC}

7. Net National Product at Market Price (NNP_{MP})

Net National Product at Market Price (NNP_{MP}) can be defined as the value of all final goods and services produced by the normal residents of a country during an accounting year estimated on the basis of their prices prevailing in the market in the accounting year minus the depreciation cost or the value of capital consumption. It is estimated by deducting depreciation cost (D) and adding the Net Factor Income from abroad to the value of Gross Domestic Product at Market Price (GDP_{MP}).

Symbolically,

$$NNP_{MP} = GDP_{MP} - D + NFIa \Rightarrow NNP_{MP} = GNP_{MP} - D$$

$$\Rightarrow NNP_{MP} = NDP_{MP} + NFIa$$

The value of NNP_{MP} is always less than GNP_{MP} ($NNP_{MP} < GNP_{MP}$) but may be greater than or equal to or less than NDP_{MP} depending upon the value of NFIa. *i.e.* –

(i) If NFIa is positive, $NNP_{MP} > NDP_{MP}$

(ii) If NFIa is zero, $NNP_{MP} = NDP_{MP}$, and

(iii) If NFIa is negative, $NNP_{MP} < NDP_{MP}$

8. Net National Product at Factor Cost (NNP_{FC})

Net National Product at Factor Cost (NNP_{FC}) can be defined as the value of all final goods and services produced by the normal residents of a country during an accounting year estimated on the basis of the payments made to the factors of production involved in producing those final goods and services after deducting the depreciation cost and net indirect taxes and adding net factor income from abroad. NNP_{FC} actually reflects the national income of a country.

Symbolically –

$$NNP_{FC} = GDP_{MP} - D - NIT + NFIa$$
$$= NDP_{MP} - NIT + NFIa$$
$$= NDP_{FC} + NFIa$$

It is to be noted that the formula related to the estimation of different aggregates mentioned in the above discussion can be manipulated to compute different aggregates. For this it is important to remember the following relations between different aggregates –

1. GDP_{MP} = Volume of final goods and services × their market price
2. $GDP_{FC} = GDP_{MP} - NIT$
3. $GNP_{MP} = GDP_{MP} + NFIa$
4. $GNP_{FC} = GDP_{MP} + NFIa - NIT \Rightarrow GNP_{MP} - NIT$
5. $NDP_{MP} = GDP_{MP} - D$
6. $NDP_{FC} = GDP_{MP} - D - NIT \Rightarrow NDP_{MP} - NIT$
7. $NNP_{MP} = GDP_{MP} - D + NFIa \Rightarrow NDP_{MP} + NFIa$
8. $NNP_{FC} = GDP_{MP} - D - NIT + NFIa \Rightarrow NDP_{MP} - NIT + NFIa$

   $\Rightarrow NDP_{FC} + NFIa$

To be noted that –

(i) To change FC to MP, add NIT
(ii) To change MP to FC, deduct NIT
(iii) To change Gross to Net, deduct D
(iv) To change Net to Gross, add D
(v) To change Domestic to National, add NFIa
(vi) To change National to Domestic, deduct NFIa

Components of National Income

Broadly speaking the national income of a country has two components –

(i) Domestic Factor Income, and
(ii) Net Factor Income from abroad

Domestic Factor Income

Domestic factor income refers to the income generated to the owners of different factors of production which help in production of goods and services (output) inside domestic territory of a country. It includes income earned by the owners of factors of production such as land, labour, capital etc. for producing output during an accounting year.

It has three broad components –

(i) Compensation of employees

(ii) Operating surplus, and

(iii) Mixed-income of self-employed

Compensation of Employees

Compensation of employees refers to the payments made by the producers to their employees or workers for rendering their services in the process of production. This is paid in terms of salaries and wages and contributions to the social security schemes in favour of these employees and workers.

Operating Surplus

Operating surplus as a part of national income can be defined as the sum total of income earned by the owners of property, i.e. land and capital and from the entrepreneurship in the process of production. This is the sum of rent, interest and profit.

Mixed-Income of the Self-employed

Income of the self-employed persons from which the property income and labour income cannot be separated is called mixed-income. Income of doctors, lawyers, shop-keepers etc. are the examples of mixed-income. Such income includes rent, wage, interest and profit but cannot be separated.

Thus, Domestic Factor Income = Compensation of Employees + Operating Surplus + Mixed-income of the Self-employee

N.B. = Domestic Factor Income = NNP_{FC}

Net Factor Income from Abroad (NFIa)

Net Factor Income from abroad is the difference between the income earned by the factors owned by the normal residents of a country from abroad and income earned by the factors owned by the non-residents from the home country during an accounting year. This may either be positive or zero or negative.

National income is obtained by adding the domestic factor income and net factor income from abroad. Since the domestic factor income is equal to the net domestic product at factor cost (NDP_{FC}) so –

National Income = Domestic factor income + Net factor income from abroad

$= NDP_{FC} + NFIa$

$= NNP_{FC}$

$\therefore$ National income = NNP_{FC}

Other Aggregates

Other aggregates related to national income accounting are –

(i) National Disposable Income (Gross and Net)

(ii) Private Income

(iii) Personal Income

(iv) Personal Disposable Income

(v) Nominal National Income (Nominal GDP)

(vi) Real National Income (Real GDP)

National Disposable Income

National disposable income refers to the sum of the disposable or spendable income of all residents, institutional units and sectors during an accounting year. It is calculated by adding all current transfers received by resident institutional units from non-resident institutional units to the national income at market price and then subtracting all current transfers paid by resident institutional units to non-resident institutional units during an accounting year. It is to be noted that current transfers include current taxes on income, wealth, social security contributions, social benefits and other current transfers.

National disposable income can be put under two categories-

(i) Gross National Disposable Income

(ii) Net National Disposable Income

Gross National Disposable Income (GNDI)

Gross National Disposable Income is the sum of the gross disposable incomes of all resident institutional units of a country during an accounting year.

It is estimated as –

Gross National Disposable Income = Gross National Income at market price + All current transfers received by resident institutional units from the rest of the world – All current transfers paid by resident institutional units to the rest of the world.

Gross National Disposable Income is also defined as the sum total of Net National disposable income and Depreciation cost of the whole economy in an accounting year.

That is –

Gross National Disposable Income = Net National Disposable Income + Depreciation Cost

= Gross National Income at factor cost + NIT + Net Current transfers from abroad.

GNDI represents the income available to the nation for final consumption and gross saving.

Net National Disposable Income

Net National Disposable Income is the sum of the net disposable incomes of the resident institutional units of a country during an accounting year. It is estimated as –

Net National Disposable Income = Net National Income at Market Price + All current transfers received by resident units from the rest of the world – All current transfers paid to non-resident units

It is the net income at marker price available in the country for disposal during an accounting year. It can also be present as –

Net National Disposable Income = National Income + Net Current transfers from abroad + NIT

= Net Domestic Product at Factor Cost + NFIa + NIT + Net Current transfers from abroad

Private Income

Private income can be defined as the total income which accrues to private sector from all sources both within the domestic territory as well as from the rest of the world. Thus it does not include income of the government sector.

Private income is estimated as –

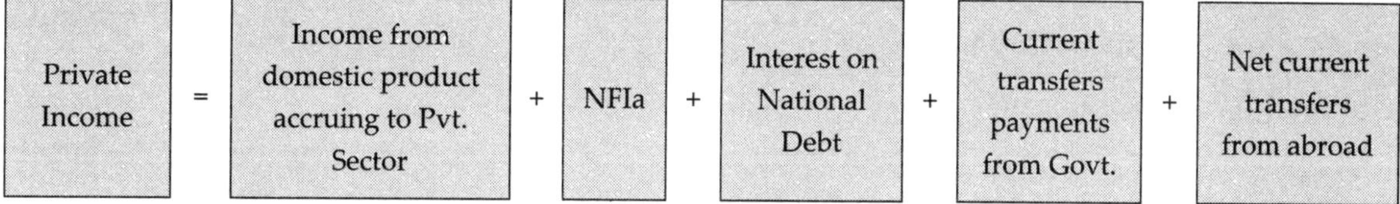

From National Income it can be calculated as –

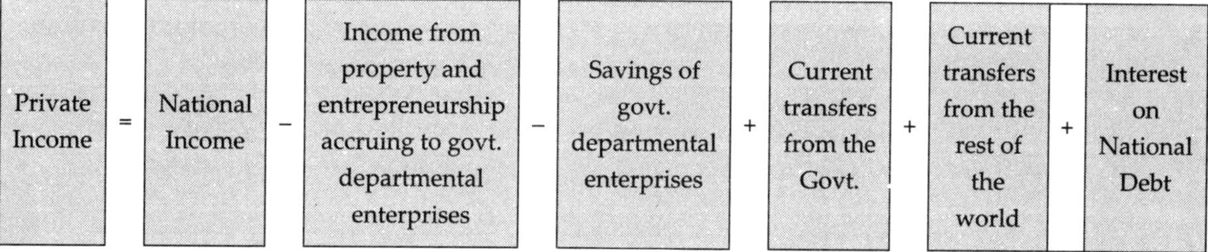

Distinction between National Income and Private Income

National Income	Private Income
1. National Income includes only factor payments	1. Private Income includes both factor payments and transfer payments.
2. National income = NDP_{FC} + NFIa	2. Private Income = NDP_{FC} – Surplus of Public Sector + NFIa + All transfer incomes + Interest on national debts
3. Interest on national debt is not included in national income.	3. Interest on national debt is included in private income.

Personal Income

Personal income refers to that part of private income which is received by the household only. Like private income it includes both factor income and transfer payments but does not include that part of the income of the corporate sector which does not accrue to the households, i.e. the corporate tax and saving. Personal income can be calculated both from National Income and Private Income.

Personal Income from National Income = National Income – Income from domestic product accruing to Public Sector – Corporate Tax – Corporate Savings + Transfer earnings from all sources + Interest on national debt

Personal Income from Private Income = Private Income – Corporate Tax – Corporate Savings

Distinction between Private Income and Personal Income

Private Income	Personal Income
1. Private income is a broad concept which includes the income of both private enterprises and households.	1. Personal income is a narrow concept which includes the actual income received by the household only.
2. It includes factor incomes, transfer incomes, corporate tax and corporate savings.	2. It includes factor incomes and transfer incomes but not corporate tax and corporate savings.
3. Private Income = Domestic Income accruing to Private Sector + NFIa + All transfer payments + Interest on national debts.	3. Personal Income = Private Income – Corporate Tax – Corporate Savings.

Personal Disposable Income

Disposable income refers to spendable income which can be actually consumed and saved. The income that is actually received by a persons or households, i.e. personal income, in an accounting year are not available to them for disposal or consumption. This is because government levy some personal taxes such as income tax, wealth tax etc on the personal income received by the household. So personal disposable income is that part of personal income which the individuals or households can actually spend, i.e. consume and save.

Personal disposable income is calculated by deducting personal taxes, fees and fines and all other payments made to the government from the personal income.

Thus, Personal Disposable Income = Personal Income – Personal Taxes Fees and Fines and Other government payments.

Since Personal Disposable Income (PDI) can either be consumed or save or both, PDI = C + S

Distinction between Personal Income and Disposable Personal Income

Personal Income	Personal Disposable Income
1. Personal income is a wider concept than personal disposable income which includes actual income received by the household but may not be spent.	1. Personal disposable income is a narrow concept as it includes only that part of personal income which can actually be spent, i.e. consumed or saved.

2. Personal income is calculated both from national income and private income.	2. It can be calculated directly from the personal income deducting taxes and other payments that is to be paid to the government.
3. Personal Income = National income – Corporate tax – Corporate saving – Social Security contributions + All transfer payment or, Personal Income = Private Income – Corporate Tax – Corporate Savings	3. Personal Disposable Income = Personal Income – Tax and all other governments.

How we get personal income and personal disposable income from National Income is shown below –

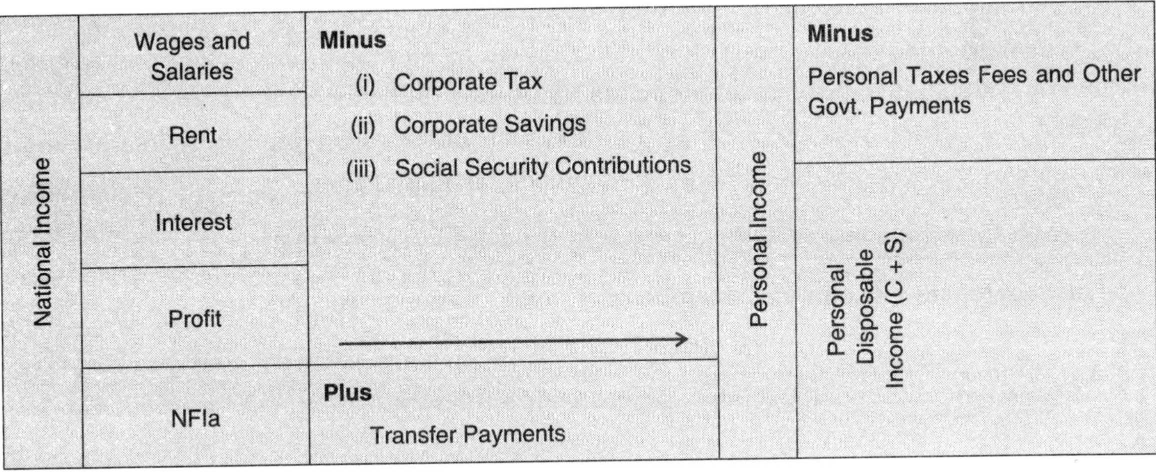

Nominal National Income (Nominal GDP)

National income refers to the sum of total income generated to the factors of production in the production of output with in the domestic territory and the net factor income from abroad during an account year. Thus-

National Income = Domestic Income + NFIa

National income can be evaluated in two ways –

(i) At the current prices, i.e. prices prevailing in the accounting year, which is termed as Nominal National Income.

(ii) At any previous year's prices of the commodities, taken as base year price, which is termed as Real National Income

Nominal National Income

Nominal national income or National income at current prices refers to the sum of total domestic income and net factor income from abroad estimated in terms of prices of goods prevailing in the market in the current year, i.e. in the year of accounting national income.

Thus –

Nominal National Income = GDP_{MP} – D – NIT + NFIa

Remember – When the Gross Domestic Product of a country during an accounting year is estimated at the prices prevailing in the market during the current or accounting year, it is called as Nominal GDP or GDP at current prices.

Real National Income

When the national income of a country during an accounting year is estimated in terms any previous year's prices of the commodities, taken as base year, it is called real national income or national income at constant prices. Thus, it is the value of the domestic products produced in a current year but estimated on the basis of the prices prevailing in a previous year, called as the base year. Real national income is calculated as –

Real National Income = GDP at Constant Prices – D – NIT + NFIa

This aggregate of national income, i.e. Real National Income reflects the actual performance of the economy over a period of time.

Remember – When the Gross Domestic Products are estimated on the basis of constant price or base year price, it is called Real GDP or GDP at constant price.

Conversion of Nominal National Income or National Income at Current Price into Real National Income or National Income at Constant Price

The real rational income or national in come at constant prices reflects the actual performance of an economy. Because the economic development or welfare depends upon the increase in the real output not its nominal value. The nominal value of the national output might have gone up due to rise in prices which will not reflect the actual performance. So to know the actual performance of an economy estimation of real national income bears much significance. For this we convert the nominal national income into real national income. For this conversion the formula is –

$$\text{Real National Income} = \frac{\text{National Income at Current Prices}}{\text{Current Year Price Index}} \times 100$$

$$\text{Current Year Price Index} = \frac{\text{Current Year Price}}{\text{Base Year Price}} \times 100$$

Example

Let the current year (2023) national income is ₹ 520 crore and the current year price index is 300 as against the national in come of 2018 (base year) was ₹ 100 crore. Then the real national income in 2023 will be –

$$\text{Real National Income} = \frac{\text{National Income at Current Prices}}{\text{Current Year Price Index}} \times 100$$

Here, National income at current prices = ₹ 520 crore

Current Year Price Index = 300

$$\therefore \text{ Real National Income} = \frac{₹\,520}{300} \times 100 = ₹\ 130 \text{ crore}$$

The base year index is always taken as 100.

From the example it is clear that though the national income at current prices in 2023 is 5.2 times than that of 2018 yet the real national income is only 1.3 times. The massive increase in the current year's nominal national income is due to increase in prices in the current year 3 times the prices in the base year.

Thus, the nominal national income does not reflect the actual performance of an economy. It is the real national income or national income at constant price which reflects the actual performance of an economy.

Distinction between Nominal and Real National Income

Nominal National Income	Real National Income
1. The sum of total domestic income and net factor incomes from abroad when estimated in terms of prices of goods and services prevailing in the market in the current or accounting year is called nominal national income.	1. The sum of total domestic income and net factor incomes from abroad of a current year is estimated in terms of a previous year or base year's price then it is called real national income.
2. Nominal National Income = GDP_{P1} – D – NIT + NFIa (P_1 = Current Year Price = MP)	2. Real National Income = GDP_{P0} – D – NIT + NFIa (P_0 = base year price)

3. It does not reflect the actual performance of an economy.	3. It reflects the actual performance of an economy.
4. It is also called National Income at Current Price.	4. It is also called National Income at constant price.

Remember –The distinction between Nominal GDP or GDP at Current Price and Real GDP or GDP at Constant Price is same as the distinction between Nominal National Income and Real National Income, as made above. Only the other components (D, NIT and NFIa) are not taken into account.

WHAT WE LEARNT

1. National income is the value of all final goods and services produced by the normal residents of a country during an accounting year including the NFIa.
2. Normal residents of a country include the citizens, institutions living and working in a country, one who is residing in a country for a period of more than one year having centre of interest there and rationals of a country residing in a foreign country temporarily.
3. Domestic territory of a country includes the political boundary, territorial waters of the country, her embassy or consulate and military establishments abroad, oil and natural gas rigs of the country in international water, air and water ways.
4. Accounting year refers to a financial year not a calendar year.
5. Factor income refers to the income received by the factors of production in the form of rent, wage, interest and profit.
6. Transfer income refers to the income received by individuals or institutions from government or from any sources, internal or external, without providing any productive service.
7. While estimating national income only factor incomes are included not the transfer income.
8. The cost incurred in the production process on the capital goods to keep them in working condition is called depreciation cost or cost of capital consumption.
9. Net Indirect Tax (NIT) is the difference between Indirect Tax and Subsidy (NIT = IT – S)

10. Net Factor Income from abroad (NFIa) is the difference between the factor incomes received from the rest of the world and the factor income paid to the rest of the world.
11. Net Factor Income from abroad can be either positive or zero or negative.
12. GDP_{MP} is the value of domestic output estimated in terms at market price. (GDP_{MP} = Domestic Output × Market Price)
13. GDP_{FC} is the difference between the value of domestic output at market price and net indirect tax. ($GDP_{FC} = GDP_{MP} - NIT$)
14. NDP_{MP} is the difference between the value of Gross Domestic Product at market price and the depreciation cost. ($NDP_{MP} = GDP_{MP} - D$)
15. NDP_{FC} is the difference between the value of net domestic product at market price and the net indirect tax. ($NDP_{FC} = NDP_{MP} - NIT$)
16. GNP_{MP} is the sum of the value of domestic output at market price and the net factor income from abroad. ($GNP_{MP} = GDP_{MP} + NFIa$)
17. GNP_{FC} is the difference between the value of Gross National Product at market price and net indirect tax. ($GNP_{FC} = GDP_{MP} - NIT$)
18. NNP_{MP} is the sum of the value of net domestic product at market price and the net factor income from abroad. ($NNP_{MP} = NDP_{MP} + NFIa$)
19. NNP_{FC} is the sum of the value of net domestic product at factor cost and the net factor income from abroad. ($NNP_{FC} = NDP_{FC} + NFIa$)
20. NNP_{FC} is the actual measure of National Income ($NNP_{FC} = NY$)
21. National income of a country has two components – (i) Domestic Factor Income, and (ii) Net Factor Income from abroad.
22. Domestic Factor Income is the sum of compensation of employees, operating surplus and mixed-incomes of self-employed.
23. Operating surplus is the sum of rent, interest and profit.
24. The income in which the share of property and labour cannot be separated is called mixed income.
25. Domestic factor income is equal to NDP_{FC}
26. National Disposable Income is the sum of the disposable or spendable incomes of all residents, institutional units and sectors during an accounting year.

27. The total income of private sectors from all sources both within the domestic territory and from the rest of the world is called as the private income.
28. National income includes only factor payments, not transfer payments.
29. Private income includes both factor payments and transfer payments.
30. That part of private income which is received by the household only is called personal income.
31. That part of personal income which is actually consumed and saved is called personal disposable income.
32. National income of an accounting year estimated on the basis of the current price or prices prevailing in accounting year is called Nominal National Income or National Income at Current Prices.
33. National income of an accounting year estimated on the basis of a previous year (base year) prices is called Real National Income or National Income at constant prices.
34. Real National Income reflects the actual economic performance of a country.

QUESTIONS FOR REVIEW

A. *Choose the correct answer from the given alternatives in each question. (Each Carrying 1 Mark)*

1. Which one is a significant part of macroeconomics ?

(i) Consumption (ii) Production

(iii) National Income (iv) Distribution

2. Who is a normal resident of a country ?

(i) A citizen

(ii) One who is residing is the country for more than 1 year

(iii) One whose centre of interest lies in the residing country

(iv) All the above

3. Which one of the following is not a factor income ?

(i) Mixed income (ii) Rent

(iii) Wage (iv) Interest

4. **Which one of the following is not an earning concept ?**

   (i) Factor income (ii) Transfer income

   (iii) Mixed income (iv) None of the above

5. **Which one is received without rendering any productive service ?**

   (i) Transfer income (ii) Factor income

   (iii) Mixed income (iv) None of the above

6. **Old age pension is an example of –**

   (i) Factor income (ii) Mixed income

   (iii) Transfer income (iv) None of the above

7. **Which one is deducted from the gross value to get the net value ?**

   (i) Net Indirect Tax (ii) Depreciation Cost

   (iii) Net Factor Income from abroad (iv) Subsidy

8. **Which one is added to the value at factor cost to get the value at Market Price ?**

   (i) Depreciation Cost (ii) Net Factor Income from abroad

   (iii) Net Indirect Tax (iv) Indirect Tax

9. **Which one of the following may either be positive or zero or negative ?**

   (i) Net factor income from abroad (ii) Factor cost

   (iii) Net Indirect tax (iv) Depreciation cost

10. **Which one is deducted from National Income to get Net Factor Income from abroad ?**

    (i) Compensation of the employees (ii) Domestic income

    (iii) Transfer income (iv) Private income

11. **Value at domestic output when multiplied with the prices prevailing in the market is called -**

    (i) National Income (ii) GDP_{MP}

    (iii) GDP_{FC} (iv) GNP_{MP}

12. **When Net Indirect Tax is deducted from the Gross Domestic Product at market price it gives to -**

    (i) GDP_{MP} (ii) GNP_{MP}

    (iii) GDP_{FC} (iv) None of the above

13. **Which one is deducted from GDP_{MP} to get NDP_{MP}?**

(i) NFIa (ii) Depreciation Cost
(iii) NIT (iv) All the above

14. **Which one is added to GDP_{MP} to get GNP_{MP} ?**

(i) NFIa (ii) NIT
(iii) Depreciation Cost (iv) All the above

15. **When NFIa is positive which one is true ?**

(i) $GNP_{MP} > GDP_{MP}$ (ii) $GDP_{MP} > GNP_{MP}$
(iii) $GNP_{MP} = GDP_{MP}$ (iv) None of the above

16. **When NFIa is added to NDP_{MP} it gives –**

(i) GNP_{MP} (ii) NNP_{FC}
(iii) NDP_{FC} (iv) NNP_{MP}

17. **Which one is equal to national income ?**

(i) GDP_{MP} (ii) NNP_{FC}
(iii) NNP_{MP} (iv) NDP_{FC}

18. **If GDP_{MP} = ₹ 5,000 cr. D = 50 cr. IT = 250 cr. S = 80 cr. NFIa = –70 cr. Then what is NNP_{FC}?**

(i) ₹ 4710 cr. (ii) ₹ 4550 cr.
(iii) ₹ 4690 cr. (iv) ₹ 5190 cr.

19. **Which one is not a component of domestic factor income ?**

(i) Compensation of employees (ii) Transfer payments
(iii) Operating surplus (iv) Mixed income of self-employed

20. **The sum of rent, interest and profit is called –**

(i) Mixed-income of self-employed (ii) Transfer payments
(iii) Operating surplus (iv) None of the above

21. **Domestic factor income is equal to which one ?**

(i) NDP_{FC} (ii) GDP_{FC}
(iii) GNP_{FC} (iv) NNP_{FC}

22. **The sum of the disposable income of all residents, institutional units and sectors during an accounting year is called –**

(i) Disposable income (ii) Personal disposable income
(iii) National income (iv) National disposable income

23. Total income which accrues to private individuals and private sectors from all sources is called –

(i) National Income (ii) Personal Income

(iii) Private Income (iv) None of the above

24. Which one includes both factor payments and transfer payments ?

(i) Private Income (ii) Personal Income

(iii) National Disposable Income (iv) All the above

25. Which one is not included in the national income ?

(i) Factor Income (ii) Interest on national debt

(iii) Operating Surplus (iv) Mixed-income of Self-employed

26. Corporate Tax and Corporate Savings are not included in which one ?

(i) National Income (ii) Private Income

(iii) Personal Income (iv) All the above

27. The income which an individual can actually spend or save is –

(i) Personal Income (ii) National Disposable Income

(iii) Personal Disposable Income (iv) Private Income

28. Which one reflects the actual performance of an economy ?

(i) Gross Domestic Product (ii) Real Gross Domestic Product

(iii) Real National Income (iv) Nominal National Income

29. National income at constant price is estimated on the basis of the prices of _____

(i) Current Year

(ii) Base Year

(iii) Average of Current and Base Year

(iv) None of these

30. Which one is equal to nominal national income ?

(i) GDP_{MP} (ii) GNP_{MP}

(iii) NNP_{MP} (iv) NNP_{FC}

B. *Correct the statement, if necessary, without changing the underlined portions. (Each Carrying 1 Mark)*

1. National income refers to the income received by the factors of production.
2. When national income is estimated on the basis of factor payments it is called as national income at market price.

3. Income received by individuals without providing any productive service is called transfer income.
4. Old-age pension is an example of factor income.
5. Depreciation cost is added to the gross value of output to get the net value.
6. Net Indirect Tax is the sum of the indirect taxes and subsidies.
7. Net indirect tax is always supposed to be negative.
8. If factor income from abroad is greater than factor income paid to abroad, then Net Factor Income is negative.
9. When net factor income from abroad is negative Gross National Product is greater than Gross Domestic Product.
10. While estimating national income net factor income from abroad is deducted from the domestic income.
11. Gross Domestic Product at market price is always greater than Gross Domestic Product at factor cost.
12. The sum of Gross Domestic Product and Net Factor Income from abroad is called Net Domestic Product.
13. The sum of rent, interest and profit is called mixed income.
14. The income in which rent, wage, interest and profit cannot be separated is called operating surplus.
15. Net National Product at factor cost is called domestic income.
16. Private income includes factor income and transfer income.
17. Interest on national debt is included in national income.
18. Personal disposable income is more than personal income.
19. Personal income can be actually consumed or saved.
20. Real national income reflects the performance of an economy.

C. *Answer the following questions in 2-3 sentences each. (Each question carries 2 Marks)*

1. What is national income ?
2. What do you mean by normal residents ?
3. What do you mean by domestic territory in a national income accounting ?
4. What is an accounting year ?

5. What is factor income ?
6. What is transfer income ?
7. What is depreciation cost ? (Cost of capital consumption)
8. What is factor cost ?
9. What is net indirect tax ?
10. What is net factor income from abroad ?
11. What are the components of net factor income ?
12. What is Gross Domestic Product ?
13. What is Gross National Product ?
14. What is Net Domestic Product ?
15. What is Net National Product ?
16. What is domestic factor income ?
17. What is compensation of employees ?
18. What is Operating surplus ?
19. What is Mixed-income of self-employed ?
20. What is national disposable income ?
21. What is private income ?
22. What is personal income ?
23. What is personal disposable income ?
24. What is nominal national income ?
25. What is real national income ?

D. *Distinguish between the following in Six Sentences each. (Each Carrying 3 Marks)*

1. Factor Income and Transfer Income.
2. GDP_{MP} and GDP_{FC}
3. GNP_{MP} and GNP_{FC}
4. NDP_{MP} and NDP_{FC}
5. NNP_{MP} and NNP_{FC}
6. Gross National Disposable Income and Net National Disposable Income.

7. National Income and Private Income.
8. Private Income and Personal Income.
9. Personal Income and Personal Disposable Income
10. Nominal National Income and Real National Income

E. Long Answer Type Questions (Carrying 7½ Marks)

1. Discuss different concepts related to national income accounting.
2. Briefly discuss different aggregates related to national income accounting.
3. What is National Income ? Discuss the components of National Income.

Answer to Q. N. A

1.	(iii)	2.	(iv)	3.	(i)	4.	(ii)	5.	(i)	6.	(iii)	7.	(ii)	8.	(iii)
9.	(i)	10.	(ii)	11.	(ii)	12.	(iii)	13.	(ii)	14.	(i)	15.	(i)	16.	(iv)
17.	(ii)	18.	(i)	19.	(ii)	20.	(iii)	21.	(i)	22.	(iv)	23.	(iii)	24.	(i)
25.	(ii)	26.	(ii)	27.	(iii)	28.	(iii)	29.	(ii)	30.	(iii)				

Answer to Q. N. B

1. Factor Income	2. Factor Cost	3. Correct
4. Transfer Income	5. deducted from	6. difference between
7. Positive	8. Positive	9. Positive
10. added to	11. correct	12. Gross National Product
13. Operating Surplus	14. Mixed-income	15. National Income
16. Correct	17. Personal Income	18. less than
19. Personal disposable income	20. Correct	

❑❑❑

INCOME DETERMINATION

(AGGREGATE DEMAND AND AGGREGATE SUPPLY AND THEIR COMPONENTS, SIMPLE KEYNESIAN THEORY OF INCOME DETERMINATION)

The study of income determination is a vital part of macroeconomics. The classical economists, in fact, did not propounded any systematic theory on income determination. Broadly speaking, they were not concerned with the determination of income, output and employment. They assumed full employment of resources including labour and were more concerned with the efficient allocation of resources through free forces of market mechanism, *i.e.*, without state intervention. They believed that full employment is a normal situation and any deviation from this was regarded as temporary as the automatic market mechanism will soon lead the economy towards full employment. The classical theory of employment and output was based on the idea of J.B. Say and A.C. Pigou, in the name of **'Say's Law of Market'** and **'Pigou's Wage Price Flexibility Theory'**.

However, the Great Depression of 1930s (1929–33) proved the classical theories and their full employment assumption wrong as they failed to revive the global economies from the crisis of the Great Depression. This made J.M. Keynes to have a deeper study of the economic crisis, its causes and what could be the solution. His efforts were published in the form of a book named, **"The General Theory of Employment, Interest and Money"**, in the year 1936. In his book he refuted the classical postulates and theories and brought a revolutionary change in the economic thinking strengthening the study of macroeconomics. In his book he presented a comprehensive theory of income determination which later became the core of macroeconomic analysis in the name of "Principle of Effective Demand'.

According to Keynes employment in an economy and hence income depends on the effective demand which is determined by the equality between the aggregate demand and aggregate supply (AD = AS). To him an increase in the level of effective demand will tend to raise the volume of employment and income. Thus aggregate demand and aggregate supply are the two main determinants of the level of employment and income. Moreover, in short-run since the aggregate supply is more or less stable, it is the aggregate demand which plays a crucial role in determining the level of employment and income in an economy. On this backdrop, let us first understand what is aggregate demand and what is aggregate supply.

Aggregate Demand

Aggregate demand refers to the total demand for goods and services produced in an economy during a given period of time at a given level of employment. In other words, aggregate demand can be defined as the total amount of money which all the buyers in different sectors of an economy are ready to spend on various goods and services produced in an economy during a given time period at a given level of employment at the given price level. In a 4-sector economy the aggregate demand of economy consists of four components.

There are –

1. Household Consumption Demand (C)
2. Private Investment Demand (I)
3. Government demand for Goods and Services (G)
4. Net-Export Demand (X–M)

Let us discuss these components of aggregate demand (AD)

1. Household Consumption Demand (C)

Household consumption demand or expenditure refers to the total volume of final goods and services demanded or the expenditure on total volume of final goods and services incurred by all the households in the economy for consumption purpose during a given time period. The household consumption demand depends upon the disposable income of the households. The functional relationship between consumption expenditure (C) and personal disposable income (Y) is stated as consumption function or **propensity to consume.** It states that as income increases consumption expenditure also increases but less than proportionately.

Symbolically if the consumption function is –

$$\left.\begin{aligned} C &= f(Y) \\ MPC &= \frac{\Delta C}{\Delta Y} < 1 \end{aligned}\right\} \quad \begin{aligned} &Y = \text{disposable income} \\ &MPC = \text{Marginal propensity to consume} \end{aligned}$$

Consumption function in a schedule form shows different amounts of consumption expenditure at different levels of disposable income.

This is presented below.

Consumption Function

Personal Disposable Income (Y) (₹)	Consumption Expenditure or Demand (C) (₹)	Saving (S) (₹)	MPC	APC
0	100	–100	–	–
100	175	–75	0.75	1.75
200	250	–50	0.75	1.25
300	325	–25	0.75	1.08
400	400	0	0.75	1
500	475	25	0.75	0.95
600	550	50	0.75	0.92
700	625	75	0.75	0.89

The schedule shows the consumption expenditure is positive (₹ 100) even when the personal disposable income is zero (Y = 0). This is called as **autonomous consumption,** *i.e.* consumption independent of the level of income. Then when income starts increasing from ₹ 100 cr. to ₹ 200 cr., ₹ 300 cr., ₹ 400 cr. and soon the consumption expenditure is also increasing from ₹ 175 cr. to ₹ 250 cr., ₹ 325 cr., ₹ 400 cr. and so on respectively, but less than increase in income. Thus the consumption expenditure and disposable income are positively related. Since the disposable income is the sum of consumption expenditure and saving, saving has been negative upto the equality between the disposable income and consumption expenditure. Then the saving has become positive with further increase in the disposable income.

In the schedule we have shown two more concepts related to consumption function, they are –

(i) Marginal Propensity to Consume (MPC)

(ii) Average Propensity to Consume (APC)

Marginal Propensity to Consume (MPC)

Marginal propensity to consume can be defined as the rate of change in consumption expenditure with respect to a given change in disposable income. In other words it is the ratio of change in consumption expenditure (ΔC) to change in disposable income (ΔY).

That is $\boxed{MPC = \frac{\Delta C}{\Delta Y}}$

On the basis of Keynesian Fundamental Psychological law of consumption which states that as income increases consumption expenditure also increases but less than proportionately. That is $\Delta C < \Delta Y$.

So $MPC = \frac{\Delta C}{\Delta Y} < 1$

In the table drawn above, in the MPC column we have shown the value of MPC at different level of income as 0.75, *i.e.,* less than 1 (<1). Of course it may not be the same for all levels of disposable income, we have shown it as the same for the sake of simplicity in determining the slope of the consumption function when presented graphically.

Average Propensity to Consume (APC)

Average propensity to consume can be defined as the ratio of consumption expenditure (C) to the disposable income (Y).

That is – $\boxed{APC = \frac{C}{Y}}$

The APC column in the table shows the fraction of income that is devoted to consumption expenditure. The column shows as the income increasing the average propensity to consume is constantly decreasing.

We know the disposable income is the sum of consumption expenditure and saving. As shown in the saving column, it is negative till the equality between disposable income and consumption expenditure (Y = C), which is called **the break-even point,** where saving is zero. Before the break-even income APC > 1, at the break-even level of income APC = 1 and after the break-even level of income APC < 1.

In the figure personal disposable income is presented on the OX-axis and consumption expenditure and saving are presented on the OY-axis. OZ is the income consumption equality (Y = C) line. The consumption function C = f(Y) starts from point 'a' on the Y-axis representing 'oa' is the autonomous consumption. The consumption function moving upward indicates consumption expenditure increases with the increase in income but the slope of the consumption function C = f(Y) indicates the increase in consumption expenditure is less than the increase in income. Point 'E' is the break-even point where Y = C. Right below this point the saving function 'S' intersects the base line indicating zero saving. The slope of the consumption function represents the MPC < 1. Prior to the breakeven point the saving function is in negative zone indicating negative saving.

Consumption function is graphically presented in the figure drawn below :

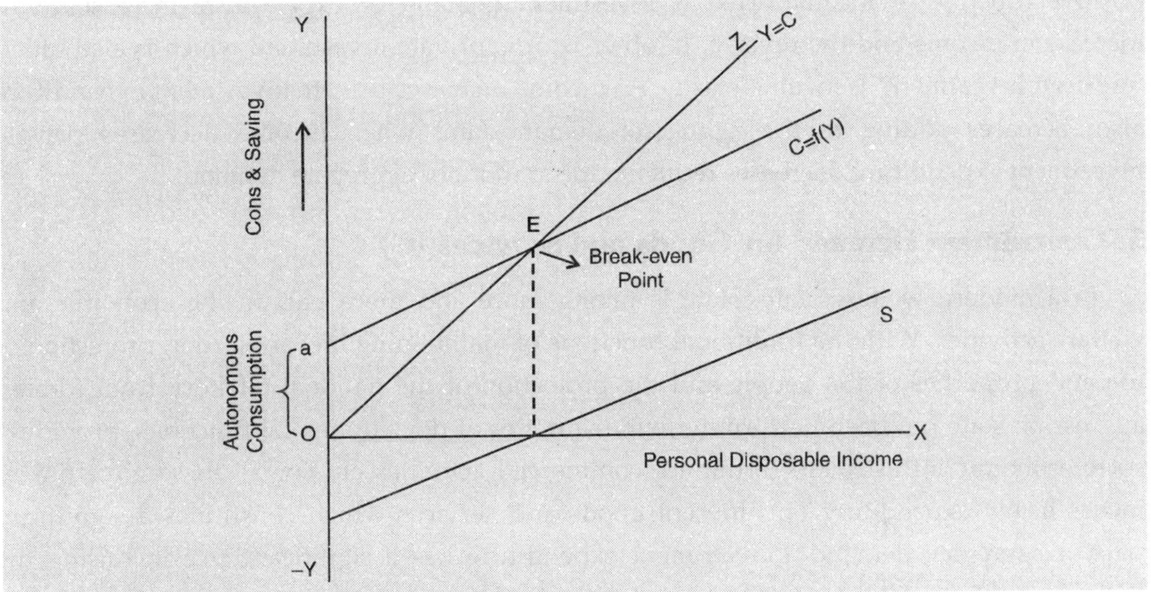

Consumption is a direct function of disposable income of course several other factors also influence consumption expenditure but according to Keynes such factors do not change in short-run. So, he assumed consumption function to remain stable in short-run. This is the reason why we have shown a constant MPC on the consumption schedule drawn earlier.

2. Investment Demand (I)

Private investment demand as a component of aggregate demand can be defined as the expenditure incurred by the private sector on the creation of new capital assets, such as machines, plants, factory building, tools and inventories etc.

The amount of private investment expenditure depends upon the level of income, marginal efficiency of capital (MEC) and rate of interest (r). Of these three important factors so long as the MEC is greater than rate of interest (MEC > r) the prospective yield from investment remains positive and encourage private investment and hence aggregate demand or expenditure will increase. The equilibrium amount or optimum amount of investment is reached at that level where MEC = r.

However, the rate of interest is policy disciplined and remains more or less stable in short-run. So it is MEC which is an important determinant of investment expenditure. But MEC is determined by the prospective yields from the investment and the price of capital which again depends upon the state of business activities which is determined by the level of demand and hence income. So like consumption expenditure investment expenditure is a positive function of income. That is investment demand or expenditure increases with increase in income and the reverse. In other words, private investment which is also called **'induced investment'** is income-elastic. As income increases private investment expenditure also increases adding to the aggregate demand and when income decreases private investment expenditure decreases reducing the amount of aggregate demand.

3. Government Demand for Goods and Services (G)

In a modern welfare state, state is taking more and more part in the economic and welfare activities. With the traditional functions of maintaining law and order, protection of life and properties of the people and the protection of the national territory from foreign aggression state has been performing wide varieties of developmental functions, providing socio-economic infrastructure, running commercial activities etc For all these government incurs heavy expenditure on different goods and services which constitutes a significant part of aggregate demand. Government expenditure has a significant role in raising the level of aggregate demand, particularly during the depressionary situations.

4. Net Export Demand (X-M)

In the present days almost all the economies are open economies have trade relations with each other. So Foreign trade plays a significant role in the working of an economy. Every country exports a number of things to the rest of the world (X) and imports a number of things from the rest of the world (M). Net export is the difference between exports and imports (X-M) of a country during a given period. This also constitutes a part of the aggregate demand. Net export is the only component of aggregate demand which may either be positive or zero or negative, accordingly affecting the aggregate demand.

Thus the aggregate demand or expenditure is the sum of consumption demand (c), private investment demand (I), government demand for goods and services (G) and the net export demand (X-M). That is :

$$AD = C + I + G + (X-M)$$

AGGREGATE SUPPLY

Aggregate supply refers to the flow of final goods and services in the economy during a given period of time. In other words, it refers to the total amount of final goods and services produced by all the producing enterprises in an economy during a given period of time at different level of employment, offened for sale at given prices.

Aggregate supply depends upon two factors :

(i) The general price level, and

(ii) The extent of capacity utilization.

The general price level determines the desire to supply. i.e. more will be supplied at higher price level and the reverse. On the other hand the extent of capacity utilization affects the capacity to supply. The capacity to supply i.e. the potential output is affected by two factors :

(i) availability of factors of production i.e. land, labour, capital and entrepreneurs, and

(ii) productivity or efficiency of the factors of production.

When we express the volume of aggregate supply in terms of prices, i.e. the prices at which all the producers are willing to sell their products that is called as **aggregate supply price.** In this sense aggregate supply price refers to the proceeds or income that all the producers must expert to receive by selling their products produced at different level of employment. In other words the aggregate supply price of different amount of aggregate supply is equal to the sum of factor costs for producing the given amount of output which the producers must expect to get while supplying or offering for sale. Since the value of output at factor cost is equal to national income aggregate supply depends on the level of income which is the basis of proceeds from sale of output. This also implies that aggregate supply at different level of employment is directly and proportionally related to national income. This direct relationship between national income (at factor cost) and the aggregate supply in terms of money (aggregate supply price) is shown in the table – Aggregate supply schedule, drawn below.

National Income ₹ Cr.	Aggregate Supply ₹ Cr.
0	0
100	100
200	200
400	400
800	800
1600	1600
3200	3200

The aggregate supply schedule shows a direct relationship between national income and aggregate supply and the figures are shown same in both the columns as the aggregate supply are shown at factor costs and national income is equal to the sum of the factor cost for producing different level of output.

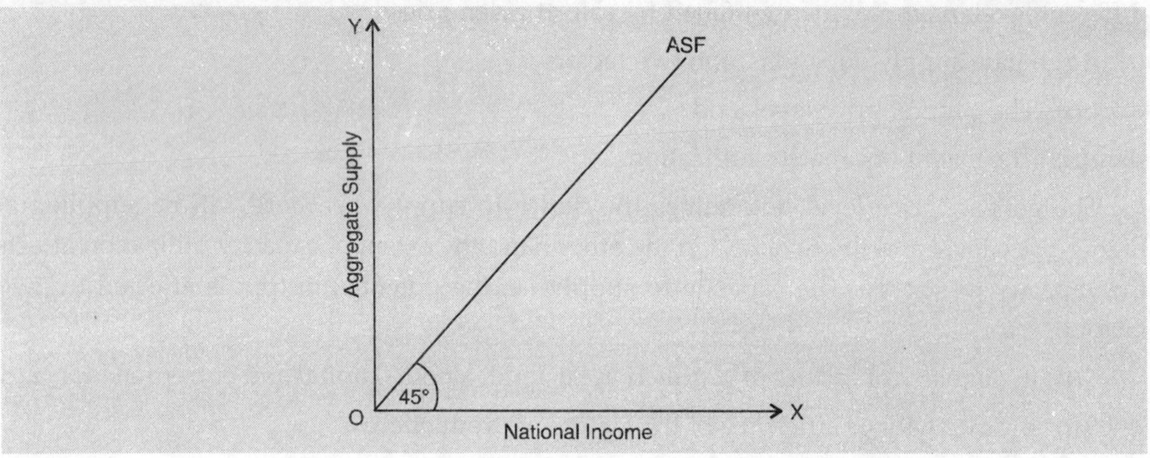

The aggregate supply presented graphically gives us the aggregate supply function (ASF). The ASF) line drawn with a 45° angle represents a linear direct relationship between national income and aggregate output supplied for sale at the given prices. That is at all points on the aggregate supply function (ASF) line the national income and the aggregate output are the same.

SIMPLE KEYNESIAN THEORY OF INCOME DETERMINATION

Simple Keynesian theory of income determination is related to his theory of employment determination and states that in short-run the level of income of a country will change as a result of change in the level of labour employment. In the short-run when capital stock, techniques of production, efficiency of labour, size of population, forms of business organizations etc. remain unchanged, income is a function of labour employment. In fact, both income and employment go together, that is the higher the level of employment, the higher will be the level of income and the reverse.

As the level of employment is determined by aggregate demand (AD) and aggregate supply (AS), the level of income, according to Keynes, is also determined by aggregate demand and aggregate supply. However, he explained his simple theory of income determination through his income-expenditure analysis, in which income is refered to aggregate supply and expenditure is refered to aggregate demand, relating to a two-sector economy comprising of household sector and business sector. To him, **the equilibrium level**

of national income in a two sector economy, with a fixed price level, is determined where the aggregate output (i.e. income or aggregate supply) equals the aggregate expenditure on goods and services by both the sectors (i.e. the aggregate demand). Of course this simple theory of income determination can be extended to explain income determination in a modern four-sector economy, which includes government sector and foreign-trade sector.

Now let us discuss his simple theory.

Assumptions

Keynesian simple theory of income determination is based on the following assumptions :

1. There are two sectors in the economy-household sector and business sector.
2. Aggregate expenditure has two components-household consumption expenditure (C) and private investment expenditure (I). Thus AE = C + I (AD = C + I).
3. Capital stock, state of technology, size of population, efficiency of labour etc. are constant.
4. Planned investment expenditure remains constant.
5. Business sectors are non-corporate type, i.e. all profits are distributed since there is no government sector to impose tax on business sectors.
6. National income is the same as the sum of personal income and sum of personal disposable income as there is no taxes, no subsidies or transfer payments in the absence of government intervention.
7. The economy has unemployed labour forces and other resources.
8. The theory is related to short-run analysis.

With the above assumptions Keynes's simple theory states that equilibrium national income is determined at that point where aggregate expenditure (AE) or aggregate demand (AD) is equal to aggregate output or aggregate supply (AS).

Aggregate Expenditure or AD

Aggregate demand (AD) or aggregate expenditure (AF) in a two sector economy is comprised of household consumption demand (or, expenditure) (C) and the expenditure made by the business sector on investment, i.e. invest demand (I).

That is AD = C + I or AE = C + I.

Consumption Demand (C)

In Keynesian analysis consumption demand (C) depends on the propensity to consume and the level of national income (Y). In short-run the propensity to consume is assumed to be constant. So, given the autonomous consumption and propensity to consume consumption expenditure or demand is a direct function of income, i.e. consumption expenditure will increase with the increase in income.

The short run consumption function is :

$$c = a + bY$$

Where c = consumption demand

a = autonomous consumption

b = propensity to consume (MPC)

Y = current disposable income

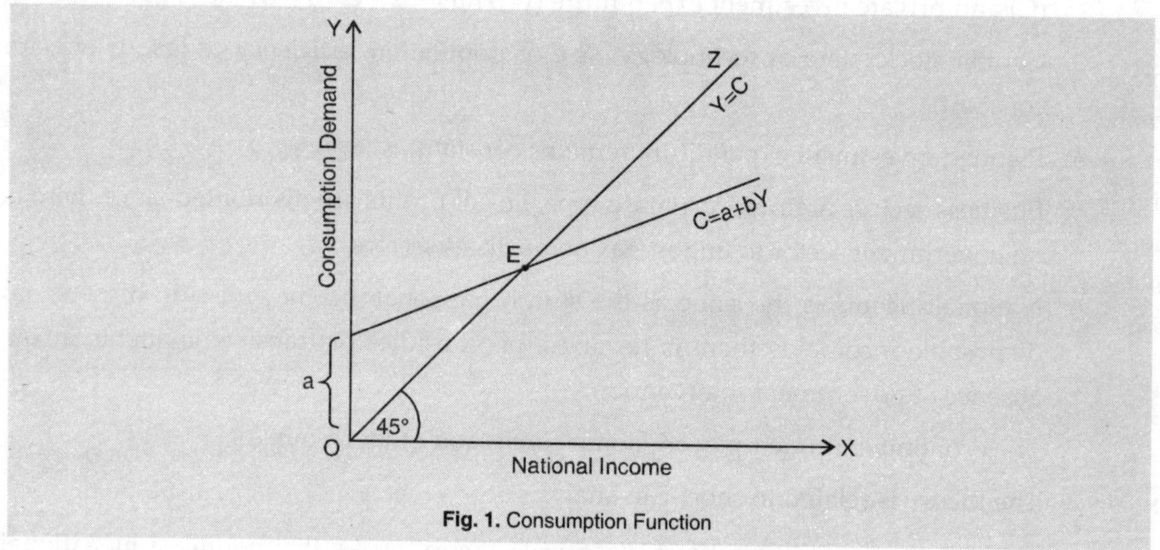

Fig. 1. Consumption Function

In Fig. 1 the national income is presented on the OX-axis and the consumption expenditure on the OY-axis. OZ line drawn with 45° angle represents income consumption equality line (Y = C). The c = a + bY line represents the consumption function which starts from above the origin indicating 'a' as autonomous consumption, which is independent of income. As income increases the consumption function c = a + bY also moves upward but its slope is flatter than the slope of OZ line indicating MPC < 1. Point 'E' is the income consumption equality point (break-even point). The gap between the OZ line and c = a + bY line, prior to break-even pint represents negative saving and after the break-even point represents saving. This shows an another aspect of Keynesian analysis, i.e. Y = C + S.

Investment Demand (I)

Investment demand of expenditure as a component of aggregate demand refer to the expenditure incurred by the business sector on creation of capital assets. According to Keynes investment demand (I) depends upon two factors :

(i) Marginal efficiency of capital (MEC).

(ii) Rate of interest.

MEC refers to the expected rate of profit which the business sector or the investor expects to get from the investment on capital assets.

According to Keynes in short-run the rate of interest remains more or less stable. So, changes in the investment demand mainly depend upon the MEC.

MEC again depends upon two factors :

(i) Replacement cost of capital goods, and

(ii) Profit expectations.

In short-run replacement cost of capital goods remains stable as the theory assumes prices are fixed. So it is profit expectations which are more important because they often change even in short-run and cause changes in the investment demand. However according to Keynes in short-run there will be a given level of investment demand as shown in the figure-2, drawn below which is determined by MEC and rate of interest and does not depend on the level of income. That is in Keynes's income-expenditure analysis investment is treated as autonomous, independent of income and so investment demand remains constant in short-run at all levels of income.

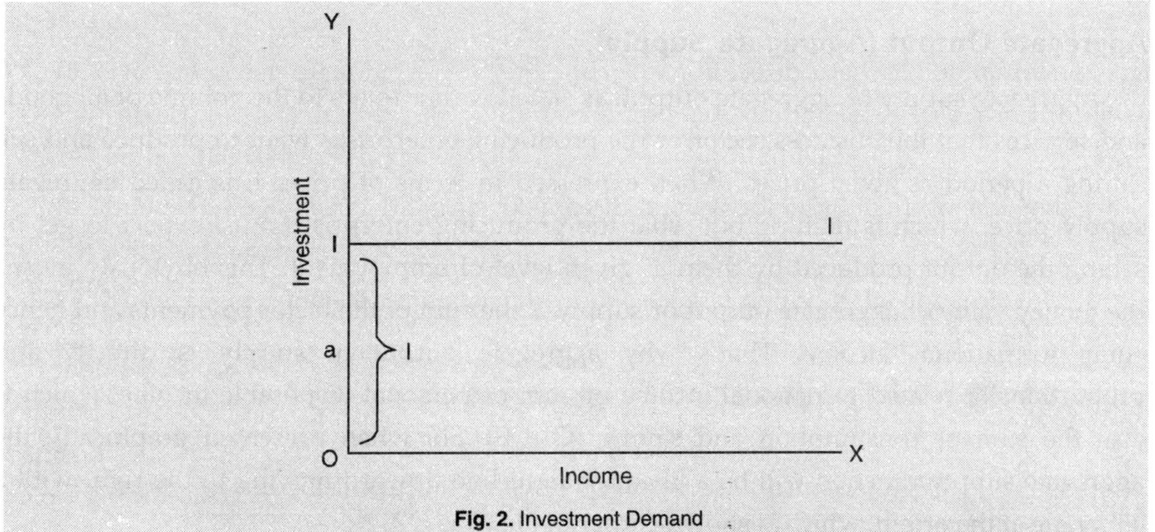

Fig. 2. Investment Demand

Now we can determine the aggregate demand function by adding its both the components, i.e. C = a + bY and I. Diagramatically we have presented this in Fig. 3 drawn below :

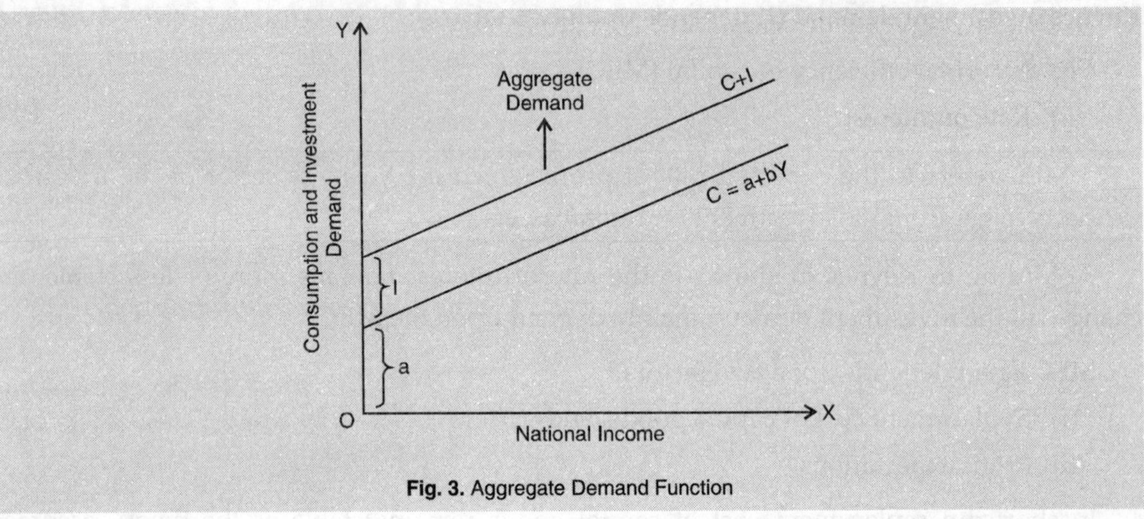

Fig. 3. Aggregate Demand Function

In the figure c = a + bY is the consumption function representing consumption expenditure (or consumption demand), i.e. C. drawn on the basis of autonomous consumption 'a' and given propensity to consume along with the increase in income. Since investment is autonomous of income the investment function is drawn parallel to the consumption function to show the aggregate demand function C + I. The vertical distance between c = a+ bY and C + I is equal throughout indicating in short-run investment is independent of level of income.

Aggregate Output (Aggregate Supply)

Aggregate supply or aggregate output, as stated earlier refers to the volume of all goods and services that the business sector or the producing enterprises want to produce and sell during a period at given prices. When expressed in terms of prices it is called aggregate supply price, which is nothing but what the producing enterprises must expect to get by selling the output produced by them at given level of employment. This obviously means the money value of aggregate output or supply is the sum of the factor payments and hence equal to national income. That's why aggregate output or supply is directly and proportionally related to national income or sum of personal disposable income, which is also the sum of consumption and saving (C + S). So, when presented graphically the aggregate supply function will be a linear straight line upward moving to the right with a 45° angle at the origin, which is shown earlier in Fig. 1 as OZ.

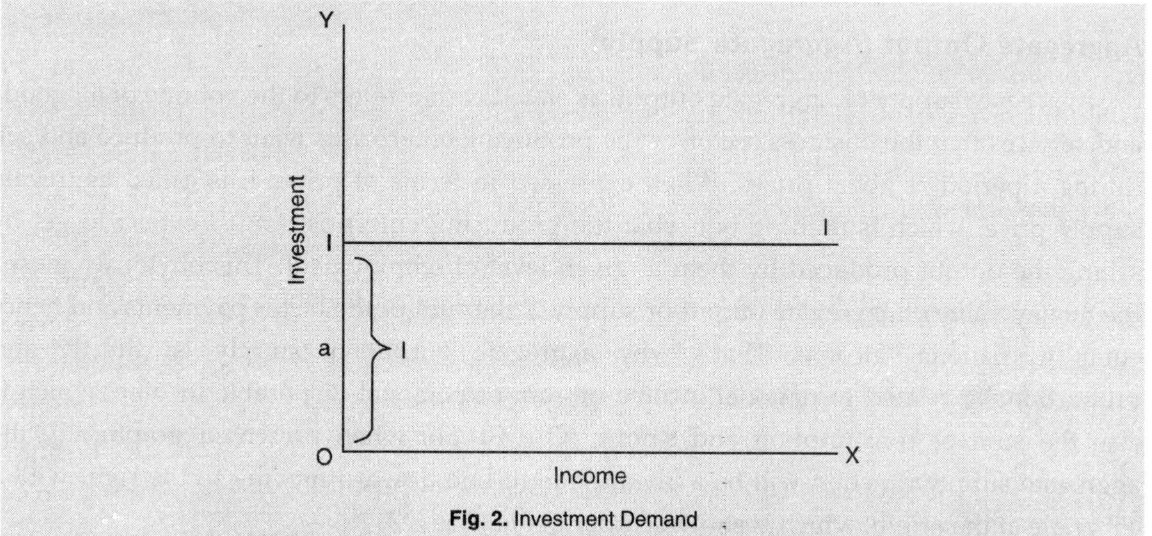

Determination of Equilibrium Level of Income

After getting the aggregate demand function and the aggregate supply function now we can present the determination of equilibrium level of income graphically through the intersection of aggregate demand curve (C + 1) and the aggregate supply curve OZ as shown in Fig. 4 drawn below :

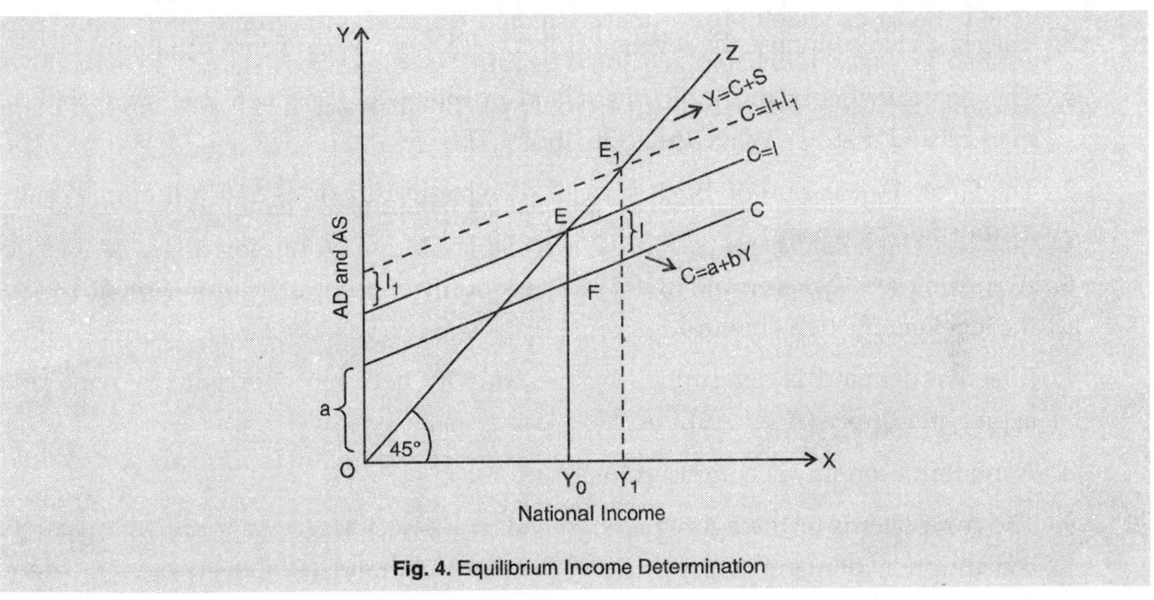

Fig. 4. Equilibrium Income Determination

In the figure C + I line represents the aggregate demand or aggregate expenditure and the OZ line represents aggregate supply. The aggregate demand function C + I intersects the aggregate supply, function OZ (C + S) at point 'E', showing the equality between aggregate demand and aggregate supply (AD = AS). The perpendicular drawn from point E touches the base line, representing national income, at point Y_0 and thus determines the equilibrium level of national income OY_0.

At this level of income aggregate demand = aggregate expenditure = value of aggregate output (GDP) = National income

$$\boxed{AD = AE = GDP = Y}$$

However, OY_0 is not the full employment equilibrium income. Keynes believed that full employment is a myth. The equilibrium level of income determined above is rather an underemployment equilibrium income. Because aggregate supply and hence aggregate demand and national income can be raised by generating more employment opportunities via raising investment, as is shown by the dotted investment function I_1, by which the equilibrium level of income has increased by OY_1.

WHAT WE LEARNT

1. The study of income determination is a subject matter of macroeconomics.
2. The classical economists did not propound any systematic theory of income determination.
3. The classical economists believed in full employment as a normal situation.
4. The classical theory of employment and output was based on the 'says' 'law of market' and 'Pigou's Wage Price Flexibility Theory'.
5. The Great Depression of 1930s proved the classical theories and full employment assumption as wrong.
6. According to Keynes employment in an economy and hence income depends upon the level of effective demand.
7. Effective demand is determined by the equality between aggregate demand and aggregate supply (AD = AS).
8. A modern economy is comprised of 4-sectors.
9. The components of the aggregate demand in a 4-sector economy are – Household consumption demand (C), private investment demand (I), Government demand for goods and services (G) and Net-export demand (X-M).

   Thus AD = C + I + G (X-M)
10. Consumption demand or expenditure and disposable income are positively or directly related.
11. The functional relationship between consumption expenditure (C) and disposable income (Y) is called consumption function or propensity to consume.
12. The marginal propensity consume refers to the ratio of change in consumption expenditure (ΔC) to change in disposable income (ΔY), i.e. MPC = $\Delta C/\Delta Y$.
13. The MPC is always less than unity (1), i.e. MPC < 1.
14. The MPC determines the slope of the consumption function (Consumption expenditure curve).
15. Average propensity to consume is the ratio of consumption expenditure (C) to the disposable income (Y), i.e. APC = C/Y.
16. Disposable income (Y) is the sum of consumption expenditure (C) and savings(S), i.e. Y = C + S.

17. The point of equality between consumption expenditure (C) and disposable income (Y) is called break-even point (Y = C).
18. Prior to the break-even point saving is negative.
19. At the break-even point of consumption expenditure and disposable income, i.e. at Y = C, saving is zero (0).
20. After the break-even point of income, saving is positive.
21. The expenditure incurred by the business sector on creation of new capital assets is called private investment demand.
22. The private investment expenditure depends upon MEC, rate of interest and level of income.
23. So long as the MEC is greater than the rate of interest (r) i.e. MEC > r, the prospective yield from investment is positive.
24. The equilibrium amount of investment is reached where MEC = r.
25. In short-run 'MEC' and 'r' remain more or less constant so level of income is the main determinant of investment demand.
26. Investment demand and level of income are positively (directly) related.
27. Government demand for goods and services or government expenditure has a significant role in raising aggregate demand during depression.
28. The difference between the export earning (X) and imports expenditure (M) is called net export demand (X-M).
29. The flow of final goods and services in the economy during a given period of time is called aggregate supply (AS).
30. Aggregate supply depends upon – the general price level and the extent of capacity utilization.
31. Aggregate supply expressed interms of the prices at which the producers are willing to sell their products is called aggregate supply price (ASP).
32. ASP is what the producing enterprises must expect to get from the sale of the products produced at different level of employment, and hence equal to sum of factor costs and equal to national income.
33. The aggregate supply curve slopes upwards to the right from the origin with a 45° angle.
34. Keynes's simple theory explains income determination in a two-sector economy- Household sector and Business sector.

35. According to Keynesian simple theory equilibrium level of national income is determined by the equality between the aggregate income (or output or supply) and aggregate expenditure (or, demand) incurred by the household sector and business sector on different goods and services (AD = AS).

36. Keynes theory of income determination is developed on his income-expenditure analysis.

QUESTIONS FOR REVIEW

A. Choose the correct answer from the given alternatives in each question. (Each Carrying 1 Mark)

1. The classical economists believed which one as a normal situation ?

(i) Full employment (ii) Unemployment

(iii) Underemployment (iv) Involuntary Unemployment

2. According to Keynes level of employment and hence income in an economy depends upon:

(i) Aggregate demand (ii) Aggregate supply

(iii) Level of effective demand (iv) None of the above

3. The point at which aggregate demand is equal to aggregate supply is called point of :

(i) Equilibrium demand (ii) Effective demand

(iii) Aggregate demand (iv) Full employment demand

4. A modern economy is comprised of :

(i) Two-sectors (ii) Three-sectors

(iii) Four-sectors (iv) None of the above.

5. Consumption expenditure and disposable income are related :

(i) Positively (ii) Inversely

(iii) Proportionately (iv) Linearly

6. The marginal propensity to consume is always :

(i) Equal to 1 (ii) Greater than 1

(iii) Less than 1 (iv) Zero.

7. **Which one of the following determines the slope of consumption function ?**

   (i) Consumption expenditure (ii) Marginal propensity to consume

   (iii) Average propensity to consume (iv) Aggregate expenditure

8. **The ratio of consumption expenditure to disposable income is :**

   (i) Average propensity to consume (ii) Break-even point

   (iii) Marginal propensity to consume (iv) Consumption function

9. **The sum of consumption expenditure and savings is equal to :**

   (i) Personal income (ii) Nominal income

   (iii) Real income (iv) Disposable income

10. **The point at which the consumption expenditure and disposable income are equal is called :**

    (i) Equilibrium point (ii) Break-even point

    (iii) Point of inflexion (iv) None of the above

11. **Prior to break-even point on consumption function saving is :**

    (i) Positive (ii) Negative

    (iii) Zero (iv) None of the above

12. **The expenditure incurred by the business sector on creation of new capital assets is called :**

    (i) Investment demand (ii) Capital formation

    (iii) Stock of capital (iv) Cost of production

13. **Private investment demand depends upon :**

    (i) Marginal efficiency of capital (ii) Rate of interest

    (iii) Level of income (iv) All the above

14. **So long as the Marginal Efficiency of capital is greater than the rate of interest the investment will :**

    (i) Increase (ii) Remain constant

    (iii) Decrease (iv) None of the above

15. **According to Keynes in short run the rate of interest :**

    (i) Increases (ii) Decreases

    (iii) Remains constant (iv) None of the above

16. **Investment demand and level of incomes and related :**
    (i) Inversely (ii) Directly
    (iii) Proportionally (iv) None of the above

17. **The flow of final goods and service in the economy during a given period of time is called :**
    (i) Aggregate supply (ii) Aggregate demand
    (iii) Effective demand (iv) Stock of output

18. **The aggregate supply curve slopes :**
    (i) Downwards to the right (ii) Horizontally
    (iii) Vertically (iv) Upwards to the right

19. **The slope of the aggregate supply curve indicates that the relationship between aggregate output and level of income is :**
    (i) Inverse (ii) Linear
    (iii) Non-linear (iv) Not correlated

20. **Keynes's theory of income determination is developed on his :**
    (i) Income-expenditure analysis (ii) Saving-investment analysis
    (iii) Input-output analysis (iv) None of the above

B. *Correct the statement, if necessary, without changing the underlined portions. (Each Carrying 1 Mark)*

1. Keynes believed that full employment is a normal situation.
2. The classical theory of employment was based on principle of effective demand.
3. According to Keynes an increase in the level of effective demand will tend to raise the volume of employment and income.
4. The study of income determination is a subject matter of macroeconomics.
5. Effective demand is determined at that point where aggregate demand is greater than aggregate supply.
6. Consumption demand and disposable income are inversely related.
7. The functional relationship between consumption expenditure and disposable income is called effective demand.
8. Average propensity to consume is always less than one.
9. The APC determines the slope of the consumption function.

10. Personal income is the sum of consumption demand and savings.
11. After the break-even point of income and expenditure saving is negative.
12. The optimum amount of investment is reached where MEC is greater than rate of intertest.
13. The sum of the export earnings and import expenditure is called net export demand.
14. Aggregate supply depends upon the general price level and the extent of capacity utilization.
15. Keynes's simple theory of income determination is related to a four-sector economy.

C. *Answer the following questions in 2-3 sentences each. (Each question carries 2 Marks)*

1. What is aggregate demand ?
2. What are the components of aggregate demand ?
3. What is consumption demand ?
4. What is private investment demand ?
5. What is government demand for goods and services ?
6. What is net-export demand ?
7. What is propensity to consume ? (What is consumption function ?)
8. What is marginal propensity to consume ?
9. What is average propensity to consume ?
10. What is aggregate supply ? (What is aggregate output ?)
11. What is marginal efficiency of capital ?
12. What the Keynesian simple theory of income determination states ?

D. *Distinguish between the following in Six Sentences each. (Each Carrying 3 Marks)*

1. Aggregate demand and aggregate supply.
2. Household consumption demand and private investment demand.
3. Marginal propensity to consume and average propensity to consume.

E. Long Answer Type Questions (Carrying 7½ Marks)

1. What is aggregate demand ? Discuss the components of aggregate demand.
2. Explain Keynes simple theory of income determination.

Answer to Q. N. A

1.	(i)	2.	(iii)	3.	(ii)	4.	(iii)	5.	(i)	6.	(iii)	7.	(ii)	8.	(i)
9.	(iv)	10.	(ii)	11.	(ii)	12.	(i)	13.	(iv)	14.	(i)	15.	(iii)	16.	(ii)
17.	(i)	18.	(iv)	19.	(ii)	20.	(i)								

Answer to Q. N. B

1. Classical economists	2. The Keynesion	3. Correct
4. Correct	5. Equal to	6. Directly
7. Consumption Function or propensity to Consume	8. MPC	9. MPC
10. Disposable Income	11. Positive	12. Equal to
13. The difference between	14. Correct	15. Two-sector

❑❑❑

UNIT – VIII

10. MONEY AND BANKING

11. PUBLIC FINANCE

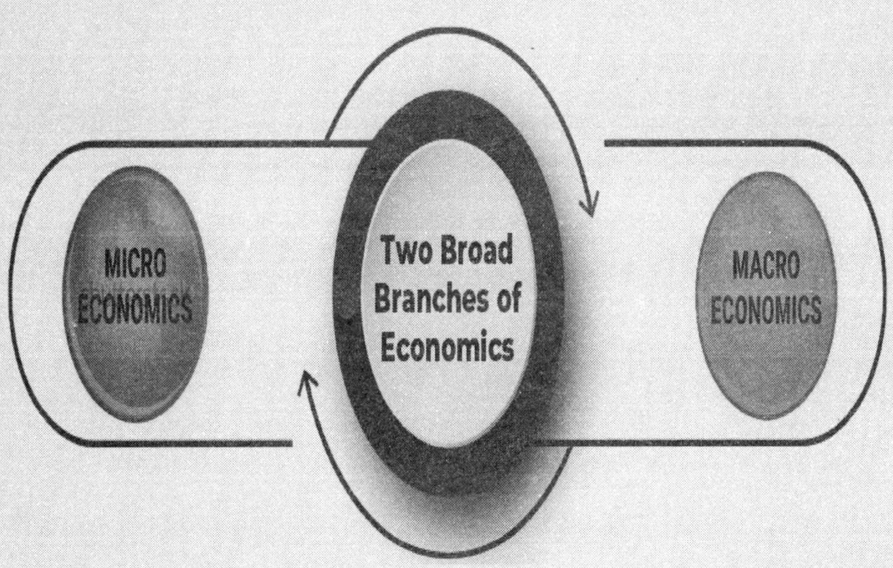

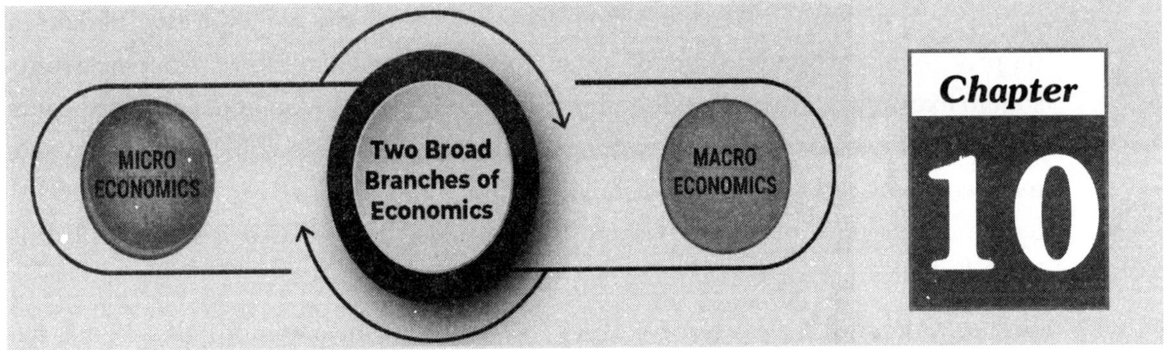

MONEY AND BANKING

'Money is one of the most wonderful inventions that man has ever made. It has become so much important in man's life that his life cannot be imagined without 'money'. It's importance in economic and business transaction can be compare with the importance of the invention of fire in physics, invention of wheel in transportation and implementation of universal adult suffrage in democracy etc. That's why Adam Smith, the father of economics said, "In the whole Commercial side of man's social existence money is the essential invention on which all the rest is based."

Prior to the invention of money wants in the Primitive Society were few and man living in the lap of nature was self sufficient. Gradually with the progress of civilization his wants increased. Man could not satisfy all his wants and started depending upon each other and felt the need of trade and transactions. During those early days of transactions the system was direct exchange of goods against goods or goods against services or services against services and the system was known as **barter system**. The system was alright till the wants were few and economic activities were simple and limited. But with the further advancement of civilization men's wants multiplied and became diversified, economic activities became complex, mode of production, relations of production and transactions became too complex to comply with the prevailing barter system giving rise to a number of difficulties.

Difficulties of Barter System

Barter system involves a number of difficulties and inconveniences. The major difficulties of barter system are :

1. **Lack of Double Coincidence of Wants:** A double coincidence of wants is required

for any transaction to be materialized. In other words the wants of two person in the process of exchange of goods must coincide. For example, if a person wants cloth in exchange of his wheat then he must find a person who had cloth and wants wheat in its exchange. Under barter system such a double coincidence of wants involved great difficulty and wastage of time. With the increase in wants lack of double coincidence of wants became more intense and needed a solution to this difficulty.

2. **Lack of Common Measure of Value:** The value of all commodities are not the same. So it is obvious that one will compare the value of his commodity with the value of the commodity that he wants in exchange of this. But under barter system there was the lack of a common measure of value to determine the magnitude of one commodity in exchange of an another commodity, as it is difficult to compare the commodities of different nature and features. Even in the presence of coincidence of wants it was difficult to determine the rate of exchange. That is, the farmer and the weaver are ready to exchange their commodities, but the difficulty was how much cloth the weaver will provide to farmer for how much wheat ? So the necessity of a common measure of value was felt very much.

3. **Indivisibility of Goods:** An another difficulty of the barter system of exchange was on account of indivisibility of goods. There are so many goods which are indivisible, i.e., they are required or available as a whole and cannot be divided into parts or units. For example, a horse or a goat are indivisible and hence cannot be divided into parts to exchange for any divisible good like rice or wheat or fruits etc. Thus under barter system trade between divisible and indivisible goods was not possible without a loss of value. W. S. Jevons rightly says, **"In a barter system, smooth exchange operations are impossible for want of a means of sub-dividing and distributing values according to people's varying requirements."** Hence, there was the necessity of a means of sub-dividing the values of indivisible goods to facilitate their exchange for divisible goods.

4. **Lack of Store of Value:** By instinct man always wants to save a part of his present income to meet the uncertainties of future. Saving present income means to save the purchasing power. But under barter system since the present income is in the form of goods that one produces, it cannot be a general purchasing power. People can store value for future use by storing their products which is expensive and involves chances of damage, loss due to natural calamities, attack of sects and insects etc. It is also not possible to store the perishable goods for a long time. This

implies that barter system lacks the presence of a generalized purchasing power or store of value. This also needed a solution.

5. **Lack of Standard of Deferred Payments:** Deferred payments is involved with credit transaction i.e. transactions taking place with the contract of making payments on a future date. Simply speaking, deferred payments is related to the act of lending and borrowing. Barter system lacks a standard of deferred payments, so that transactions involving future payments cannot take place with ease. Under barter system credit transactions involve so many controversies and risks. There are chances of controversies over the quality of goods to be repaid in future, over the mode of repayment, chances of high risks to both the parties as the real value of the goods to be repaid may increase or decrease in future etc. Thus, barter system was not suitable for credit transactions and made people to ponder over its solution.

For the above discussed difficulties and many more practical and conceptual inconveniences barter system was considered as the most inefficient system of transaction and was rejected in different places and at different times. Gradually, people in different places and at different times started accepting different commodities even animals and metal as medium of exchange and ultimately 'money' the most wonderful invention of man came into existence.

Money – Evolution and Definition

With the progress of civilization human wants diversified leading to the expansion of economic activities. However, from the very early stages of economic expansion the difficulties and inconveniences of barter system became more pronounced. To remove those difficulties the thing that man brought into lime light is non other, rather 'money'. However, 'money' was not brought into lime light all at sudden. The evolution of money has been a secular process. Before reaching at its present form it has passed through several phases and developed through centuries. That's why writers like **Spalding** say, **"Money seems to have been discovered rather than invented in the progress of economic civilization of mankind."**

However, money is considered as an invention of man as it involves conscious reasoning power of man to take the step from simple barter to money accounting. Of course the development of money has passed through various stages in accordance with time, place and circumstances with the progress of economic civilization of mankind.

In the process of evolution of money economists have recognized six stages such as :

1. Animal Money
2. Commodity Money
3. Metallic Money
4. Paper Money
5. Credit Money
6. Plastic Money

1. Animal Money

The concept of animal money is too primitive. In the primitive hunting stage of human civilization animals were used as the common medium of exchange. History of human civilization states that in the early primitive society cattle were considered as wealth and regarded as the most standard unit of barter for quite a long period of time. However, because of too much primitivity the concept of animal money is not discussed much in the evolution of money.

2. Commodity Money

During the early stages of civilization in many communities to carry out the simple exchange of goods for goods the terms of exchange were fixed with reference to one standard commodity and the values of other commodities were measured in terms of that commodity. A number of commodities were accepted as the medium of exchange, in different regions and in different times.

However, the commodity money suffered a number of draw backs like lack of uniformity and standardization, inefficient store of value, lack of easy transferability and indivisibility.

3. Metallic Money

Discovery of precious metals like gold, silver, copper etc. displaced the commodity money from circulation and these precious metals in various shapes, size and weight were used as medium of exchange. Use of metals as money in the course of time paved the way for the development of coinage system in different economies. In this sense the metallic money refers to the coins made of various metals like gold, silver, bronze, nickel etc. A coin is a piece of metal of a given size, shape, weight and fineness whose value is determined by the monetary authority or the government of the concerned country.

Metallic money is further classified under two heads :

1. **Standard Money or Standard Coin** or full-bodied money which refers to that money or coin whose face value is equal to its intrinsic value, i.e. the worth of the metallic content of the coin. It is unlimited legal tender and has free coinage.

2. **Token Money or Token Coin,** which refers to that coin whose face value is greater than its intrinsic value. Token coins are made of cheap metals like nickel, copper, alminium etc. and are used primarily as a form of subsidiary money for the payment of small amounts. Token coins are limited legal tender as payments through token coins can be made up to a limited amount.

   However, metallic money has the following drawbacks :

   - Because of bulkiness a large sum of money in terms of coins is not easily portable.
   - In the form of precious metals like gold and silver it was not safe to carry.
   - Quick transaction is not possible with coins as the mode of payment.
   - Physical depreciation of precious metallic coins was creating illusion and distrust.

4. Paper Money

In modern economies paper money has become popular. Initially it came as paper receipts against metallic money which was not safe to carry. But with the shortage of metals it took the shape of money in the name of paper money. Paper money consists of the currency notes issued by the monetary authority of a country or by the government of the country or both. In modern era the use of paper money is wide spread as it is economical, convenient to carry, easy to store and adjustable to the need of the country.

Paper money can be classified under four heads :

(i) Representative Paper Money
(ii) Convertible Paper Money
(iii) Inconvertible Paper Money
(iv) Fiat Money

Representative Paper Money is 100 percent backed up and fully redeemable in some commodity such as gold, silver etc. **Convertible Paper Money** is that which can be converted in to standard coins at the option of the holder. A less that 100 percent reserve in metallic form is maintained for this kind of paper money. The basic principle underlying the system is that all the notes are not simultaneously presented by the people for encashment. Therefore, the value of gold and silver is less than the value of notes issued by the monetary authority. **Inconvertible Paper Money** is that money which cannot be converted into full-bodied money. **Fiat money** is an another type of inconvertible paper money which circulates in the economy under extra-ordinary circumstances, on the demand of the state. It is issued generally at a time of crisis, without any backing reserve.

5. Credit Money

In modern economic system with the development in the banking activities, along with paper money an another form of convertible money has been developed in the form of credit money or bank money. Credit money is nothing but the additional purchasing power created by the Commercial banks in the process of credit creation or advancement of loans. Derivative deposits, cheque system of payment etc. have started functions as money. Cheques are now conventionally accepted as a mode of payments by the business community in general. In a modern economy, bank notes (currencies) and bank money (credit money) together constitute the total money supply. However, credit money are not legal tender.

6. Plastic Money

This is the latest form of money which includes credit cards, debit cards and all other forms of digital payment modes. Plastic money are now widely used in various transactions of all denominations and thus have overcome the risks of carrying transactions in cash.

The above discussed evolution of money can be presented as the classification of money in the manner presented below :

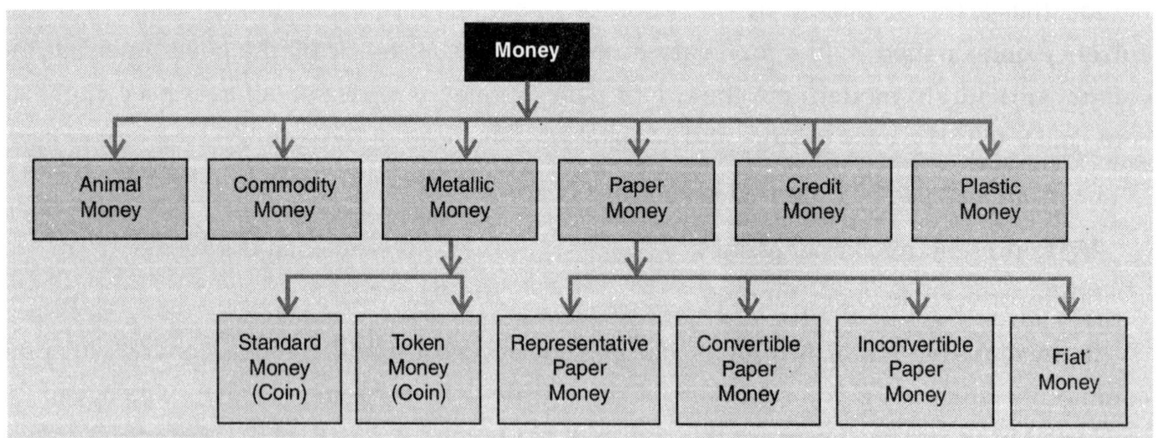

Definition of Money

We all are very familiar with money as it is an important and indispensable element of our life. But the question is do we know the exact meaning of the term 'money' ? In our simple understanding we refer money to what we pay to purchase any thing and more particularly in India 'rupee' is the money. In America it is 'dollar', in England it is 'pound' and so on. But this is not enough to present the meaning of the term 'money'. The simple way to know what something is to look into its definition (s). But in case of money the task is too difficult. Because the difficulty in defining money lies in its forms and in the diversified functions that it is performing. So, we can have a broad idea about what money is only by discussing on its functions.

Yet, different economists have given different definitions of money but on the basis of different criteria. Some of them are on the basis of its functions, some are on the basis of its general acceptability and some are on the basis of its legal aspects. Below we have quoted some of the definitions given by some renowned monetary economists.

The term 'money is supposed to be derived from the Latin word 'Moneta', the name of the Roman Goddess Junomeneta, the Goddess of Heaven, in whose temple coins were being minted.

According to ***Prof. Crowther*** *money is, "anything that is generally acceptable as a means of exchange and at the same time acts as a measure and store of value."*

According to ***D. H. Robertson***, *"anything which is widely accepted in payment for goods or in discharge of other kinds of business obligation is called money."*

According to ***Prof. Seligman*** *money is "anything that possesses general acceptability."*

According to ***Prof. Ely***, *"Money is anything that passes freely from hand to hand as medium of exchange and is generally received in final discharge of debts."*

From the ***view*** *point of legal aspect* ***Prof. Hawtrey*** *says, "Only legal means of payment should be accepted as money." Similarly, Prof. Knapp points out, "Any commodity assigned by the state the role of setting debt shall be deemed as money."*

Thus, no single definition covers all the aspects of money compelling the economists like ***Francis Walker*** *to say, "Money is what money does."*

However, From among the definitions given above, ***Crowther's*** *definition emphasizes the most important functions of money for which it was originally invented.*

Functions of Money

Basically money was invented to remove the difficulties of barter system of exchange, i.e. the lack of double coincidence of wants, absence of a common measure of value, lack of a standard of deferred payments and lack of store of value. But in this present days' modern economies money has gone much ahead besides removing the difficulties of the barter system of exchange. To-day there is hardly any aspect of life of man which has not been affected by money. Now a days money in its different forms is performed diversified functions. The most important functions of money, for which it was originally invented, have been rightly summarized by **Jevons** in a famous couplet :

"Money is a matter of functions four,

A medium, a measure, a standard, a store."

However, the functions of money can be put under three broad categories :

1. Primary functions
2. Secondary functions and
3. Contingent functions.

Primary Functions

1. **Money Acts as a Medium of Exchange:** Acting as a medium of exchange money has removed the lack of double coincidence of wants' difficulty of the barter system. Under the barter System the exchange pattern was C → C, i.e. Commodity against commodity. But it was too difficult to carry out this pattern of transactions. Because one had to find out a person who had the commodity required by the first person and ready to exchange that for what the first person had. But with the invention of money the exchange pattern has become C → M → C, i.e. commodity against money then money against commodity. Now anything can be exchanged for money and with the help of money anything can be purchased and money acts as a medium of exchange. With money acting as a medium of exchange John is no more looking for Charlie who will take his cloth and give him paddy, what he wants. This function of money is facilitating transactions and making transactions easy, time and cost saving.

2. **Money Acts as a Measure of Value:** Under barter System it was very difficult to determine the value of different commodities. Because there was no common measure of value and the relative values of different commodities are not the same. People had to remember innumerable relative values of different goods with different features, which was too difficult. The problem was acute in case of indivisible goods and services. Simply speaking, determination of rate of exchange of different goods was too difficult. But invention of money has removed this difficulty by acting as a measure of value. Now the value of all goods and services

are expressed in terms of money, which is called as price and with the introduction of money it has become easier to compare the value of two goods and to determine their exchange rate.

Secondary Functions

1. **Money Acts as a Standard of Deferred Payments:** Deferred Payments are related to credit transactions. Whenever credit transactions take place involving lending and borrowing, the question of deferred payments arises. It means goods and services are exchanged or provided on the present against promises to pay on a future date. In modern economic communities credit transactions are being carried widely with money acting as a standard of future payments for the present transactions. Under barter system there was the danger of loss to one party on the credit transactions due to the changes in the value of the commodity concerned in future. But money acting as a standard of deferred payments has reduced this danger. Of course there is the chance of change (decrease) in the value of money in future, but that is negligible and if significant can be mitigated to a large extent charging interest on the deferred payments.

   Money acting as a standard of deferred payments has simplified the credit transactions, leading and borrowing and promoted trade and commerce and all other economic activities.

2. **Money Acts as a Store of Value:** By instinct every individual wants to store or save something or a part of his present earning to meet the unforeseen emergencies or to make future safe. This can only be imagined with the help of money. Under barter system storing value on terms of goods was difficult, expensive and risky and storing of perishable commodities was not possible. But value of goods in terms of money can be stored easily. Money being the general purchasing power, by holding money one can store the value of other goods as well. There is less risk in storing value in terms of money and storing value in terms of money is less expensive. Even storing value in terms of money may generate income in the form of interest. That's why Prof. Crowther rightly remarks, " Money is round so that it can circulate and is so flat that it can be piled up." Thus by acting as a store of value money has removed the difficulties of storing values under barter System. Of course there is the possibility of the fall in the value of money in future but that loss is negligible in comparison to the loss under the barter system.

Contingent Functions

Besides the above discussed functions, in the present days monetary economies money is also performing a number of functions which are ancillary to its primary and secondary functions. Those functions are put under the category of contingent or ancillary functions.

Such functions include :

(i) Money acts as a means of transfer of value from one place to another or from one person to another.

(ii) By enabling Commercial banks and other financial institution to create credit, money acts as a foundation of credit system in the economy.

(iii) Money acts as a basis of price mechanism to facilitate transactions.

(iv) Money acts as an equaliser of marginal utilities on the consumption process and marginal productivities in the production ventures.

(v) Money acts as a measuring rod of national income of a country and facilitates distribution of rational income, both at macro and micro level.

Thus, money plays a key role in the working of an economy and the working of the global economy. We cannot imagine our lives relating to business, trade, other economic activities and even our lives relating to other aspects of life.

Near Money

The total money supply in an economy is comprised of the currencies issued by the monetary authority, i.e. the bank notes or legal tenders and some other financial assets which can be easily converted into money, but not legal tender, which are called as near-money. The near-money is considered as a component of the total money supply as they do have direct impact on the economic activities of an economy.

Near-money as the title suggest are very close to money and act as money-substitute, of course not perfect substitutes of money, as they are not legal tender. In this sense we can define near money as **the liquid financial assets which can be easily converted into money without any loss of value and are accepted in most business transactions and discharge of other obligation but are not legal tender.** Money in the form of cash and demand deposits are the most liquid assets, where as the near-money have a high degree of liquidity or moneyness. Fixed deposits and savings deposits with Commercial banks, post-offices and other non-banking financial institutions, treasury bills, bills of exchange, securities, share, stock, bond, debentures, cheque etc. are very close to money and hence are included in the category of near-money. In the modern economic transaction and in facilitating trade and commerce and in accelerating economic activities and hence in economic development near-money are playing significant role.

Money	Near-Money
1. Money is legal tender.	1. Near money is not legal tender.
2. Money includes currency notes, coins and the demand deposits.	2. Near money includes the liquid financial assets like fixed and saving deposits, treasury bills, shares, debentures, cheque etc. which can be easily converted into money.
3. Money acts as unit of account.	3. Near money cannot act as unit of account.
4. Money possesses hundred percent liquidity.	4. Liquidity of near money is high but not hundred percent.
5. It is the principal legal tender.	5. It is substitute to legal tender.
6. The legal tender are money proper.	6. Near money are optional money.

Money of Account and Money Proper

Money of account refers to that money in terms of which the value of everything is expressed. In other words it refers to the name of currencies of different countries in which the countries concerned express the value of different commodities in their countries. This also refers to unit of account. For example, Rupee in India, Dollar in the USA, Pound in England, Rouble in Russia etc. are the money of account or unit of account in the respective countries. Money Proper on the other hand refers to the currency notes and coins with which actual payments are made.

Commercial Banks – Meaning and Functions

The term 'bank' is more probably derived from the Greek word 'banque' or the Italian word 'banco', both meaning a 'bench'. So far as the evolution of banking is concerned, it is an age-old phenomenon which started since the beginning of the early civilization. The evolution of Commercial banking is related to the practice of safe keeping of gold and other valuables by the people with the merchants or goldsmiths or money lenders. In those early days the money lenders and money-changers used to display their coins on 'banque' or 'banco', which mean 'bench' and transact business in the market places, facilitating the transactions of goods and services. The Commercial banks of the present days have emerged from those 'banque' or 'banco' transactions. However, in those days banking was confined to the business of money changing.

The emergence of institutional bank dates back to 1157 when in Italy the first bank called the **'Bank of Venice'** was established to fulfill the financial needs of the authorities of the State of Venice facing crisis due to war. However, the initiative to start modern banking was taken by the banks of Lombardy in England and Commercial banking began there only after 1640 when some goldsmiths started receiving deposits from the public for safe custody and issued receipts for the acknowledgments. That's why Prof. Crowther considers the merchants, the money-lenders and the goldsmiths as the three ancestors of modern Commercial banking system.

The 'Bank of England', which is considered as the mother of all Commercial banks was established in 1694, of course in Italian lines to support the government at the time of financial crisis. Otherwise the modern joint-stock Commercial banking system came into existence with the passage of the Banking Act, 1833 in England. In India, the modern banking started when the English agency houses in Kolkata and Mumbai started serving as the bankers to the East India Company and the Bank of Hindustan established in 1770, was the first banking institution with its headquarters in Kolkata.

Meaning and Definitions

In present days economies we come across several types of banks such as Central bank, Commercial bank, Agricultural bank, Industrial bank, Development bank, Co-operative bank etc. But here we are concerned with the Commercial bank.

Broadly speaking a Commercial bank is an institution which deals with money and credit. As the name suggests the Commercial banks like Joint-Stock Companies work in profit seeking manner. However in the present days economies Commercial banks are performing multifarious activities and influencing directly and indirectly the working of an economy and the economic activities. Because of this it is not an easy task to present the meaning of Commercial bank in a sentence or two or in the form of definition. Yet, different economists and institutions have tried to define a Commercial bank. We have quoted some of those definitions below.

*According to **Prof. Crowther**, "a bank collects money from those who have it to spare or who are saving it out of their incomes, and it lends this money to those who require it."*

*According to **Prof. Sayers**, "a bank is an institution whose debts, i.e. bank deposits, are widely accepted in settlement of other people's debts to each other."*

In the words of ***Prof. Kenley****, "A bank is an establishment which makes to individuals such advances of money as may be required and safely made, and to which individuals entrust money when not required by them for use."*

According to the ***Indian Companies Act****, 1949, banking means "the accepting for the purpose of landing or investment, of deposits of money from the public, repayable on demand or otherwise and withdrawable by cheque, draft, order or otherwise."*

However, all the above discussed definitions and many more definitions given by economists and institutions are not complete to give a clear understanding of what a Commercial bank is ? For this we must go through the multifarious functions that a modern Commercial bank is performing which is discussed below.

Functions of Commercial Bank

In the present days economies Commercial banks perform a large variety of functions and are taking active part in the promotion of trade and commerce and the overall development of an economy. Some of the functions of the present day's Commercial banks are hereditary as they are inherited from their ancestors, i.e. the merchants, goldsmiths and the money lenders. These functions of Commercial banks are called as their primary functions. Besides those primary functions the other functions that the modern Commercial banks are performing now a days are considered as their secondary functions. Let us discuss those functions under the following heads :

A. Primary Functions

The most fundamental functions of Commercial banks that they have inherited from their ancestors are called the primary functions. These include :

(i) Acceptance of deposits, and

(ii) Advancement of loans

(i) Acceptance of Deposits

Acceptance of deposits from those who have the capacity to save but cannot utilize their saving's profitably is the most fundamental function of a Commercial bank.

Usually people save money in the banks due to the reasons like :

- to meet the unforeseen emergencies of future,
- to avoid the risk of having cash in hand,

- to earn in the form of interest, as they cannot utilize their savings profitably themselves.

The Commercial banks accept different types of deposits such as –

Current or Demand Deposits – Current deposit or account refers to that deposit or account from which the depositor or the account holder can withdraw money at any time during the banking hours on demand, i.e. without giving any prior information, issuing cheque only. That's why this deposit is also called demand deposit. Having money in current or demand deposit by a depositor is like having money or cash in hand. A bank could not make any profitable use of the money deposited in this account. Se a very negligible or no interest is paid by the bank on this deposit. Rather bank may charge a meagre service charges from the depositors. Usually traders and businessmen prefer such deposit.

Fixed Deposit Or Time Deposit – Fixed deposit or account refers to that deposit or account in which money is deposited for specific period of time, say 1 year or 2 years or 5 years and so, and cannot be withdrawn before the expiry of the stipulated time period. So bank can make profitable use of money deposited in this account. That's why highest rate of interest is paid on this deposit. Of course the rates of interest on this deposit vary on the basis of time period for which money is deposited. This deposit is also called 'term deposit'.

Savings Deposit – The deposit accepted by the bank to encourage and mobilize small savings of the public is called savings deposit or savings account. In this account money can be deposited in small denominations. Money can be withdrawn from this about at any time during the banking hours either by voucher or cheque but with certain restrictions regarding the number of times a depositor can withdraw money per week or month, the maximum amount of money that can be withdrawn at a time etc. These conditions vary from bank to bank. A low rate of interest is paid to the depositors of this account.

Recurring Deposit – The deposit in which money is deposited in regular intervals or in equal instalments, i.e. monthly or quarterly or half-yearly or annually, for a specific period of time, before the expiry of which time period money cannot be withdrawn is called recurring deposit. After the expiry of the stipulated time period the principal along with the interest, at the pre-determined rate, is repaid to the depositor. The rate of interest on recurring deposits is comparatively less than the fixed deposits but higher than the saving deposits. People of fixed income group usually prefer this deposit.

Home Safe Deposit – This deposit is more or less same as the saving deposit and meant to encourage the marginal Savers belonging to lower income group like the wage earners to save in small denomination. In such deposit a safe is provided to the depositors to keep it at home and to put their small savings in it. Then periodically, on a stipulated date the safe is taken to the bank where the amount in the safe is credited to their accounts.

(ii) Advancement of Loans

The second primary function of a Commercial bank is the advancement of loans. This in fact is the most profitable function of a Commercial bank. The Commercial banks do not let the money accepted by them from the people in the form of deposits to lay idle in the bank. After keeping certain cash reserves the bank's lend the excess reserves to the needy borrowers and earn interest. They give loans in different forms Such as cash credit, discounting bells of exchange, Overdraft, direct Loans, money at call etc. Let us have a brief discussion on these forms of loans advanced by the Commercial banks.

Cash Credit – The loans given by the banks to the borrowers against current assets such as shares, stock, bonds etc. with two guaranters are called as cash credit. In such cases of credit bank opens a current account in the name of the borrower and credits the sanctioned loan amount on the account and allows the borrower to withdraw money as per his requirement issuing cheque. In case of cash credit interest is charged only on the amount withdrawn not on the amount sanctioned. This type of credit is preferred by the traders and businessmen.

Discounting Bills of Exchange – Discounting bills of exchange is also a popular way of giving loans by the Commercial bank. When the holders of bills of exchange need money before the maturity date of the bills, they can pledge the bills before the Commercial bank. The bank gives loan against the bill, which is called discounting bills of exchange. While discounting a bill bank deducts certain amount from its face value as commission. After maturity the bank collect's the full value of the bill from the debtor. Thus, the loans given on the bills of exchange are self-liquidating.

Overdrafts – Overdraft as a system of advancement of loan refers to the facility provided by a bank to its reliable customers to withdraw more than their actual deposit. In such case interest is charged on the overdrawn amount. This facility is provided on the basis of prior agreement. Mostly the governments, established business enterprises avail such facility.

Direct Loan – Such loan is sanctioned to individuals and businessmen against collateral security such as land, building, gold, vehicle etc. In case of such loan the amount sanctioned is either paid or credited to the account of the borrower. The interest in such case is charged on the entire amount of the loan sanctioned and the loan is repaid either in maturity of in instalments. Personal loan, house building loan, gold loan etc. are the examples of such loan.

Money at call and short Notice – The Commercial banks provide such loans for a very short period of time which may be for one day to fourteen days and can be called back by the bank at a very short notice. These loans are generally made to other banks or financial institutions.

B. Secondary Functions

The secondary functions of Commercial banks include –

1. Creation of Credit
2. Promotion of Cheque
3. Agency Functions
4. General Utility Functions

Creation of credit – Creation of credit is a unique function of the modern Commercial banks. In fact, credit creation is a natural outcome of the process of advancing loans as adopted by the banks. By this function the Commercial banks create invisible money in the circulation, which are called '**bank money'.** When a Commercial bank advances loan to its customer, usually it does not led in cash rather opens an account in the name of the borrower and credits the loan amount to his account. By this, an equal amount of deposit is created, adding to the purchasing power of the economy, which is called **derivative deposit.** By this the actual money supply or cash in the hands of the bank does not increase, only the purchasing power is increased in the economy. This helps in increasing trade and commerce and hence the economic development of the country.

Promotion of cheques – The Commercial banks also promote a useful medium of exchange on the form of cheques. By this the risks of cash transactions are reduced. Cheque is a credit instrument issued by the bank which has become much convenient in settling obligations in modern business transactions. Through a cheque a depositor directs his bank to pay the mentioned amount to the bearer of the cheque or in whose name the cheque is issued. However in case of crossed or account payee (A/c) cheque the amount is credited to the account of the person in whose name it is issued.

Agency Functions – The modern Commercial banks also perform various agency functions for and on behalf of their customers, such as –

- The Commercial banks help their customers in transferring funds from one place to another through drafts against certain commission.

- Banks also collect and pay various credit instruments like, cheques, drafts, bills of exchange, promissory notes on behalf of the customers.
- Banks also execute the standing instructions of their customers for making various periodic payments and subscriptions like rents, interest, electric bills, telephone bills, insurance premiums etc. on behalf of them.
- Banks also collect dividends, interest and other receipts for their customers.
- Banks also undertake the functions of brokers in purchasing and selling of various shares, securities, stocks, bonds etc. on behalf of the customers.
- Banks also act as the trustee and executer of the property of their customers.
- Sometimes the banks also act as representatives and correspondents of their customers in settling various financial and non-financial matters etc.

General Utility Functions – The modern Commercial banks also perform certain general utility services which include –

- Bank's provide locker facilities to the customers to keep their valuables and important documents in safe custody.
- Banks also issue traveller's cheques to help their customers to travel without the risk or fear of losing money.
- Banks also issue letter of credit in the names of their customers certifying their creditworthiness.
- Banks also collect and publish statistics relating to agriculture, industry, trade, commerce and various financial matters for the knowledge of the public and the government which help them in taking policy decisions.
- As a part of the financial sector of the country the Commercial banks also underwrite the securities issued by the government, public sector and private sector enterprises for the greater interest of the investors.

From the above discussion on the functions of the Commercial banks we can conclude that the banks are to be considered not merely as dealers in money but also leaders in economic development of a country. The modern Commercial banks are playing a significant role in the economic development of a country by facilitating capital formation, encouraging entrepreneurial ability, promoting trade and commerce, influencing various economic activities, removing referral on equalities and above all helping on the implementation of the monetary policies adopted by the monetary authority from time to time, so we can say that a well - developed banking system is a necessary condition for the economic development of a country.

Central Bank – Meaning and Functions

The concept of Central banking is comparatively of recent origin and related to 19th and 20th centuries. Of course prior to these dates certain Central banking functions were performed by Certain institutions in different countries. The evolution of Central bank started only after the International Financial Conference meeting held in Brussels in 1920 which suggested for the opening of Central banks in all countries. Of course some major countries like England, France, Netherlands, Russia, Germany etc. had established their Central Central banks in the 19th century. The Federal Reserve of America was established in 1913 and Reserve Bank of India was established in 1935 and became nationalized in 1949.

Meaning

Broadly speaking the bank which stands at the apex of the banking and monetary structure of a country is called the Central bank. It is called the Central bank as it occupies a pivotal position in the monetary and banking system of a country. It is the leader of the money market of a country and on that capacity it supervises, controls and regulates the functioning of the Commercial banks and other non-banking financial institutions working within the country. It acts as a supreme financial authority without any profit seeking motive rather to protect the economic interest of the country.

Definitions

Since as the supreme institution of the financial sector of a country the Central bank plays such a pivotal role in the monetary and banking system of the country that it is too difficult to define a Central bank in precise. Yet different economists have defined Central bank differently. We have quoted some of the definitions below.

According to ***De Kock****, "a bank which constitutes the apex of the monetary and banking structure of the country and performs a number of important functions in the economic interest of the country concerned, is the Central bank."*

According to ***Kent****, "The Central bank is an institution charged with the responsibility of managing of the expansion and contraction of the volume of money on the interest of general public welfare."*

Simply speaking, Central bank is an apex institution that controls, operates, regulates and directs the entire banking and monetary structure of the country and also helps the government in implementing its economic policies successfully.

Functions of Central Bank

The Central bank of a country is its apex financial institution controlling and regulating the economic and financial structure of the concerned country. We know the economic and financial structure of all countries are not the same. So the Central banks of different countries are performing diversified functions. Yet most of the functions performed by the Central banks of almost all countries are common which are discussed under the following heads.

1. **Monopoly of Note Issue** – Central bank of a country has the monopoly power of issuing currency notes. The currency notes issued by the Central bank are unlimited legal tender throughout the country. In some countries like the USA, England their Central banks have complete monopoly of note issue as they issue currency notes and coins of all denomination circulating in their countries. However, in India, the RBI has partial monopoly as the currency notes of one Rupee denomination are issued by the Government of India. Monopoly power of note issue is assigned to the Central bank mainly due to three reasons. They are :

   (i) To ensure uniformity in the currency notes circulated in the country.

   (ii) To enable the Central bank to implement its credit control methods effectively, and

   (iii) To prevent the issue of too much currency and thus helps in maintaining stability is the economy.

   While issuing currency notes the Central banks follow certain principles or systems like - Fixed Fiduciary System, Maximum Fiduciary System, proportional Reserve System and Maximum Reserve System. In the present days most of the Central banks including the Reserve Bank of India, are following the minimum reserve system of note issue. Under this System the Central banks are allowed to issue currency notes keeping a minimum reserve of gold or foreign exchange. The RB] issues currency with a minimum reserve of gold worth ₹ 115 crores and foreign exchange reserve of worth ₹ 85 crores and thus a total minimum reserve worth ₹ 200 crores.

2. **Banker to the Government** – Central bank of a country acts as the banker, agent and adviser to the government of the concerned country. As a banker to the government the Central bank performs the same functions for the government what the Commercial banks perform for their customers. It maintains the accounts of the Central government as well as state governments, receives deposits from different government departments and gives loans and advances to the government, collects cheques and drafts deposited in government accounts etc.

   As an agent of the government the Central bank collects taxes and other payments on behalf of the government. It raises loans from money markets for the government and manages public debts.

   As the financial adviser of the government the Central bank gives advices to the government on economic, monetary and financial matters such as deficit financing, devaluation of currency, trade policy, foreign exchange policy etc

3. **Banker's Bank** – The Central bank of a country acts as the bankers bank or the bank of the Commercial banks working in the country and affiliated to it in three respects –

   (i) It acts as the custodian of the Cash Reserve Ratio (CRR) of the Commercial banks.

   (ii) It acts as the lender of last resort for the Commercial banks.

   (iii) It acts as the clearing house for the Commercial banks in settling the inter-bank obligations.

   It is a legal obligation for all Commercial banks to keep a stipulated percentage of the primary deposits accepted by them from the people with the Central bank. This is called as the **Cash Reserve Ratio (CRR).** The CRR with the Central bank acts as a general credit-control device. On the ground of such reserves the Commercial banks also get financial support from the Central bank at the time of their financial crisis. When the Commercial banks need cash and fail to arrange cash from other sources they borrow from the Central bank. The Central bank gives loans to the Commercial banks either by rediscounting the bills of exchange or giving loans against government securities. Thus the Central bank acts as the lender of last resort for the Commercial banks.

4. **Controller of Credit** – Controlling credit, created by the Commercial banks, is the most important function of the Central bank of a country. Because in the modern economies credit created by the Commercial banks which are called 'bank money'

constitute a major part of the total money supply in the circulation. The price stability in the economy mainly depends upon the magnitude of the bank money or credit created by the Commercial banks. We know, the Commercial banks are the profit seeking institution and advancement of loans is their most profitable functions. But if the Commercial banks go on creating credit indiscriminately it will increase the supply of money and inflationary rise in prices. The fluctuations in the price level is not good for the economic health of the country. As the custodian of the national economy the Central bank is assigned the task of controlling the credit created by the Commercial bank. For this the Central banks adapt broadly two types of credit control methods - General or Quantitative credit control methods which include bank rate policy, open market operation and variable cash reserve ratio; and Selective or Qualitative Credit Control methods which include regulation of margin requirements, regulation of consumer's credit, rationing of credit, Moral Suation, publicity and even direct action. The quantitative credit control methods are intended to control the volume of credit without any consideration of the purpose of credit. On the other hand the qualitative credit control methods aim at controlling the quality or purpose of credits created by the Commercial banks and by these the Central bank tries to encourage the productive credits and discourage the unproductive credits created by the Commercial bank. By this the price stability is maintained in the economy.

(A detailed discussion on the quantitative and qualitative credit control methods is made later in this chapter.)

5. **Custodian of Foreign Exchange Reserves** – The Central bank acts as the custodian of the foreign exchange reserves of the country. All foreign exchange, earnings are deposited in the Central bank to regulate the use of foreign exchanges. By this the Central bank tries to maintain stability in the foreign exchange rates and overcome the balance of payments difficulties of the country. In the capacity of the custodian of the foreign exchange reserve the Central bank determines the rate of exchange of domestic currency with the foreign currencies, of course with the confirmation of the International Monetary Fund (IMF). In this capacity also the Central bank regulates the demand and supply of foreign currencies in the domestic country and regulates the volume of foreign trade.

6. **Execution of Monetary Policy** – As the supreme monetary authority of the country the Central bank formulates, implements and makes time to time reviews of the monetary policy of the country. Through the monetary policy the Central bank tries to manipulate the rate of interest according to the changing economic

activities and, the need of the time, regulate the activities of the banking and non-banking financial intermediaries, supply of money, etc. to achieve various macroeconomic objectives like stability in the prices, stability in the exchange rates, equilibrium is the balance of payments position of the country, increase in the level of employment, economic development and growth etc.

7. **Developmental Functions** – Besides the above discussed functions the Central banks of developing countries perform various developmental and promotional functions. To promote economic development via sectoral development the Central bank establishes various specified financial institutions to facilitate credit and investment to the priority sectors. For example, in India the Reserve Bank of India has created Small Industries Development Bank of India (SIDBI) for catering credit to Small Scale Industries, cottage industries and Small business etc, Industrial Development Bank of India (IDBI) to facilitate credit for the industrial development in the country; National Bank for Agriculture and Rural Development (NABARD) to facilitate credit to the agricultural sector and rural infrastructural sector etc. Moreover, as an agent of economic development the Central banks of the developing countries also play a significant role in developing the money and capital markets to promote saving and investment and capital formation for the rapid economic development.

Moreover, the Central bank of a country also maintains relations of the concerned country with international institutions like the IBRD (World Bank), the IMF etc. It collects and publishes various statistical data relating to different sectors of the economy regarding their performance and progress. It organises various surveys and seminars and publishes reports on economic matters etc. The Central bank of country performs all these functions without any profit motive.

Distinction Between Central Bank and Commercial Bank

The distinction between the Central bank and the Commercial Banks can be summarized as :

Central Bank	Commercial Bank
1. Central bank at the apex of the banking and monetary structure is the supreme institution to control and regulate the financial system of the country without any profit motive.	1. Commercial bank working under the supervision and control of the Central bank deals with cash and credit creation and works with profit motive

2. A country has only one Central bank and that is nationalised or state-owned.	2. There are several Commercial banks in a country and in some countries there are both nationalised and private Commercial banks including some foreign banks.
3. Central bank issues currency notes, acts as the banker of the government and of the Commercial banks, custodian of the country's foreign exchange reserves and works for public welfare and faster economic development.	3. Commercial bank accepts deposits from the public, advances loans to the public and business organisations, creates bank money, provides agency services and general utility services but on business lines, i.e. to make profit.
4. Central bank does not directly deal with public rather issues guidelines for the Commercial banks and non-banking financial institutions for the smooth working of the financial sector of the country.	4. Commercial bank directly deals with the public in accordance to the guidelines issued by the Central bank and plays a significant role in the expansion of the trade and commerce, capital formation and overall economic development.

Credit Control Methods Adopted By Central Bank

Credit control is one of the most significant functions of the Central bank of a country. Commercial banks as the profit seeking institutions may go on creating credit indiscriminately in the economy in order to earn profit in the form of interest. But this indiscriminate credit creation by the Commercial banks may lead to inflationary rise in the price level, instability in the exchange rate and above all instability in the economy, which is not conducive to economic development. That's why as the apex bank and as the custodian of the national economy the Central bank has to control the creation of credit by the Commercial banks to maintain stability in the economy.

There are several methods that the Central bank adopts to control credit. These methods can be put broadly under two categories –

(i) General or Quantitative credit control methods

(ii) Selective or Qualitative Credit Control methods

It is to be noted that credit control means contraction of credit when there is excess credit created in the economy causing inflationary rise in prices and expansion of credit when there is the need to increase money supply to activate the economy from the state of recession.

Quantitative Credit Control Methods

The general or quantitative credit control methods, as the name suggests are intended to control the quantity or volume of credit created in the economy by the Commercial banks, without considering the purpose of credit, i.e. whether the credits are productive or unproductive. The methods that come under this category are discussed below.

Bank Rate Policy – Bank rate is the official minimum rate at which the Central bank rediscounts the first class bills of exchange or lends the Commercial banks on approved securities such as treasury bills, bills of exchange etc. There is an intimate, direct and proportional relationship between the bank rate and interest rate prevailing in the money market. When the bank rate increases the rate of interest in the money market also increases and vice versa. When the Central bank raises the bank rate, rate of interest in the money market also increases and credit becomes costlier and hence is contracted reverse happens when the Central bank decreases bank rate. Thus through bank rate policy the Central bank contracts and expands the volume of credit as per the need of the time.

Open Market Operation – Normally, the Central bank does not operate in the open market. But in order to control the credit creation process it operates in the open market by purchasing and selling various credit instruments like government bills, securities, bonds and other promissary notes. The logic is when the Central bank sales the financial assets in the open market the buyers having greater faith on Central bank withdraw money from Commercial banks to purchase the assets. As a result the cash reserves of the Commercial banks on which their credit creation power depends, decreases and hence creation of credit contracts. On the other hand when the Central bank purchases these financial assets the supply of money in circulation increases which also increases the cash reserves of the Commercial banks and their credit creation power.

Variable Cash Reserve Ratio – By legal obligation all Commercial banks are required to keep a certain percentage of the amount of money accepted by them as primary deposits with the Central bank, which is called Cash Reserve Ratio (CRR). By varying this CRR the Central bank can affect the cash reserves of the Commercial banks and their credit creation power. The logic is when the Central bank well raise the CRR it will leave less amount of money (excess reserve) with the Commercial banks to the extent of increased CRR. As a result of which the credit creation power of the Commercial banks will decrease to its multiple extent. Reverse will happen if the Central bank decreases the CRR. Thus by manipulating the CRR the Central bank can control the credit created by the Commercial banks.

Qualitative Credit Control Methods – Qualitative or Selective credit control methods, as the name suggests, are intendent to control the quality or purpose of credit, i.e. by discriminating between the productive and unproductive credits created by the Commercial banks. Different methods adopted under this category are discussed below.

Fixation of Margin Requirements – Margin requirement means the difference between the market value of a security and its maximum loan value, which is determined by the Central bank. When the Central bank increases the margin requirement the loan value of a security decreases and thus the unproductive credits are discouraged leading to contraction in the credit creation. On the other hand credit creation can be encouraged by decreasing the margin requirements for productive credits.

Regulation of Consumers' Credit – Under the consumers' credit system for purchasing durable goods a certain percentage of the price is paid by the consumer on cash, which is called down payment and the rest is financed through bank credit which is repayable by the consumer in instalments. The Central bank can regulate such credit by determining the amount of down payment (in percentage of the price of the goods) by changing the number of instalments etc. This method is meant to discourage excessive demand for consumer durable goods and thereby controlling the inflationary rise in their prices.

Rationing of Credit – The Central bank applies this method to the Commercial banks which create credit. Rationing of credit may assume two forms – (i) The Central bank may fix its rediscounting facilities for any particular bank, (ii) It may fix the minimum ratio regarding the capital of a Commercial bank to its total assets. In other words credit rationing aims at limiting the maximum loans and advances to the Commercial banks and fixing the ceiling for specific categories of loans and advances. This also discourages Commercial banks to create excessive loans.

Moral Suasion – Moral Suasion means moral pressure or influence which includes advising, requesting and persuading the Commercial banks to co-operate with the Central bank on implementing its general monetary policy. Through this method the Central bank merely uses its moral influence to make the Commercial banks to follow its policy. The success of this method depends on the leadership quality of the Central bank.

Publicity – The Central bank can also use the method of publicity to put psychological pressure on the Commercial banks to control the creation of credit. Through this it tries to influence the credit policy of the Commercial banks, educate the people about the economic and monetary condition of the country, to influence the public opinion in favour of its monetary policy and against the Commercial banks defying its monetary policy.

Direct Action – This is the ultimate method to control the credit creation power of the Commercial banks adopted by the Central bank. Direct action may take different forms like refusing to discount bills of exchange pledged by the Commercial banks, charging penalty rate of interest, refusing to grant more credit etc. Even under this method the Central bank can go to the extent of withdrawing recognition and affiliation of the Commercial banks whose credit policy is not in the line of the Central bank.

WHAT WE LEARNT

Money –

1. In the whole Commercial side of man's social existence money is the essential invention on which all the rest is based.
2. Prior to the invention of money transactions were carried out on barter line, *i.e.* Commodity against Commodity (C→C).
3. The major difficulties of barter system were – lack of double coincidence of wants, lack of common measure of value, and lack of indivisibility of goods and lack of store of value and lack of standard of deferred payments.
4. Money as a commonly accepted thing to measure the value in business transaction was invented to remove the difficulties of barter transactions.
5. Money in its present state has evolved through different stages, *i.e.* from animal money to plastic money.
6. The evolution of money has recognized through six stages – Animal money, commodity money, metallic money, paper money, credit money and plastic money.
7. The term 'money' is derived from the Latin word "Moneta', the name of Roman Goddess 'Junomeneta', the Goddess of Heaven.
8. Money can be defined as anything that is generally acceptable as a means of exchange and at the same time acts as a measure and store of value. **– Crowther.**
9. Francis Walker said, "Money is what money does."
10. The primary functions of money are – (i) It acts as a medium of exchange, and (ii) It acts as a measure of value.

11. The secondary functions of money are – (i) It acts as a standard of deferred payments, and (ii) It acts as a store of value.
12. The contingent functions of money includes – transfer of value, foundation of credit creation, basis of price mechanism, measuring rod of national income etc.
13. The liquid financial assets which can be easily converted into money without any loss of value and are accepted in most business transactions, though are not legal, are called near money.
14. The money in terms of which the value of everything in a country is expressed is called 'Money of account' or 'unit of account'. e.g. Rupee in India.
15. Money proper refers to the currency notes and coins with which actual payments are made.
16. The money whose face value is equal to its intrinsic value is called 'Standard money' or 'Standard Coin'.
17. The money whose face value is greater than its intrinsic value is called 'Token money' or 'Token coin'

Banking –

1. The term 'bank' is derived from Greek word 'banque' or Italian word 'banco', both meaning 'bench'.
2. First institutional bank was established in Italy named 'Bank of Venice' in 1157.
3. Modern Commercial banking originated in England in 1640 by the merchants, the money-lenders and the goldsmiths.
4. Bank of England, the mother of all commercial banks was established in 1694.
5. Joint-Stock Commercial Banking System started in England in 1833.
6. Bank of Hindustan established in 1770 with its head- quarters in Kolkata, was the first banking institution on India.
7. A commercial bank is a profit seeking financial institution which deals with money and credit.
8. Acceptance of deposits and advancement of loans are the main functions of the Commercial banks.
9. Current or demand deposit refers to that deposit from which money can be withdrawn at any time during the banking hours issuing cheque only.
10. Current deposits are preferred by the traders and businessmen.
11. No interest or a very negligible interest is paid on the current deposit.

12. Bank cannot use money deposited in current deposit profitably.
13. The highest interest rate is paid on the fixed or time deposits.
14. Bank can make profitable use of money deposited is fixed deposits.
15. Saving deposits are meant to encourage saving habits among the small income earners.
16. Recurring deposits are preferred by fixed income earners.
17. In recurring deposits money is deposited in instalments for a specific time period.
18. Advancement of loans is the most profitable function of the Commercial banks.
19. Cash credit is preferred by the traders and businessmen.
20. In case of cash credit interest is charged only on the amount withdrawn.
21. In case of direct loan interest is charged on the amount of loan sanctioned.
22. Creation of credit, promotion of cheque, agency and general utility functions are the secondary functions of the Commercial banks.
23. The bank which stands at the apex of the monetary and banking structure of a country is called Central bank.
24. Reserve Bank of India is the Central bank in India.
25. The RBI was established in 1939 and nationalized in 1949.
26. The Central bank of a country has the monopoly power of note issue.
27. The RBI has partial monopoly over note issue.
28. The Central bank acts as banker, agent and adviser to the government.
29. The Central bank acts as the bankers bank in three respects :
    - as the custodian of the CRR
    - as the lender of last resort
    - as the clearing house in settling inter-bank obligations.
30. The Central bank acts as the controller of credit.

QUESTIONS FOR REVIEW

A. Choose the correct answer from the given alternatives in each question. (Each Carrying 1 Mark)

1. **Direct exchange of goods against goods is called :**

   (i) Barter System (ii) Market System

   (iii) Exchange Mechanism (iv) None of the above

2. **Who said 'Money is what money does' ?**
   (i) Crowther (ii) Robertson
   (iii) Francis Walker (iv) A. C. Pigou
3. **The money whose face value is equal to its intrinsic value is called :**
   (i) Token Money (ii) Standard Money
   (iii) Fiat Money (iv) Near Money
4. **Which one is a unlimited legal tender ?**
   (i) Standard Money (ii) Token Money
   (iii) Near Money (iv) None of these
5. **Which one is more popular ?**
   (i) Animal money (ii) Commodity Money
   (iii) Near Money (iv) Paper Money
6. **Which one has 100 percent back up of precious metals ?**
   (i) Representative Paper Money (ii) Convertible Paper Money
   (iii) Inconvertible Paper Money (iv) All the above
7. **Which money is circulated in the economy under extra-ordinary circumstances ?**
   (i) Convertible Paper Money (ii) Fiat Money
   (iii) Near Money (iv) None of the above
8. **The additional purchasing power created by the commercial banks is called :**
   (i) Bank notes (ii) Cash credit
   (iii) Bank Money (iv) All the above
9. **The bank notes and which of the following together constitute the total money supply ?**
   (i) Bank Money (ii) Near Money
   (iii) Plastic Money (iv) All the above
10. **Which one is the latest form of money ?**
    (i) Paper Money (ii) Credit Money
    (iii) Plastic Money (iv) None of the above
11. **Which one of the following is a primary function of money ?**
    (i) Medium of exchange (ii) Standard of deferred payment
    (iii) Store of value (iv) None of the above
12. **Which one of the following is a contingent function of money ?**
    (i) Measure of value (ii) Medium of exchange
    (iii) Basis of Price mechanism (iv) Standard of deferred payments

13. Who summarised the functions of money is a famous couplet ?

(i) Walker (ii) Jevons

(iii) Crowther (iv) Robertson

14. Which function of money made transaction easy, time and cost saving ?

(i) Measure of value (ii) Medium of exchange

(iii) Store of value (iv) All the above

15. Value expressed in terms of money is called :

(i) Exchange value (ii) Cost

(iii) Price (iv) All the above

16. Which function of money facilitates credit transactions ?

(i) Medium of exchange (ii) Measure of value

(iii) Store of value (iv) Standard of deferred payments

17. Who said 'Money is round so that it can circulate and it is so flat that it can be piled up.' ?

(i) Crowther (ii) Francis Walker

(iii) Robertson (iv) Kent

18. The financial assets which can be easily converted in to money are called :

(i) Bank Money (ii) Near Money

(iii) Representative Money (iv) Standard Money

19. Which one of the following is a legal tender ?

(i) Cheque (ii) Currency note

(iii) Bond (iv) Share

20. Which one of the following is a near money ?

(i) Share (ii) Fixed Deposit

(iii) Bond (iv) All the above

21. Which one is also called optional money ?

(i) Bank Money (ii) Token Money

(iii) Near Money (iv) None of the above

22. Which one of the following is the unit of account in India ?

(i) 2000 Rupee note (ii) 500 Rupee Note

(iii) 100 Rupee Note (iv) Rupee

23. The currency notes and coins with which actual payments are made, are called :

(i) Money of account (ii) Money Proper

(iii) Currency Notes (iv) None of the above

24. The first institutional bank was established in which country ?

(i) England (ii) The USA

(iii) Italy (iv) India

25. Which one of the following is called the mother of all commercial banks ?

(i) Bank of Venice (ii) Bank of England

(iii) Bank of Hindustan (iv) None of the above

26. Which one of the following is a primary function of commercial bank ?

(i) Acceptance of deposits (ii) Promotion of cheque

(iii) Creation of bank money (iv) All the above

27. From which deposits money can be withdrawn at any time during the banking hour ?

(i) Fixed deposit (ii) Current deposit

(iii) Saving deposit (iv) All the above

28. From which deposit money is withdrawn issuing cheque only ?

(i) Time deposit (ii) Demand deposit

(iii) Saving deposit (iv) Recurring deposit

29. On which deposit no interest or a negligible rate of interest is paid ?

(i) Demand deposit (ii) Fixed deposit

(iii) Savings deposit (iv) None of the above

30. Which deposits are preferred by the traders and businessmen ?

(i) Savings deposit (ii) Fixed deposit

(iii) Current deposit (iv) All the above

31. Money in which deposit is like cash in hand ?

(i) Fixed deposit (ii) Saving deposit

(iii) Home safe deposit (iv) Current deposit

32. The highest rate of interest is paid on which deposit ?

(i) Fixed deposit (ii) Savings deposit

(iii) Current deposit (iv) Recurring deposit

33. In which deposit money can be deposited in small denominations ?

(i) Recurring deposit (ii) Saving deposit

(iii) Current deposit (iv) Fixed deposit

34. In which deposit money is deposited in instalments for a fixed period of time ?

(i) Fixed deposit (ii) Current deposit

(iii) Savings deposit (iv) Recurring deposit

35. Which one of the following is the most profitable function of the commercial bank ?

(i) Acceptance of deposits (ii) Advancement of loans

(iii) Promotion of cheque (iv) None of the above

36. Interest is paid only on amount of money withdrawn in case of :

(i) Direct loans (ii) Overdraft

(iii) Cash Credit (iv) Discounting bills of exchange

37. Which bank provides agency function to its customers ?

(i) Central bank (ii) Development bank

(iii) Commercial bank (iv) Industrial bank

38. Which bank provides locker facilities to its customers ?

(i) Commercial bank (ii) Central bank

(iii) Co-operative bank (iv) None of the above

39. The bank which stands at the apex of the banking system of a country is called :

(i) World bank (ii) Central bank

(iii) Commercial bank (iv) Lead bank

40. Which one of the following stands at the apex of India's banking system ?

(i) Central Bank of India (ii) State Bank of India

(iii) Reserve Bank of India (iv) Bank of India

41. Which of the following has the monopoly power of issuing notes ?

(i) Central Bank (ii) World Bank

(iii) Commercial Bank (iv) Development Bank

42. Reserve Bank of India's monopoly power of note issue is :

(i) Absolute (ii) Partial

(iii) Complete (iv) None of the above

43. Monopoly power of note issue is assigned to the Central bank to :

(i) Maintain uniformity in currency notes

(ii) Avoid over issue

(iii) Implement the credit control methods effectively

(iv) All the above

44. Which bank provides short-term loans and advances to the government ?

(i) World Bank (ii) Foreign Exchange Bank

(iii) Central Bank (iv) Commercial Banks

45. Which bank acts as the lender of last resort for the Commercial banks ?

(i) World Bank
(ii) Central Bank
(iii) Nationalised Banks
(iv) Co-operative Banks

46. The Reserve Bank of India was established in the year :

(i) 1913
(ii) 1935
(iii) 1949
(iv) 1969

47. Which bank acts as the controller of credit ?

(i) Central Bank
(ii) Commercial Bank
(iii) Foreign Exchange Bank
(iv) None of the above

48. Which bank determines the foreign exchange rate of the currency of the country ?

(i) Foreign Exchange Bank
(ii) World Bank
(iii) Central Bank
(iv) Commercial Bank

49. Which bank acts as the custodian of the CRR of commercial banks ?

(i) Commercial bank
(ii) Foreign Exchange Bank
(iii) World Bank
(iv) Central Bank

50. The rate at which the Central bank provides loans to the commercial bank is called :

(i) Interest rate
(ii) Bank rate
(iii) Repo rate
(iv) Exchange rate

B. *Correct the statement, if necessary, without changing the underlined portions. (Each Carrying 1 Mark)*

1. The money whose face value is equal to its intrinsic value is called token money.
2. In case of convertible paper money 100 percent reserve in metallic form is maintained.
3. Convertible paper money cannot be converted in to full-bodied money.
4. Fiat money is circulated in the economy under extra-ordinary circumstances.
5. Standard money are not legal tender.
6. Measure of value is a secondary function of money.
7. Near money acts as money substitute.
8. Near money acts as unit of account.

9. Value of everything is expressed in terms of near money.
10. Fixed deposit is an example of near money.
11. The money with which actual payments are made is called money of account.
12. The 'Bank of Venice' is called as the mother of all commercial banks.
13. Advancement of loans is a secondary function of commercial bank.
14. Acceptance of deposit is the most profitable function of commercial bank.
15. Highest interest is paid on the demand deposits.
16. The bank can make profitable use of money deposited in fixed deposits.
17. The loans given by commercial banks on overdraft are self-liquidating.
18. In case of cash credit interest is charged on sanctioned amount.
19. Creation of credit is a primary function of the commercial banks.
20. Derivative deposits increases the cash in hand of the commercial bank.
21. Commercial bank stands at the apex of the banking structure of a country.
22. The Reserve bank of India was established in the year 1949.
23. The Reserve bank of India was nationalised in the year 1935.
24. The Commercial Banks provide short-term credits to the government.
25. The Central Bank of India stands at the apex of Indian banking and monetary structure.
26. The RBI has absolute monopoly over issuing currency notes.
27. The Central bank acts as the creator of credit.
28. The Central bank acts as the lender of last resort for the government.
29. The Central bank acts as the clearing house for the Commercial banks.
30. The Foreign Exchange Bank acts as the custodian of the foreign exchange reserves of the country.
31. The Central bank of a country directly deals with the public.
32. Bank money is created by the Central bank.
33. The Central bank works with profit seeking motive.
34. Commercial bank works in the interest of the national economy.
35. Bank rate and interest rate in the money market are inversely related.
36. Commercial banks maintain stability in the economy.
37. The Central Bank of India is a commercial bank.

38. The Central bank raises the bank rate to expand credit creation in the economy.
39. The rate at which the Central bank lends money to commercial banks is called repo rate.
40. Bank rate is a quantitative credit control method.

C. Answer the following questions in 2-3 sentences each (Each Carrying 2 Marks)

1. What is barter system ?
2. Point out the major difficulties of barter system.
3. What is money ?
4. What is standard money ?
5. What is token money ?
6. What is representative paper money ?
7. What is convertible paper money ?
8. What is credit money (or Bank money) ?
9. What are the primary functions of money ?
10. What are the secondary functions of money ?
11. What are the contingent functions of money ?
12. What is near money ?
13. What is money of account ?
14. What is money proper ?
15. What is commercial bank ?
16. What are the primary functions of commercial bank ?
17. What are the secondary functions of commercial bank ?
18. What is demand (current) deposit ?
19. What is fixed (term or time) deposit ?
20. What is savings deposit ?
21. What is recurring deposit ?
22. What is primary deposit ?
23. What is derivative deposit ?
24. What is cash-credit ?
25. What is direct loan ?

26. What is discounting bills of exchange ?
27. What is overdraft ?
28. What is money at call and short notice ?
29. What are agency functions of commercial banks ?
30. What are the general utility functions of commercial banks ?
31. What is Central bank ?
32. Why monopoly power of note issue is assigned to the Central Bank ?
33. Why Central bank is called the bankers' bank ?
34. Why Central bank is called banker to the government ?
35. What is bank rate ?
36. What is open market operation ?
37. What is variable cash reserve ratio ?
38. What is legal tender ?

D. *Distinguish between in six sentences each (Each Carrying 3 Marks)*

1. Standard coin and Token coin
2. Money and Near Money
3. Money of account and Money Proper
4. Demand deposit and Fixed deposit
5. Cash Credit and Direct Loan
6. Primary Deposits and Derivative Deposits
7. Central Bank and Commercial Bank
8. Quantitative and Qualitative Credit Control Methods

E. *Long Answer Type Questions (Each Carrying 7½ Marks)*

1. What is Barter system ? Discuss the difficulties of the barter system.
2. Define Money. Discuss the functions of money.
3. Discuss the functions of Commercial bank.
4. Discuss the functions of Central Bank.
5. Discuss the Credit Control methods adopted by Central bank.

Answer to Q. N. A

1.	(i)	2.	(iii)	3.	(ii)	4.	(i)	5.	(iv)	6.	(i)	7.	(ii)	8.	(iii)
9.	(i)	10.	(iii)	11.	(i)	12.	(iii)	13.	(ii)	14.	(ii)	15.	(iii)	16.	(iv)
17.	(i)	18.	(ii)	19	(ii)	20.	(iv)	21.	(iii)	22.	(iv)	23.	(ii)	24.	(iii)
25.	(ii)	26.	(i)	27	(ii)	28.	(ii)	29.	(i)	30.	(iii)	31.	(iv)	32.	(i)
33.	(ii)	34.	(iv)	35.	(ii)	36.	(iii)	37.	(iii)	38.	(i)	39.	(ii)	40.	(iii)
41.	(i)	42.	(ii)	43.	(iv)	44.	(iii)	45.	(ii)	46.	(ii)	47.	(i)	48.	(iii)
49.	(iv)	50.	(ii)												

Answer to Q. N. B

1. Standard Money	2. Representative	3. Incovertible
4. Correct	5. Token money	6. Primary
7. Correct	8. Money of account	9. Money
10. Correct	11. Money proper	12. Bank of England
13. Primary	14. Advancement of loans	15. Fixed deposit
16. Correct	17.Discounting bills of exchange	18. Withdrawn amount
19. Secondary	20. Primary	21. Central bank
22. 1935	23. 1949	24. Central bank
25. Reserve Bank of India	26. Partial	27. Controller
28. Commercial banks	29. Correct	30. Central bank
31. Commercial banks	32. Commercial banks	33. Commercial banks
34. Central bank	35. Directly	36. Central bank
37. Correct	38. Reduces	39. Bank rate
40. Correct		

❑❑❑

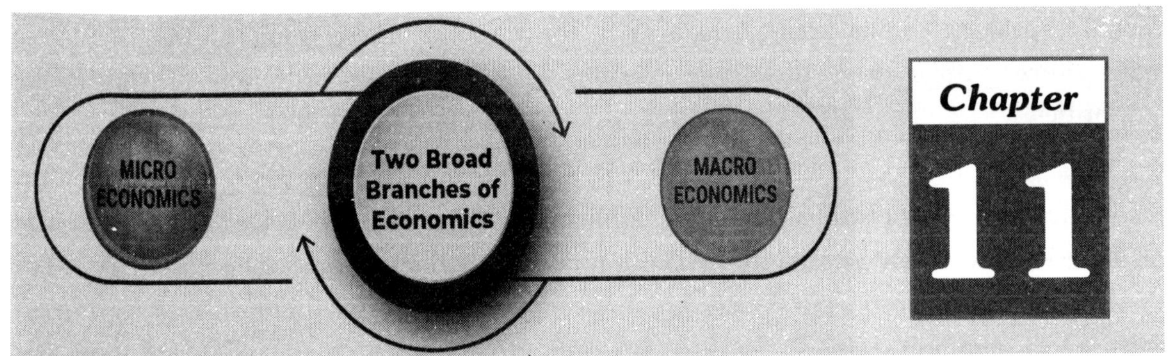

PUBLIC FINANCE

Public finance refers to that branch of economics which deals with the income and expenditure of the public authorities, i.e. the government. The importance of the study of Public finance has been receiving priority since the publication of Keynes's 'General Theory in 1936, in which he suggested for government intervention into economic activities through its budgetary policy for the revival of the depression-stricken economies. Prior to the Keynesian revolution in the economic thinking the perception of the classical economists on the public finance was very much confined. The classicals believed in the laissez-fair Principle and favoured limited activities of the state confined to maintenance of law and order in the society, protection of life and property of the people and protection of national territory. They strictly prohibited state intervention into economic activities and favoured a small income and expenditure plan, i.e. Small and balanced budget of the government. But the Great Depression of 1930s and the Keynesian revolution brought through his General Theory changed the perception of the economists on the importance of public finance and the concept of welfare state also added twist to the new perception on public finance. Now a days, almost all states as the welfare states are performing increasing activities along with their traditional activities. Accordingly the purview of the income and expenditure of the public authorities i.e. the purview of public finance has been expanding constantly.

Meaning

'Public finance' is a composite word in which 'public' means public authorities which include the Central government, State governments and local governments, and 'finance' means matter related to money. In this sense public finance refers to that branch of economics which studies the monetary matter and its management of the public authorities.

Broadly speaking public finance deals with the receipts of the public authorities, their expenditure, public debt, their management and fiscal administration of the public authorities.

Thus public finance on the one hand deals with the monetary affairs which is related to economics and on the other hand the public authorities, i.e. the governments which is related to political science. That's why **Dalton** has rightly remarked, "Public finance is one of those subjects that lie on the border-line between economics and politics. It is concerned with the income and expenditure of public authorities with the adjustment of one to the other."

*In the words of **Bastable**, "Public finance deals with expenditure and income of public authorities or the state and their mutual relation as also with the financial administration and control."*

*According to **Prof. Findlay Shiras**," Public finance is the study of principles underlying the spending and raising of funds by public authorities."*

Broadly speaking Public finance is the study of income and expenditure of the public authorities including public debt management, fiscal administration of the public authorities and the fiscal federation of a federal set up, which are included in the fiscal policy of the government of a country to achieve certain macroeconomic objectives.

Subject Matter of Public Finance

From the above discussed meaning and definitions of public finance we can discuss the subject matter of public finance broadly under the following heads.

1. **Public Revenue:** Public revenue refers to those receipts of the government which come from revenue sources like earned sources and unearned sources. It includes receipts from public domains, receipts from commercial activities undertaken by government, i.e. the Public Sector undertakings and unearned sources like tax revenue, revenue from administrative sources like fees, fines, penalties etc. However, public revenue is not equal to public income as the later includes public borrowing and receipts from the sale of public assets. The study of public revenue which deals with the method of raising funds, classification of public revenue, canons and justification of taxations, effects of taxation, the incidence and shifting of burden of taxation etc. come under the subject matter of public finance.

2. **Public Expenditure:** Public expenditure is the study of the principles and problems related to the allocation of public receipts. In this section of the public finance we study the principles governing the flow of public funds into different channels. Here we study public. Spending in the form of revenue expenditure, capital expenditure, developmental expenditure, non-developmental expenditure, planed and non-planed expenditure etc. In this section of public finance we also study the expenditure policy of the government, effects of public expenditure on consumption, production and distribution of income including the measures adopted by the government for the general welfare of the people and economic stability.

3. **Public Debt:** The matter of public revenue and public expenditure give rise to this section of the public finance, particularly when the public expenditure exceeds public revenue. When the government faces a deficit budget to bridge up the gap between expenditure and receipts the government borrows through different sources, both from domestic or internal and external sources. So under this section of public finance we study the sources of public debt, the methods of redemption of public debt, the effects of public debt on consumption, production and other economic activities including the burden created by the public debt both on the present generation and the posterity.

4. **Financial Administration:** In this section of public finance we study the organisation and functioning of the financial machinary of the government in raising funds and allocating public funds into different channels. For this the budget is the master financial plan of the government which reflects the efficiency of the financial administration of the government. The financial administration prepares and executes the budget and hence come under the subject matter of public finance.

5. **Fiscal Federation:** In a federal set up there is division of power among the central and state governments. There is legislative, executive and financial relations between the union government and state governments. The fiscal relations between the centre and the state governments relating to collection of revenue, determination of the shares of the centre and states in the collected revenue, allotment of national revenue to different developmental projects, imposition of taxes on different goods and services by the centre and the states, financial aids of the union government to the state governments and their utilization etc. refer to fiscal federalism and hence constitutes a part of the study of public finance.

From the above discussion we can say that public finance is a dynamic subject. That's why it's scope cannot be confined to any limited areas of study. It's scope is widening day-by-day and hence its subject matters are also subject to change. The government can alter the subject matter of this branch of economics for the greater interest of the economy.

Distinction Between Public Finance and Private Finance

As discussed above public finance is the study of income, expenditure and borrowings of the public authorities, i.e. the government. On the other hand private finance deals with the income, expenditure and debt of an individual or a private institution or organisation or a business firm. Since both the concepts are related to money matters both have some similarities as well as some differences.

From the view point of similarities we can say that both have the same objectives, i.e. satisfaction of want and maximization of satisfaction. In case of private finance the objective is to satisfy individual wants and maximization of individual satisfaction and in case of public finance the objective is to satisfy social or collective wants and the maximization of social welfare. Both are based on the concept of rationality. Because both private individual and government have limited resources and both want to make the rational use of the resources at their disposal. Moreover, as an individual may be tempted by circumstances to act foolishly and irrationally similarly some of the decisions of the government regarding utilization of resources may be unwise and unproductive. Both the private individual and the government resort to borrowing at the time of crisis and both have to repay their loans. Tentatively, both Private individual and the government try their level best for the efficient management of their financial matters.

However, the dissimilarities between the public finance and private finance are quite sharp. They can be discussed under the following heads.

1. Adjustment of Income and Expenditure

*According to **Prof. Dalton**, "While an individual's income determines his expenditure, a public authority's expenditure determines it's income."*

This implies the government first decides the nature and the magnitude of its expenditure and accordingly finds out the sources to obtain the income to meet the decided expenditure. But in case of private finance an individual or a business organization adjusts its expenditual to its income. That's why it is rightly said that an individual cuts his coat according to the cloth that he has, where as a public authority arranges cloth according to the size of the coat. So we can differentiate public and private finance as in case of public finance income is adjusted to expenditure where as in case of private finance expenditure is adjusted to income.

2. Motives of Expenditure

In case of public finance the motive of government expenditure is guided by the welfare of the community as a whole not any particular individual or group of individual. On the other hand in case of private finance the motive of an individuals or an institution's expenditure is guided by individual interest, i.e. maximization of personal or individual interest, which may go against the social interest. There is no such apprehension in case of public expenditure.

3. Sources of Resources

The Sources of resources of an individual or private institution are limited and confined to what he or it has at his disposal. An individual or an institution cannot use force to enhance his or its sources of income. On the other hand in case of public finance the sources of income of the government are enormous and the government can draw upon the entire wealth of the community by using force, if necessary. The government may raise tax rates or impose additional taxes and compel its citizens to save more etc. to increase its income. But such coercion cannot be used by the private individuals or institutions.

4. Principle of Equi-Marginal Utility

In case of private finance an individual plans his expenditure on the basis of the law of equi-marginal utility to maximize his satisfaction from his limited resources. Because he can spend his income on the basis of utility derived from different heads of expenditure. But in case of public finance it is not possible on the part of the government to compare the welfare from different heads of public expenditure. Because State expenditure is decided keeping in view some political expedience, non-economic considerations, distributive justice etc.

5. Compulsory Character

In case of public finance it is to be noted that the government cannot postpone or avoid certain expenditure. In the words of Prof. Findlay Shirras, 'an important characteristic of public expenditure is its compulsory character.' The expenditure on defence, maintenance of law and order and protection of life and properties of the people etc are of compulsory nature. Likewise in modern welfare state the public expenditure on the provisions for the basic amenities of life is also of compulsory nature. The government cannot avoid or postpone expenditure on these heads. On the other hand, in case of private finance an individual can avoid or postpone expenditure on any head.

6. Budgeting Difference

In the matter of budgeting there is a clear cut difference between the government budget and private or individual buffet. A government prepares its budget usually for one year, where as an individual prepares his budget keeping in view the time lag of receiving income which may be a day or a week or a month. An individual believes in surplus budget to ensure saving and always tries to avoid deficit budget. On the other hand a government prepares its budget keeping in view the economic stability in the country. Though the government prepares surplus budget to curb inflationary situations and deficit budget to uplift the economy from depressionary state, now a days almost all governments are preferring deficit budget for the expansion of the economic activities and economic development. Because the government has several ways to mitigate the budgetary deficit. But no private individual or business organisation prefers deficit budget.

7. Scope of Borrowing

In case of deficit the scope of borrowing for a private individual is limited as he can borrow either from friends or relatives or from self-help groups or co-operative societies or at best from commercial banks. But the scope of borrowing for the government is wide spread. In case of deficit the government can borrow from internal sources like its citizens, banks and Central bank. It can also borrow from external sources like foreign governments, from regional and international institutions like IMF, World Bank and other international agencies.

8. Secrecy

Private finance is subject to secrecy. No private individual or business organisation likes to disclose his or its financial matters to other. On the other hand in case of public finance the government gives higher publicity to its budget proposals. People are entitled to know and criticised the income and expenditure proposals of the government. The budget of the government is widely discussed in the legislature before it is passed. It is also widely discussed in the press. The openness of the income and expenditure proposals of the government is necessary for transparency and effective execution.

9. Sanction and Audit

In case of public finance any proposal relating to income and expenditure of the government requires prior approval of the cabinet and subject to audit by constitutional authorities. But no such approval is required for earning and spending of a private individual or business organisation and are also not subject to any audit.

Besides the above discussed differences there are also some other points of differences between public finance and private finance on the grounds of elasticity of income, long-term confederations of expenditure, solvancy etc. The income of an individual is relatively inelastic where as the income of a government is relatively more elastic as it can raise its income by a simple strike of pen. It can also print more currency notes and resort to deficit financing to raise funds. An individual while making expenditure or investment keeps in mind the short-run considerations or immediate returns, where as the government's consideration is both for short-run and long-run returns. Moreover, a state cannot afford to be insolvant where as an individual may go bankrupt.

Budget – Meaning and Definitions

The term 'Budget' is derived from the French word 'Bougette' which literally means 'a small leather bag'. In the study of public finance the bag itself is not vital, what is vital is what the bag contains. In this sense budget contains the financial plan of the government which is vital. It is presented in the parliament by the Finance Minister for elaborate discussion on the proposals of the government on taxation, public expenditure on various heads, sources of raising funds. etc contained in the budget. The proposals contained in the budget have far reaching effects on various aspects of the economy for which the bag or the briefcase that contains the proposals is not important rather those proposals are important. The government of a country tries its level best to maximize the welfare of the community through its budgetary policy, that's why it is important for the common people to have some knowledge about the budget.

From the above discussion, we can say that 'budget is a statement of the anticipated receipts and proposed expenditure of the government of a country for a fixed period of time, usually a year called a financial year.'

*In the words of **Prof. F. Taylor**, "Budget is the master financial plan of the government. It brings together estimates of anticipated revenue and proposed expenditure for the budget year."*

*According to **Prof. W.E. Willoughby**, "The budget has come to mean the financial arrangements of a given period, with the usual implication that they have been submitted to the legislature for approval."*

*According to **Prof. Rene Stourn**,"Budget is a document containing a preliminary approved plan of public revenue and expenditure."*

From the above discussed meaning and definitions we can say that a government budget contains the following features.

1. It is an annual financial statement of the government containing the anticipated revenue and proposed expenditure of the government.
2. It is an approved statement of the public authority.
3. It reflects the financial plan of the government of the previous year, current year and to some extent that of the succeeding year.
4. It presents the procedure in which revenue is to be collected and expenditure is to be executed.
5. It reflects the relative status and importance of different sectors of the economy as per the resources allotted to them.
6. It reflects the macroeconomic goals of the government and hence is an instrument of economic policy of the government.

Objectives of Budget

In modern times budget is considered as an important instrument of economic policy of the national government. The budget is not simply a proposal of estimates but a comprehensive plan and programme for the future on the basis of the past experience, expressing the economic and social policy of the government and its ideology. Through budget the government tries to achieve various socio-economic objectives. So it is not merely an estimate of anticipated revenue and proposed expenditure rather a document of fundamental importance for the country as a whole. Keeping in view the importance of budget for the whole economy, Prof. D.T. Lakhawala has rightly said –

> *"Budget is an instrument of economic policy meant to guide and regulate the course of the economy on the desired direction at an optimum pace."*

The importance of budget can be better understood from the discussion on the objectives of budget made below.

1. Allocation of Resources

Optimum allocation of scarce resources is the prime odjective of a government budget. By allocating resources to different lines of production in different sectors the government tries to achieve the goal of maximum social advantage. Under this objective utmost care is taken to allocate resources for the provision of social goods which cannot be provided through market mechanism, like defence, public health, education, sanitation, environmental protection and other socio-economic overheads. Socially and economically optimum allocation of resources on these heads in the budget Provides incentives to economic activities, influences industrial and agricultural production and productivity and ensures balanced growth. Optimum allocation also leads to development of human capital via education, training, better healthcare facilities etc. The government budget also aims at achieving distributive justice while determining the principles of taxation for raising resources. For optimal allocation of resources and maximization of social welfare **Prof. Pigou** and **Dalton** have suggested the principle of **Maximum Social Advantage** (MSA) which can be realised by equalising marginal social benefit from public expenditure and marginal social sacrifice due to taxation (MSB=MSS). This according to them maximize the net benefit and bring optimal allocation of resources.

2. Distribution of National Income

Equitable distribution of national income to remove or at least to decrease inequalities is an another objective of a government budget. This is highly essential for achieving distributive justice and economic development. Because inequalities in the distribution of income and wealth impades economic development and growth. Gap between the rich and the poor creates socio-economic distrust and, discontentment which is not conducive to economic development. That's why an important objective of government budget is inclusive economic development via provisions, for removal of poverty and employment, upliftment of the socio-economic status of the deprived etc. This objective of budget also includes removal of regional inequalities to ensure a balanced growth of the economy as a whole.

3. Economic Stability

For smooth economic development economic stability i.e. stability on the prices and different macroeconomic variables is an essential condition. Fluctuations in the prices either in the form of inflation or deflation destabilizes the economy and impade economic development via their adverse effects on the macroeconomic variables. So an another important objective of government budget is to maintain stability in the economy, i.e. to control inflation and deflation. The budgetary instruments like taxation, public expenditure, public debt, subsidies, deficit financing etc. can be used to ensure stability in the economy.

4. Growth Objective

Growth objective of a government budget, particularly in the developing countries, is multi-dimensional. It includes the objective to raise national saving and investment for rapid capital formation, generation of employment opportunities, provision for the expansion of socio-economic infrastructure, human development, expansion of foreign trade, development of science and technology, environmental protection etc. To achieve these objectives government budget makes provisions comprehensively.

Thus budget can be a useful instrument to touch and give shape to all aspects of the economic activities of the whole nation. Through its objectives it reflects the economic status of the country and the direction in which the economy is marching.

Types of Budget

Broadly speaking there are two types of budgets :

(i) Balanced budget, and

(ii) Unbalanced budget

Balanced Budget:

A budget is said to be a balanced budget when the anticipated revenues of the government and the proposed expenditure are shown equal. According to ***Prof. Dalton***, *" A balanced budget is that in which over a period of time, revenue does not fall short of expenditure."* Thus in a balanced budget there is neither any deficit nor any surplus. In other words, a government budget is said to be balanced when its tax revenue and its expenditure are equal.

The concept of balanced budget is an accounting concept only. It is simply a balance-sheet approach. In practice it is rather most difficult, though not impossible to have a balanced budget. The classical economists believing in the laissez-faire principle were in favour of a small and balanced budget. But in the present days economies, with the increasing importance of functional finance the balanced budget has remained only as a theoretical concept. No government, anywhere, now-a-days is adopting a balanced budget.

Merits of Balanced Budget

The classical economists favoured a balanced budget on the following merits.

1. **Effective Check:** The government always displays a tandency towards wasteful and unnecessary expenditure. But the balanced budget technique is held as an effective check in controlling extravagant expenditure of the government.

2. **Alarm against Economic problems:** Balanced budget alarms against the impediments of deficit budgeting, excess money supply, inflationary rise in prices and falling tendency of the value of money in the economy.
3. **Helps in checking Depression:** The balanced budget multiplier theory clearly states that with suitable and qualified conditions a balanced budget can raise the level of economic activities and increase national income, employment and effective demand, with the balanced budget policy depression is unlikely to creep into the economic system.
4. **Non-inflationary:** Under deficit budget the government may be tempted to print new currency notes to meet the mounting expenditure. But it may lead to inflationary rise in prices due to excess money supply. To get rid of this the safest method on the part of the government is to adopt balanced budget.
5. **Wise Economic Policy:** Government budget should not be guided by the political consideration rather on the basis of wise economic policy consistance with the need of the economy. Only the balanced budget policy is compatible to this objective.
6. **Suitable for Developed Countries:** The task before the developed countries is not to achieve economic development rather to maintain the already achieved level of development. For this there is the need to maintain stability and balanced budget policy is suitable to maintain stability in the economy.

Demerits of Balanced Budget

However the modern economist are not in favour of balanced budget on the following demerits.

1. **Not Gainful:** The advocates of balanced budget assumes that public budget must be neutral in its impact on the economy. But the truth is balanced budget is not gainful in the context of modern welfare state as it fails to accelerate economic growth.
2. **Not Effective to tackle Economic Evils:** It is argued that balanced budget is not effective to tackle the economic evils like problems of trade cycle, inflation, deflation, existence of disparities in the distribution of income and wealth etc. specially in developing countries like India.
3. **Not Suitable During Depression -** Balanced budget leads to further disincentive effects in a depression-stricken economy. Such a policy further aggravates the business prospects and weakens the Marginal Efficiency of Capital (MEC), the level

of employment, production, national income, effective demand etc. in the economy.

4. **Does not Necessarily Check wasteful Expenditures:** Balanced budget does not guarantee a disciplined and efficient management in the Financial Affairs: According to ***Prof. Arthur* Smithies,** *"It is quite possible that an effort to have a balanced budget during a given period of time may rather lead to a wasteful expenditure."* The financial discipline rather depends upon the nature of the government.

5. **Restricts Freedom of Public Authorities:** The technique of balanced budget restricts the freedom of action of the public authorities and thus restricts the extensive use of fiscal Policy. So it is very much suicidal and damaging for a developing economy like India.

An another argument against the balanced budget is in a developing country like India some deficit budgeting is needed to provide financial support to the increasing monetisation of the economy. Deficit financing, not balanced budgetary policy would promote development and growth in underdeveloped and developing countries.

Unbalanced Budget

A budget is said to be unbalanced when the government's anticipated revenue and proposed expenditure shown in the budget are not equal. The imbalance may be due to an excess of revenue over expenditure or an excess of expenditure over revenue. In this respect unbalanced budget may either be a surplus budget or a deficit budget.

Surplus Budget - Surplus budget refers to a budget proposal in which the anticipated public revenue exceeds the proposed expenditure. According to ***Prof. P.E.Taylor,*** *"If revenue receipts for the budget period are greater than costs payments, the difference is budget surplus"*

The classical economists were in favour of surplus budget on the grounds that –

- It checks inflationary rise in prices,
- It checks unproductive and unnecessary expenditure of the public authorities.
- It frees the government from the burden of debt.
- It increases the saving potentiality of the government.
- It helps the government to repay the past debts.

However, in the present day's economies surplus budget is no more preferred anywhere in the world. The concepts of welfare state and functional finance have changed the perception of the budgetary policy and made the concept of surplus budget only a theoretical one.

Deficit Budget - A deficit budget can be defined as a budget in which the anticipated public revenue falls short of the proposed public expenditure. According to ***Taylor,*** *"If revenue receipts for the budget period are less than the case payments, the difference is budget deficit".*

A deficit budget is a novel device, an effective fiscal instrument applied for making the recovery of a depression- Stricken economy. A deficit budget is the reality of the present day economies and has become the most popular budget adopted by almost all economies of the world. It is the outcome of the functional finance adopted since the recomendation of J.M. Keynes after the Great Depression of 1930s. Now a days it has become so popular when we say about unbalanced budget it usually refers to a deficit budget. The modern economists advocate in favour of deficit budget on the grounds of its following merits.

Merits of Deficit Budget

1. It is a powerful instrument for generating higher level of income and employment.
2. Deficit budget is a solution to tackle the problem of unemployment. Through the policy of functional finance it helps to provide redistributive justice and to achieve other goals of public policy.
3. Deficit budget cures deflation and bridge up the deflationary gap in the economy.
4. Deficit budget is very useful during emergencies like war, natural calamities etc.
5. Deficit budget stimulates economic grower.
6. Deficit budget enables the government to enhance its share of activities and to arrange new sources of income.
7. Deficit budget is helpful for the underdeveloped and developing countries in creating economic and social over heads by mobilising resources from internal and international sources.

Demerits of Deficit Budget

A deficit budget is subject to following demerits.

1. Deficit budget may make room for wasteful and unnecessary public expenditure and increase the liability of the government.
2. Unproductive public expenditure may lead to inflationary rise in prices and create instability in the economy.

3. Inflationary rise in price due to deficit budget may adversely affect the exports of a country and foreign exchange earnings and thus may create a balance of payments difficulty.
4. Continuous deficit in the budget may create distrust in the minds of the people and may raise questions on the efficiency of the fiscal administration of the government.
5. Excess deficit may create a situation of fiscal indiscipline in the country.
6. To meet the budgetary deficit if the government issues new currency notes it may adversely affect the exchange value of domestic currency.

However, the severity of the demerits of deficit budget is less in comparison to the necessity of its merits. That's why it is being widely adopted by the economies of the countries over the globe and has become the most popular form of budget.

Surplus Budget	Deficit Budget
1. In surplus budget government receipts are more than government expenditure.	1. In deficit budget government expenditure is more than government receipts.
2. It increases the contingency fund of the government and reduces government liabilities.	2. It decreases the contingency fund of the government and increases government liabilities.
3. It helps in curbing inflationary rise in prices.	3. It helps in curing the deflationary tendency in the economy.
4. It is not suitable during emergency.	4. It is suitable during the period of emergency.
5. It acts as a check to the wasteful and unproductive public expenditure.	5. It makes room for wasteful and unproductive public expenditure.

WHAT WE LEARNT

1. Public finance refers to that branch of economics which deals with the income and expenditure or money matters of the public authorities.
2. The subject matter of public finance includes – public revenue, public expenditure, public debt, financial administration and fiscal federalism.
3. Private finance is the study of income and expenditure or money matters of private individuals or business organizations.

4. There are certain similarities between the public finance and private finance relating to objectives, rationality and irrationality, borrowing, financial management etc.
5. The distinction between public finance and private finance is more pronounced.
6. A private individual adjusts his expenditure to his income where as the government adjusts its income to its expenditure.
7. In case of public finance the motive of government expenditure is guided by the social welfare where as in case of private finance an individual's expenditure is guided by individual interest.
8. The sources of income of an individual are limited but those of the public authorities are unlimited.
9. Some of the public expenditure are of compulsory character and cannot be avoided or postponed which is not necessarily that in case of an individual.
10. A government prepares its income and expenditure plan, i.e. budget for a specific period, normally for a year, but it varies in case of an individual which may be a day or a week or a month.
11. A private individual believes in surplus budget where as a government prefers deficit budget.
12. Private finance is secret where as public finance is open to publicity.
13. The scope of borrowing for an individual is limited but that for a government is widespread.
14. An individual cannot use force to enhance his sources of income but a government can do that.
15. The proposals relating to income and expenditure in case of public finance are subject to approval by the authorities and are auditable by the constitutional authorities which is not necessary in case of an individual.
16. Budget is the master financial plan of the government which brings together the estimates of anticipated revenue and proposed expenditure.
17. Budget is considered as an instrument of the fiscal policy of the government.
18. The broad objectives of the government budget are - optimal allocation of resources, equitable distribution of national income and wealth, economic stability, economic development and growth.
19. Budget of a government can either be balanced or unbalanced.

20. A budget is said to be a balanced budget when the anticipated revenues of the government and the proposed expenditure are shown equal.
21. A budget is said to be unbalanced when the government's anticipated revenue and proposed expenditure on the budget are not equal.
22. An unbalanced budget may either be a surplus budget or a deficit budget.
23. Surplus budget refers to a budget in which the anticipated public revenue exceeds the proposed expenditure.
24. The classical economists were in favour of surplus budget.
25. Surplus budget is useful to curb inflation.
26. Deficit budget refers to a budget in which the anticipated public revenue falls short of proposed expenditure or expenditure exceeds public revenue.
27. Modern economists are in favour of deficit budget.
28. Deficit budget helps in curing depressionary tendency.
29. Deficit budget is useful during emergency.
30. Balanced budget is suitable for developed countries.

QUESTIONS FOR REVIEW

A. *Choose the correct answer from the given alternatives in each question. (Each Carrying 1 Mark)*

1. **The study of monetary matters of the public authorities is called :**

   (i) Political economy (ii) Public finance

   (iii) Private Finance (iv) All the above

2. **Who said 'Public finance is one of those subjects which lie on the borderline between economics and politics'. ?**

   (i) Dalton (ii) Findlay Shiras

   (iii) A. C. Pigou (iv) Bastable

3. **Which one of the following is not a subject matter of public finance ?**

   (i) Public revenue (ii) Public expenditure

   (iii) Monetary Policy (iv) Financial Administration

4. Who propounded the maximum social advantage principle as a guiding principle for the state to allocate resources ?

(i) Dalton (ii) Keynes

(iii) Taylor (iv) Bastable

5. Public expenditure is guided by which motive ?

(i) Individual Interest (ii) Government Interest

(iii) Social Interest (iv) Political Interest

6. The statement showing the anticipated receipts and proposed expenditure of the government is called :

(i) Balance Sheet (ii) Budget

(iii) Performance Sheet (iv) Fiscal Policy

7. The government budget in which the anticipated receipts and proposed expenditure are equal is a :

(i) Balanced Budget (ii) Unbalanced Budget

(iii) Surplus Budget (iv) Deficit Budget

8. The government budget in which the anticipated receipts and proposed expenditure are not equal is a :

(i) Surplus Budget (ii) Deficit Budget

(iii) Unbalanced Budget (iv) None of the above

9. In a Surplus budget :

(i) Receipts fall short of expenditure (ii) Receipts exceed expenditure

(iii) Receipts equal expenditure (iv) None of the above

10. If the proposed expenditure in the budget exceeds the anticipated revenue of the government it is called a :

(i) Unbalanced budget (ii) Surplus budget

(iii) Deficit Budget (iv) Balanced Budget

11. Which budget helps in curbing inflation ?

(i) Unbalanced budget (ii) Balanced Budget

(iii) Deficit Budget (iv) Surplus Budget

12. Which budget cures depressionary tendency (deflation) ?

(i) Deficit budget (ii) Surplus budget

(iii) Unbalanced budget (iv) All the above

13. The classical economists were in favour of which budget ?

(i) Deficit Budget (ii) Surplus Budget

(iii) Unbalanced Budget (iv) All the above

14. Which one is the most popular form of budget ?

(i) Balanced budget (ii) Surplus Budget

(iii) Deficit Budget (iv) None of the above

15. Which budget is suitable for the developed countries ?

(i) Balanced Budget (ii) Surplus Budget

(iii) Deficit Budget (iv) None of the above

16. Which budget is suitable for the developing countries ?

(i) Deficit Budget (ii) Balanced Budget

(iii) Surplus budget (iv) All the above

17. Which budget checks the unproductive expenditure of the government ?

(i) Deficit Budget (ii) Balanced budget

(iii) Unbalanced budget (iv) Surplus budget

18. Which budget is suitable for emergencies ?

(i) Balanced budget (ii) Unbalanced budget

(iii) Deficit budget (iv) Surplus budget

19. Which budget increases the contingency fund of the government ?

(i) Surplus budget (ii) Deficit budget

(iii) Balanced budget (iv) None of the above

20. Which budget should be adopted during deflation ?

(i) Balanced budget (ii) Unbalanced budget

(iii) Surplus budget (iv) Deficit budget

B. *Correct the statement, if necessary, without changing the underlined portions. (Each Carrying 1 Mark)*

1. The study of income and expenditure of the public authorities is called private finance.

2. Fiscal administration constitutes a part of the study of public finance.

3. The similarities between public finance and private finance is more pronounced.

4. Government adjusts his expenditure to income.
5. The sources of income of the public authorities are limited.
6. Some of the private expenditure are of compulsory character.
7. A private individual believes in deficit budget.
8. Private finance is secrete where as public finance is open.
9. The scope of borrowing for an individual is unlimited.
10. A government cannot use force to enhance income.
11. Budget is considered as an instrument of the fiscal policy of the government.
12. In a surplus budget anticipated receipts of the government falls short of proposed expenditure.
13. A deficit budget is helpful to cure inflation.
14. Public finance is a subject matter of micro economics.
15. Balanced budget is useful to curb inflation.

C. *Answer the following questions in 2-3 sentences each (Each Carrying 2 Marks)*

1. What is public finance ?
2. What is private finance ?
3. Point out the subject matter of public finance.
4. Point out the similarities between public finance and private finance.
5. Point out three important distinctions between public finance and private finance.
6. What is budget ?
7. Point out the broad objectives of budget.
8. What is balanced budget ?
9. What is unbalanced budget ?
10. What is surplus budget ?
11. What is deficit budget ?
12. Point out any three merits of balanced budget.
13. Point out any three demerits of balanced budget.
14. Point out the merits of surplus budget.
15. Point out the demerits of surplus budget.

16. Point out any three merits of deficit budget.
17. Point out any three demerits of deficit budget.

D. Distinguish between in six sentences each (Each Carrying 3 Marks)

1. Public Finance and Private Finance
2. Balanced Budget and Unbalanced budget
3. Surplus budget and Deficit budget

E. Long Answer Type Questions (Each Carrying 7½ Marks)

1. What is public finance ? Make a distinction between public finance and private finance.
2. What is balanced budget ? Discuss its merits and demerits.
3. What is deficit budget ? Discuss its merits and demerits.
4. Make a distinction between balanced and unbalanced budget.
5. What is budget ? Discuss the objectives of a government budget.

Answer to Q. N. A

1.	(ii)	2.	(i)	3.	(iii)	4.	(i)	5.	(iii)	6.	(ii)	7.	(i)	8.	(iii)
9.	(ii)	10.	(iii)	11.	(iv)	12.	(i)	13.	(ii)	14.	(iii)	15.	(i)	16.	(i)
17.	(iv)	18.	(iii)	19	(i)	20.	(iv)								

Answer to Q. N. B

1. Public Finance	2. Correct	3. The differences
4. An individual	5. Unlimited	6. Public expenditure
7. Surplus budget	8. Correct	9. a government
10. An individual	11. Correct	12. exceeds
13. deflation	14. macro economics	15. surplus budget

❑❑❑

ANNUAL H.S. EXAM.–2023 QUESTION

ARTS/SCIENCE

SET–B

Time : 3 Hrs. *F.M. : 100*

1. Write the correct answer choosing from the alternatives given in each question. **(1 × 15)**

(a) Which of the following is not a function of commercial banks ?

(i) Acceptance of deposits (ii) Advancing loan

(iii) Credit creation (iv) Credit control

(b) Balanced budget is one in which—

(i) Proposed expenditure is equal to anticipated revenue

(ii) Proposed expenditure is greater than anticipated revenue

(iii) Proposed expenditure is less than anticipated revenue

(iv) None of the above.

(c) Who defined 'Economics as a Science of Choice' ?

(i) Adam Smith (ii) Alfred Marshall

(iii) J.S. Mill (iv) Lionel Robbins

(d) Which of the following is not a characteristics of Wealth ?

(i) Utility (ii) Scarcity

(iii) Internal quality (iv) Transferability

(e) When marginal utility is zero, total utility–

(i) decreases (ii) increases

(iii) becomes maximum (iv) becomes zero

(f) When income increases, what happens to the position of the demand curve ?

(i) Shifts to the right (ii) Shifts to the left

(iii)Remains constant (iv) Rises upward from left to right

(g) When price rise of good 'X' causes rise in the demand for good 'Y', then the two goods are–

(i) Complementary (ii) alternative

(iii) equally urgent (iv) None of the above

(h) When marginal revenue is less than average revenue, average revenue–

(i) remains constant (ii) rises

(iii) falls (iv) becomes zero

(i) Production means–

(i) Creation of matter

(ii) Creation of utility having exchange value

(iii) Satisfaction of human wants

(iv) Making factors more productive.

(j) The pain and sacrifice undergone by the owners of factors in the process of production are–

(i) explicit costs (ii) economic costs

(iii) money costs (iv) Real costs

(k) Under monopoly, the shape of the demand curve is–

(i) horizontal (ii) vertical

(iii)downward sloping (iv) upward sloping.

(l) The unique features of monopolistic competition is–

(i) Single Seller (ii) Product differentiation

(iii) Single price (iv) restricted entry into market

(m) Which of the following is associated with micro economics ?

(i) National income (ii) Theory of consumer behaviour

(iii) General Price level (iv) Aggregate employment

(n) Which of the following is a part of aggregate demand ?

(i) Private investment (ii) Household consumption

(iii) Government expenditure (iv) All of the above.

(o) Which of the following is not included in national income ?

(i) Compensation of employees (ii) Operating surplus

(iii) Transfer payment (iv) Mixed income.

2. Examine the correctness of the following statements. Correct only the incorrect statements without changing the underlined portions. (1 × 15)

(a) Aggregate supply is inversely related to employment.

(b) Demand deposits cannot be withdrawn before a stipulated time period.

(c) Medium of exchange is a Secondary function of money.

(d) In Public finance expenditure is adjusted with income.

(e) All economic goods are capital.

(f) Value of a commodity expressed in terms of money is called wealth.

(g) Demand for goods having alternative uses is relatively inelastic.

(h) Quantity demanded for Giffen good falls with the fall in its price.

(i) In the short-run, all factors of production are variable.

(j) Cost per unit of output is known as marginal cost.

(k) Under oligopoly there is restriction of entry.

(l) The law of variable proportions shows the short run Production Function.

(m) Under perfect competition, there is no distinction between firm and industry.

(n) Micro-economics studies the behaviour of aggregate economic units.

(o) If net factor income from abroad is negative, Gross National Product is greater than Gross Domestic Product.

Group –B

1. Answer any eleven of the following questions within 2 to 3 sentences each. (2 × 11)

(a) What is aggregate demand ?

(b) What is monopolistic competition ?

(c) What is money ?

(d) What is budget ?

(e) What is form utility ?

(f) What are conventional necessaries ?

(g) What is demand schedule ?

(h) What is perfectly elastic demand ?

(i) What are the Central Problems of an economy ?

(j) What is marginal revenue ?

(k) What is law of supply ?

(l) What is average costs ?

(m) What is law of equi-marginal utility ?

(n) What is personal income ?

2. Distinguish between any Six of the following. Answer the questions within 6 sentences each : **(3 × 6)**

(a) GNP and NNP

(b) Central bank and commercial bank.

(c) Public finance and private finance.

(d) Marginal utility and Total utility.

(e) Value-in-use and value-in-exchange.

(f) Fixed cost and variable cost.

(g) Marginal product and Average product.

(h) Microeconomics and Macroeconomics.

Group–C

Answer any four of the following questions **(7½ × 4)**

3. Describe the function of money.

4. Discuss the functions of central bank.

5. Discuss the characteristics of human wants.

6. Explain the law of demand.

7. Explain the law of variable proportion.

8. Explain the Simple Keynesian theory of income determination.

Answer to the Question No.–1

(a)	(iv)	(b)	(i)	(c)	(iv)	(d)	(iii)	(e)	(iii)	(f)	(i)	(g)	(ii)	(h)	(iii)
(i)	(ii)	(j)	(iv)	(k)	(iii)	(l)	(ii)	(m)	(ii)	(n)	(iv)	(o)	(iii)		

Answer to the Question No.–2

(a) directly	(b) Fixed	(c) Primary
(d) Private	(e) Wealth	(f) Price
(g) elastic	(h) correct	(i) long-run
(j) average	(k) monopoly	(l) correct
(m) monopoly	(n) Macro	(o) Positive

ANNUAL H.S. EXAM.–2023 QUESTION

COMMERCE

BSE

Time : 3 Hrs. *F.M. : 80*

Group–A
(Answer all questions serially)

1. Write the correct answer Choosing from the alternatives given under each bit. **(1 × 12)**

(a) Motor car for a busy doctor is a–

(i) Necessary (ii) Comfort

(iii) Luxury (iv) None of these

(b) The goods having exchange value are known as–

(i) Free goods (ii) Unproductive goods

(iii) Economic goods (iv) None of these

(c) The goods which satisfy human wants indirectly are called–

(i) Public goods (ii) Consumers' goods

(iii) Producers' goods (iv) Intermediate goods

(d) Health is not wealth because it has no –

(i) Scarcity (ii) utility

(iii) Marketability (iv) None of these

(e) Destruction of utility is known as–

(i) Production (ii) Distribution

(iii) Consumption (iv) Division

(f) The demand for necessaries is–

(i) Elastic (ii) Inelastic

(iii) Unitary elastic (iv) Perfectly elastic

(g) Economic cost is explicit cost plus–

(i) Variable cost (ii) Marginal cost

(iii) Average cost (iv) implicit cost

(h) What will happen to price when demand increases but supply remains constant ?

(i) Price remains constant (ii) Price increases

(iii) Price decreases (iv) None of these.

(i) In long-run–

(i) All factors of Production are variable

(ii) All factors of production are fixed

(iii) Some factors of production are fixed

(iv) Some factors of production are variable.

(j) Costs which change when output changes are–

(i) Fixed cost (ii) Variable cost

(iii) Opportunity cost (iv) None of these

(k) Under perfect competition average revenue is equal to –

(i) Marginal revenue (ii) Marginal cost

(iii) Average cost (iv) None of these

(l) Which bank creates credit ?

(i) Central bank (ii) Rural Bank

(iii) Commercial bank (iv) Cooperative Bank

2. Examine the correctness of the following statements. Correct the incorrect sentences, without changing the underlined portions. (1 ×12)

(a) The law of equimarginal utility is otherwise known as the law of substitution.

(b) Land is a variable factor.

(c) Money cost is pain and sacrifices undergone during the process of production.

(d) The shape of unitary elastic demand curve is vertical.

(e) Cash at hand is the most liquid asset of commercial banks.

(f) Salary of the watchman is variable cost.

(g) Reserve Rank of India was established in the year 1955

(h) When output increases, total fixed cost remains the same.

(i) Macroeconomics is the study of individual units.

(j) Surplus budget is more effective of control inflation.

(k) In monopolistic competition there is a single seller and large number of buyers.

(l) In a balanced budget government receipts are greater than government expenditure.

Group–B

3. Answer any ten of the following questions with in 30 words in each case. (2 ×10)

(a) What do you mean by service utility ?

(b) What are the Central Problems of an economy ?

(c) What are conventional necessary goods ?

(d) What do you mean by Giffen goods ?

(e) What is price elasticity of demand ?

(f) What is short run production function ?

(g) What do you mean by implicit cost ?

(h) What is monopolistic competition ?

(i) What is unitary elastic demand ?

(j) What do you mean by Average variable cost ?

(k) What is disposable personal income ?

(l) What is unbalanced budget ?

(m) What do you mean by Gross Domestic Production ?

4. Distinguish between any four of the following. Limit your answer to 50 words in each case. (3 × 4)

(a) Value and Price.

(b) Wealth and capital.

(c) Fixed cost and variable cost

(d) Accounting cost and Economic cost

(e) Increasing returns and Diminishing returns.

(f) Public finance and Private Finance.

Group–C

Answer any three of the following questions **(8 × 3)**

5. Explain the law of equi-marginal utility.
6. Discuss the factors influencing demand for a commodity.
7. Discuss the Functions of Central bank.
8. Explain how price is determined under perfect competition.
9. What is budget ? Discuss the objectives of budget.

Answer to the Question No.–1

(a)	(i)	(b)	(iii)	(c)	(iii)	(d)	(iii)	(e)	(iii)	(f)	(ii)	(g)	(iv)	(h)	(ii)
(i)	(i)	(j)	(ii)	(k)	(i)	(l)	(iii)								

Answer to the Question No.–2

(a) Correct	(b) Fixed factor	(c) Real cost
(d) Rectangular hyperbola	(e) Correct	(f) Fixed cost
(g) 1935	(h) Correct	(i) aggregate units
(j) Correct	(k) monopoly	(l) Surplus budget

❑❑❑